PREFACE

The King's star!
When Jesus first appeared around 2000 years ago, wise men saw the king's star from the east and followed it to the palace.

***When King Herod heard this he was disturbed and all of Jerusalem with him* (Matthew 2:3)**

The chief priests and the teachers of the law told King Herod the King was to be born in Bethlehem. So why in the world did the chief priests and the Pharisees not follow the wise men to meet the king? Even though they were full of biblical research and knowledge about the Messiah, they were indifferent towards the idea of actually meeting Him. Eventually the Messiah was crucified and killed.

In the fifth chapter of the Book of Revelation, in God's right hand, is a seven-sealed book. An angel cries out, "who is worthy to open the book and loose the seal?" At this time, the Apostle John cried out loud because no matter how hard he looked above the skies, on land, below land there was no one that could open or read the book.

We have to know this book of Revelation, which is sealed with seven seals, even if looking we cannot see, and hearing we cannot understand. Many thirsty and hungry people in this era wander to and fro to hear the words of Christ. If you do not know God's will through the Bible, nor the Revelation, which is the end of the Bible, you will fall under the spirit of delusion whether you want to or not.

The revelation of Jesus Christ was written to show His servants what must soon take place. (Revelation 1:1)

If we are His true servants, why do we not pray for God to open to us the Book of Revelation? Why do we not cry with the Apostle John's heart? Why are we afraid, try to cover up, and turn away?

When you know the Revelation, the end of the entire Bible, the purpose of faith and the purpose of life stand right.

- ○ Revelation is the conclusion of the Bible
- ○ Revelation reveals the purpose behind God's creation
- ○ Revelation reveals Satan's fate
- ○ The book of Revelation reveals God's desired overcomer in the last days.
- ○ The book of Revelation will be opened more in times of trouble and confusion. Jesus Christ gave His servants the Book of Revelation because He wanted them to know in advance what must happen so that they would be prepared to be overcomers.
- ○ The Book of Revelation is intended to be opened to those who are alive in the last days who long for grace and truth

Now here is the book sealed with the seven seals of God before you. Would you like to cry like the apostle John to open this book before you?

Those who study Revelation just with knowledge may tell others about it, but they will not be able to greet the Coming of Christ. After those who adore Christ have become aware of the Book of Revelation, they will follow in the footsteps of Christ who will come again.
They will follow the king's star to Bethlehem, and they will go to the Jordan River to meet John the Baptist and eventually meet the Messiah. They will climb the mulberry tree, throw out

their water basket and go to those who despise them, they will praise even when they are beaten and even when they are thrown into burning hot oil. They will meet our eternal king, our Messiah who will come again.

No one says 'Come, test!' Without even studying. What is the test that will come to us in the future? What is the answer to the test? The time, course, reason, and answer of the test are all found in the Book of Revelation. We must understand the gospel of this life, the gospel of heaven, and keep it to obtain the resurrection life. Becoming an overcomer is the answer to this test.

Daniel was told to seal his mystery until the time of the end, but the Revelation was not to be sealed because the time was near. Those who know the answer to this test will not keep it to themselves but will live a life of preaching and witnessing to it.

In the end, the gospel of heaven must be preached to the whole world in order for God to order the end to be upon us and say go and baptize disciples in the name of the Father and Son and Holy Spirit, teaching them to observe everything commanded by Jesus.

Will there be someone who can pray “Come, Lord Jesus”? This is a prayer of life that only overcoming disciples of Christ can offer to the heavenly throne.

[Amen. Come, Lord Jesus!]

Contents

Overview

1. The book of Revelation is **a prophetic book.**
   a. Prophecy concerning churches on the Earth
      Letters sent to seven churches (Revelation chapters 2 and 3) - symbolic meaning
   b. The prophecy of the things that must soon take place.
      Revelation of the events preceding the 2nd coming of the Lord (Rev 1:3, Rev 22:7)[1)]

2. The book of Revelation is **the concluding book** of the Bible
   a. The records of the completion of God's dispensation
      If there were no conclusion to the Bible, we wouldn't know what works God would've wanted.
   b. The Bible consists of
      1) Introduction : Genesis
      2) Body : Exodus ~ Malachi, Matthew ~ Jude
      3) Conclusion : Revelation
         God's purpose in the creation of the Universe (the New Jerusalem) is shown forth in this conclusion. In the body of the Bible, John's gospel speaks of the giving of life; John's the letters speak of the propagation and development of life, and the book of Revelation speaks of the maturing and perfection of life.
   c. The maturing and perfection of life, the harvest, take place in John's Revelation.
      God's throne: Revelation chapter 7 (group dressed in white), chapter 12 (martyrs)
      Heavenly Mt. Zion : Revelation chapter 14 (firstfruits)

---

1) Rev 1:3 Blessed is the one who reads the words of this prophecy, and blessed are those who hear it and take to heart what is written in it, because the time is near.
   Rev 22:7 "Behold, I am coming soon! Blessed is he who keeps the words of the prophecy in this book.

Rapture in the air : Revelation chapter 14 (ripe harvest)

3. The book of Revelation **reveals the completion of the salvation of Christ.**
   a. The completion of salvation: becoming heirs of God (Royal priesthood, bride of Christ)
   b. Stages of salvation
      - The salvation of the spirit (born again) (Jn 3:3～6)[2)]
      - The salvation of your souls (1Pe 1:9, 23)[3)]
      - Salvation of the body (bodily resurrection at the second coming) (1Th 4:17, 1Co 15:4, 51～ 52)[4)]

   ※ Today, our mortal bodies can enjoy glory and life (heir) through Christ to the extent that our souls have received salvation (Ro 8:11)[5)].

---

2) Jn3:3 In reply Jesus declared, "I tell you the truth, no one can see the kingdom of God unless he is born again."
   Jn3:4 "How can a man be born when he is old?" Nicodemus asked. "Surely he cannot enter a second time into his mother's womb to be born!"
   Jn3:5 Jesus answered, "I tell you the truth, no one can enter the kingdom of God unless he is born of water and the Spirit.
   Jn3:6 Flesh gives birth to flesh, but the Spirit gives birth to spirit.

3) 1Pe1:9 for you are receiving the goal of your faith, the salvation of your souls.
   1Pe1:23 For you have been born again, not of perishable seed, but of imperishable, through the living and enduring word of God.

4) 1Th4:17 After that, we who are still alive and are left will be caught up together with them in the clouds to meet the Lord in the air. And so we will be with the Lord forever.
   1Co15:4 that He was buried, that He was raised on the third day according to the Scriptures,
   1Co15:51 Listen, I tell you a mystery: We will not all sleep, but we will all be changed--
   1Co15:52 in a flash, in the twinkling of an eye, at the last trumpet. For the trumpet will sound, the dead will be raised imperishable, and we will be changed.

5) Ro8:11 And if the Spirit of Him who raised Jesus from the dead is living in you, He who raised Christ from the dead will also give

c. The redemption of Christ is to make us kings and priests to God.
   Kings : God's reign
   Priests : expresses the image of God (Rev 1:6, 5:10)[6)]

d. The office of the royal priesthood
   - Practiced in churches today
   - Reigning with Christ in the Millennial Kingdom (Rev 20:6)[7)]
   - This office continues forever in the New Jerusalem (Rev 22:5)[8)]

※The royal priesthood is for accomplishing God's original purpose in the creation of Man (Ge 1:26~28, 1Pe 2:9)[9)].

4. The book of Revelation **concludes the destiny of Satan**.
   a. The old serpent in the garden of Eden has grown over 6,000 years and will be active in the end time as a red dragon.
   b. The book of Revelation has been closed until now because this book exposes and reveals the fate and end of Satan.
   ※Satan, knowing that he will work as a red dragon and go

---

life to your mortal bodies through His Spirit, who lives in you.

6) Rev1:6 and has made us to be a kingdom and priests to serve His God and Father--to Him be glory and power for ever and ever! Amen.
   Rev5:10 You have made them to be a kingdom and priests to serve our God, and they will reign on the earth."

7) Rev20:6 Blessed and holy are those who have part in the first resurrection. The second death has no power over them, but they will be priests of God and of Christ and will reign with Him for a thousand years.

8) Rev22:5 There will be no more night. They will not need the light of a lamp or the light of the sun, for the Lord God will give them light. And they will reign for ever and ever.

9) Ge1:26 Then God said, "Let us make man in our image, in our likeness, and let them rule over the fish of the sea and the birds of the air, over the livestock, over all the earth, and over all the creatures that move along the ground."

into the Abyss in Revelation 20, and at the end of the Millennial Kingdom will deliberately deceive all the nations and enter the eternal lake of fire (Isa 14:12~17, Rev 20:10)[10], has worked to prevent access to the book of Revelation.

c. But in the time of the imminent return of the Lord, the book of Revelation will be unfolded and revealed. Now the Lord will open this book and open our hearts, spirits, eyes and ears to see the enemies of God.

※In this book, we deal with the four principal themes of Revelation, namely God's dispensation, Christ's redemption, the witness of the Church and the destiny of Satan.

5. **The composition of Revelation**

a. Introduction: (Rev 1:1~8): the Revelation of Christ and the testimony of Jesus

b. The things John has seen (Rev 1:9~20) the person having seven lampstands and seven stars

c. Contemporary affairs: (Rev 2:1~Rev 3:22) The seven churches

d. Future things to come (Rev 4:1~Rev 22:5)

1) Rev 4:1~Rev 11:19 : overview from the ascension of

---

10) Isa14:12 How you have fallen from heaven, O morning star, son of the dawn! You have been cast down to the earth, you who once laid low the nations!

Isa14:13 You said in your heart, "I will ascend to heaven; I will raise my throne above the stars of God; I will sit enthroned on the mount of assembly, on the utmost heights of the sacred mountain.

Isa14:14 I will ascend above the tops of the clouds; I will make myself like the Most High."

Isa14:15 But you are brought down to the grave, to the depths of the pit.

Isa14:16 Those who see you stare at you, they ponder your fate: "Is this the man who shook the earth and made kingdoms tremble,

Isa14:17 the man who made the world a desert, who overthrew its cities and would not let his captives go home?"

Christ to the eternal state

2) Rev 12:1~Rev 22:5 : detailed record of important future events together with the progress towards the eternal state

e. Conclusion (Rev 22:6~Rev 22:21) : The conclusion of Revelation

Chapter 1

Verse 1 The revelation from Jesus Christ, which God gave Him to show His servants what must soon take place. He made it known by sending His angel to His servant John,

1. The revelation of Jesus Christ··· (from Christ and about Christ)
   a. Other parts of the Bible are also revelation, but the distinctive nature of the book of Revelation is that it causes the apostle John to see and know the things that must soon take place.
   b. In the four gospels, we see Jesus coming to the earth, preaching the gospel for three and a half years of public ministry, dying on the cross, rising from the dead, and, in the book of Acts, ascending in front of 500 believers.
   c. What is Jesus Christ now doing from His heavenly throne?
      1) He ministers as High Priest (Heb 3:1, 4:14, 6:20, 7:26)[11].
      2) From then on, through the book of Revelation we not only receive a revelation of Christ's second coming but also a clearer and more accurate picture of Christ.
2. What must soon take place

---

11) Hev3:1 Therefore, holy brothers, who share in the heavenly calling, fix your thoughts on Jesus, the apostle and high priest whom we confess.
Hev4:14 Therefore, since we have a great high priest who has gone through the heavens, Jesus the Son of God, let us hold firmly to the faith we profess.
Hev6:20 where Jesus, who went before us, has entered on our behalf. He has become a high priest forever, in the order of Melchizedek.
Hev7:26 Such a high priest meets our need—one who is holy, blameless, pure, set apart from sinners, exalted above the heavens.

◆ In order to show His servants the things that would take place before and after His second coming, the Lord testified to John, and testifies to us today.

a. Things concerning the Millennial Kingdom (Rev 20).

b. Things concerning the eternal New Heaven and New Earth and New Jerusalem (Rev 21～22).

3. to show His servants

The book of Revelation is to show to true servants who are committed to fulfilling God's righteousness. Today we are the chosen servants if we can correctly understand and receive the words of this revelation. The chosen servants are not only clergy, but also anyone who can understand and receive the words of this book of Revelation.

Verse 2: who testifies to everything he saw--that is, the word of God and the testimony of Jesus Christ.

1. What word did John bear witness to?

a. In the spirit, he bore witness to the things that he saw with the eyes of his born-again inner man.

b. In the spirit, John directly saw all the things that were to come and bore witness to those things.

c. The eyes of the spirit means the eyes of the born-again inner man. The eyes of the inner man can transcend time and space and see the things that God has foreordained (Ro 7:22, Eph 3:16)[12].

2. Today, we too must bear witness to the things that we have seen.

Secondhand testimony has no value. Theory and knowledge is not testimony either. We must be able to see and testify with the eyes of the inner man.

---

12) Ro7:22 For in my inner being I delight in God's law;
Eph3:16 I pray that out of His glorious riches He may strengthen you with power through His Spirit in your inner being,

Verse 3: Blessed is the one who reads aloud the words of this prophecy, and blessed are those who hear it and take to heart what is written in it, because the time is near.

1. The one who reads the words of this prophecy : singular expression
   a. "he who reads" refers to a very few people who, in God's illumination, understand this word of revelation and, while reading in the light of life, receive life and digest and internalize the word.
   b. A person who does not understand this word of prophecy, despite reading it many hundreds of times, is not 'he who reads'.
2. "Those who hear it": Plural expression
   Those who hear the testimony of 'he who reads' refers to people who have received circumcised ears (Rev 2:11, Jer 6:10, Eze 3:10)[13].
3. "Those who take to heart what is written in it": Plural expression
   Reading and hearing are meaningless if we do not keep what is written. God surely made us read and hear in order to keep. Those who keep will bear fruit (Lk 8:15)[14]. Here, 'keeping' is not with fleshly methods or by human life. These things can only be kept by receiving the life of God.
4. The time is near
   Because the Lord's return and the preceding signs are imminent.

---

13)Rev2:11 He who has an ear, let him hear what the Spirit says to the churches. He who overcomes will not be hurt at all by the second death.
Jer6:10 To whom can I speak and give warning? Who will listen to me? Their ears are closed so they cannot hear. The word of the LORD is offensive to them; they find no pleasure in it.
Eze3:10 And He said to me, "Son of man, listen carefully and take to heart all the words I speak to you.

14) Lk8:15 But the seed on good soil stands for those with a noble and good heart, who hear the word, retain it, and by persevering produce a crop.

Verse 4 John, To the seven churches in the province of Asia: Grace and peace to you from Him who is, and who was, and who is to come, and from the seven spirits before His throne,

1. **to the seven churches** that are in Asia
   a. By talking of the seven churches of Asia Minor in the time of apostle John, it is a record of the condition of all churches of that time. And through the condition of those seven churches of that time, the condition of all churches is revealed
   b. Shows the history of the evolution of the Church from Christ's ascension to the time of His return.
   c. Through the seven churches, we can see the condition of all the churches on the earth today.
   d. Seven is the fundamental number of God's dispensation, ten is the complete number of going through hardship, and twelve is the complete number of God's dispensation. Seven, being the fundamental number of God's dispensation, will become twelve, the number of completion of God's dispensation, by going through number ten (hardship, tribulation).
      e.g. Seven spirits, seven lampstands, seven seals, seven trumpets, seven bowls
2. from Him who is, and who was, and who is to come: God
   a. God does not remain in heaven forever but comes down to the New Earth and to the fortress that is the New Jerusalem (Rev 22: 1~4)[15].

---

15) Rev22:1 Then the angel showed me the river of the water of life, as clear as crystal, flowing from the throne of God and of the Lamb

b. Many Christians mistakenly believe they will live in Heaven forever after their death.

3. **the seven spirits** who are before His throne (Rev 3:1, 4:5, 5:6)[16)]
   a. Seven spirits means the Holy Spirit (1 Co 12:8~11)[17)].
   b. The primary ministry of the Holy Spirit is to bring to completion the dispensation of God, namely, to establish the Kingdom and righteousness of God; for this, He

---

Rev22:2 down the middle of the great street of the city. On each side of the river stood the tree of life, bearing twelve crops of fruit, yielding its fruit every month. And the leaves of the tree are for the healing of the nations.
Rev22:3 No longer will there be any curse. The throne of God and of the Lamb will be in the city, and His servants will serve Him.
Rev22:4 They will see His face, and His name will be on their foreheads.

16) Rev3:1 "To the angel of the church in Sardis write: These are the words of Him who holds the seven spirits of God and the seven stars. I know your deeds; you have a reputation of being alive, but you are dead.
Rev4:5 From the throne came flashes of lightning, rumblings and peals of thunder. Before the throne, seven lamps were blazing. These are the seven spirits of God.
Rev5:6 Then I saw a Lamb, looking as if it had been slain, standing in the center of the throne, encircled by the four living creatures and the elders. He had seven horns and seven eyes, which are the seven spirits of God sent out into all the earth.

17) 1Co12:8 To one there is given through the Spirit the message of wisdom, to another the message of knowledge by means of the same Spirit,
1Co12:9 to another faith by the same Spirit, to another gifts of healing by that one Spirit,
1Co12:10 to another miraculous powers, to another prophecy, to another distinguishing between spirits, to another speaking in different kinds of tongues, and to still another the interpretation of tongues.
1Co12:11 All these are the work of one and the same Spirit, and He gives them to each one, just as He determines.

operates through seven spirits.

c. The work of the Holy Spirit

1) Ministry aspects of the Holy Spirit

a) Holy Spirit like a dove: (Mt 3:16, Jn 1:32)[18]

b) Holy Spirit like fire: (Lk 24:32, Ac 2:1~3, Dt 9:3)[19]

c) Holy Spirit like water: (Jn 4:13, 7:37~39)[20]

---

18) Mt3:16 As soon as Jesus was baptized, He went up out of the water. At that moment heaven was opened, and He saw the Spirit of God descending like a dove and lighting on Him.

Jn1:32 Then John gave this testimony: "I saw the Spirit come down from heaven as a dove and remain on Him."

19) Lk24:32 They asked each other, "Were not our hearts burning within us while He talked with us on the road and opened the Scriptures to us?"

Ac2:1 When the day of Pentecost came, they were all together in one place.

Ac2:2 Suddenly a sound like the blowing of a violent wind came from heaven and filled the whole house where they were sitting.

Ac2:3 They saw what seemed to be tongues of fire that separated and came to rest on each of them.

Dt9:3 But be assured today that the LORD your God is the One who goes across ahead of you like a devouring fire. He will destroy them; He will subdue them before you. And you will drive them out and annihilate them quickly, as the LORD has promised you.

20) Jn4:13 Jesus answered, "Everyone who drinks this water will be thirsty again,

Jn4:14 but whoever drinks the water I give him will never thirst. Indeed, the water I give him will become in him a spring of water welling up to eternal life."

Jn7:37 On the last and greatest day of the Feast, Jesus stood and said in a loud voice, "If anyone is thirsty, let him come to Me and drink.

Jn7:38 Whoever believes in Me, as the Scripture has said, streams of living water will flow from within him."

Jn7:39 By this He meant the Spirit, whom those who believed in Him were later to receive. Up to that time the Spirit had not been given, since Jesus had not yet been glorified.

d) Holy Spirit like oil: (1Jn 2:27, Jas 5:14)[21)]
e) Holy Spirit like wind: (Ac 2:2)[22)]
f) Holy Spirit working through clouds: (Ex 13:21, Lev 16:2)[23)]
g) Holy Spirit of light: (1Jn 2:8~11, Jn 1:4~5)[24)]

2) Quintessential aspect of the Holy Spirit

---

21) 1Jn2:27 As for you, the anointing you received from Him remains in you, and you do not need anyone to teach you. But as His anointing teaches you about all things and as that anointing is real, not counterfeit--just as it has taught you, remain in Him.
Jas5:14 Is any one of you sick? He should call the elders of the church to pray over him and anoint him with oil in the name of the Lord.

22) Ac2:2 Suddenly a sound like the blowing of a violent wind came from heaven and filled the whole house where they were sitting.

23) Ex13:21 By day the LORD went ahead of them in a pillar of cloud to guide them on their way and by night in a pillar of fire to give them light, so that they could travel by day or night.
Lev16:2 The LORD said to Moses: "Tell your brother Aaron not to come whenever he chooses into the Most Holy Place behind the curtain in front of the atonement cover on the ark, or else he will die, because I appear in the cloud over the atonement cover.

24) 1Jn2:8 Yet I am writing you a new command; its truth is seen in Him and you, because the darkness is passing and the true light is already shining.
1Jn2:9 Anyone who claims to be in the light but hates his brother is still in the darkness.
1Jn2:10 Whoever loves his brother lives in the light, and there is nothing in him to make him stumble.
1Jn2:11 But whoever hates his brother is in the darkness and walks around in the darkness; he does not know where he is going, because the darkness has blinded him.
Jn1:4 In Him was life, and that life was the light of men.
Jn1:5 The light shines in the darkness, but the darkness has not understood it.

a) The spirit of truth: (Jn 14:16～17)[25]
b) The spirit of life: (Ro 8:1-2)[26]
c) The spirit of power (Lk 24:49, Ac 1:8)[27]
d) The spirit of God (Ro 8:9)[28]
e) The spirit of Jesus (Ac 16:7)[29]
f) The spirit of Christ (Ro 8:9)[30]
g) The spirit of Jesus Christ (Php 1:19～21)[31]

---

25) Jn14:16 And I will ask the Father, and He will give you ***another Counselor*** to be with you forever--
Jn14:17 the ***Spirit of truth***. The world cannot accept Him, because it neither sees Him nor knows Him. But you know Him, for He lives with you and will be in you.

26) Ro8:1 Therefore, there is now no condemnation for those who are in Christ Jesus,
Ro8:2 because through Christ Jesus the ***law of the Spirit of life*** set me free from the law of sin and death.

27) Lk24:49 I am going to send you what My Father has promised; but stay in the city ***until you have been clothed with power*** from on high."
Ac1:8 But ***you will receive power*** when the Holy Spirit comes on you; and you will be My witnesses in Jerusalem, and in all Judea and Samaria, and to the ends of the earth."

28) Ro8:9 You, however, are controlled not by the sinful nature but by the Spirit, if the ***Spirit of God*** lives in you. And if anyone does not have the Spirit of Christ, he does not belong to Christ.

29) Ac16:7 When they came to the border of Mysia, they tried to enter Bithynia, but the ***Spirit of Jesus*** would not allow them to.

30) Ro8:9 You, however, are controlled not by the sinful nature but by the Spirit, if the Spirit of God lives in you. And if anyone does not have the ***Spirit of Christ,*** he does not belong to Christ.

31) Php1:19 for I know that through your prayers and the help given by the Spirit of Jesus Christ, what has happened to me will turn out for my deliverance.

Verse 5 and from Jesus Christ, who is the faithful witness, the firstborn from the dead, and the ruler of the kings of the earth. To Him who loves us and has freed us from our sins by His blood,

1. The faithful witness = Jesus Christ was God's faithful witness (Jn 8:26, 8:38)[32]. Also, the Holy Spirit is the witness of Jesus Christ (Jn 15:26, 16:13)[33]. Jesus Christ is the witness who represented and expressed God through His life. Through Jesus we see God (Jn 14:9)[34].
2. The firstborn from the dead = the first person to be resurrected from the dead.
3. The ruler of the kings of the earth = King of kings and Lord of lords (Isa 60:1~3, Rev 19:16)[35].

Php1:20 I eagerly expect and hope that I will in no way be ashamed, but will have sufficient courage so that now as always Christ will be exalted in my body, whether by life or by death.
Php1:21 For to me, to live is Christ and to die is gain.

32) Jn8:26 "I have much to say in judgment of you. But He who sent Me is reliable, and what I have heard from Him I tell the world."
Jn8:38 I am telling you what I have seen in the Father's presence, and you do what you have heard from your father."

33) Jn15:26 "When the Counselor comes, whom I will send to you from the Father, the Spirit of truth who goes out from the Father, He will testify about Me.
Jn16:13 But when He, the Spirit of truth, comes, He will guide you into all truth. He will not speak on His own; He will speak only what He hears, and He will tell you what is yet to come.

34) Jn14:9 Jesus answered: "Don't you know Me, Philip, even after I have been among you such a long time? Anyone who has seen Me has seen the Father. How can you say, 'Show us the Father'?

35) Isa60:1 "Arise, shine, for your light has come, and the glory of the

In the Millennial Kingdom He rules over the kings of the earth (Rev 20:6)[36]. At His first coming, He preached the gospel, died on the cross and became Christ Jesus through His resurrection (Ro 8:1,2,39)[37]. Christ Jesus, who died on the cross and rose again, became the head of earthly kings (Rev 1:5)[38]

4. Grace and peace to you (Verse 4) = Grace and peace comes because of Jesus Christ.
   a. Grace: the experience and enjoyment of God coming to us.
   b. Peace: the heart is peaceful, joyful and full of gratitude.
5. Freed us from our sins = note that 'sins' here is plural. Through the blood of Jesus, we have received forgiveness for all the sins we have committed through our behaviour (Mk 2:5)[39].

LORD rises upon you.

Isa60:2 See, darkness covers the earth and thick darkness is over the peoples, but the LORD rises upon you and His glory appears over you.

Isa60:3 Nations will come to your light, and kings to the brightness of your dawn.

36) Rev20:6 Blessed and holy are those who have part in the first resurrection. The second death has no power over them, but they will be priests of God and of Christ and will reign with Him for a thousand years.

37) Ro8:1 Therefore, there is now no condemnation for those who are in Christ Jesus,

Ro8:2 because through Christ Jesus the law of the Spirit of life set me free from the law of sin and death.

Ro8:39 neither height nor depth, nor anything else in all creation, will be able to separate us from the love of God that is in Christ Jesus our Lord.

38) Rev1:5 and from Jesus Christ, who is the faithful witness, the firstborn from the dead, and the ruler of the kings of the earth. To Him who loves us and has freed us from our sins by His blood,

Verse 6: and has made us to be a kingdom and priests to serve His God and Father--to Him be glory and power for ever and ever! Amen.

1. To serve His God and Father

   The reason why Jesus Christ ransomed us by His blood and saved us was to make us a kingdom (kings) and priests.

2. made us to be a kingdom (kings) and priests.

   The purpose in making us kings and priests is in order to rule the earth during the Millennial Kingdom (Rev 5:10, 20:6)[40]. This is to become heirs of God and to inherit His work (Ro 8:15～18, Mt 5:5)[41].

Verse 7 "Look, He is coming with the clouds," and "every eye will see Him, even those who pierced Him"; and all peoples on earth "will mourn because of Him." So shall it be! Amen.

1. He is coming with clouds

---

39) Mk2:5 When Jesus saw their faith, He said to the paralytic, "Son, your sins are forgiven."

40) Rev5:10 You have made them to be a kingdom and priests to serve our God, and they will reign on the earth."
Rev20:6 Blessed and holy are those who have part in the first resurrection. The second death has no power over them, but they will be priests of God and of Christ and will reign with Him for a thousand years.

41) Ro8:15 For you did not receive a spirit that makes you a slave again to fear, but you received the Spirit of sonship. And by Him we cry, "Abba, Father."
Ro8:16 The Spirit Himself testifies with our spirit that we are God's children.
Ro8:17 Now if we are children, then we are heirs--heirs of God and co-heirs with Christ, if indeed we share in His sufferings in order that we may also share in His glory.
Ro8:18 I consider that our present sufferings are not worth comparing with the glory that will be revealed in us.
Mt5:5 Blessed are the meek, for they will inherit the earth.

The second coming of Jesus Christ returning to the earth riding on the clouds (Ac 1:9~11)[42].

The second coming takes place in the air first and continues to the ground.

a. **The second coming in the air**

1) Coming secretly like a thief (Rev 3:3, 16:15. Mt 24:40 ~44, 1Th 5:2, 4, 2Pe 3:10)[43]

---

42) Ac1:9 After He said this, He was taken up before their very eyes, and a cloud hid Him from their sight.
Ac1:10 They were looking intently up into the sky as He was going, when suddenly two men dressed in white stood beside them.
Ac1:11 "Men of Galilee," they said, "why do you stand here looking into the sky? This same Jesus, who has been taken from you into heaven, will come back in the same way you have seen Him go into heaven."

43) Rev3:3 Remember, therefore, what you have received and heard; obey it, and repent. But if you do not wake up, I will come like a thief, and you will not know at what time I will come to you.
Rev16:15 "Behold, I come like a thief! Blessed is he who stays awake and keeps his clothes with him, so that he may not go naked and be shamefully exposed."
Mt24:40 Two men will be in the field; one will be taken and the other left.
Mt24:41 Two women will be grinding with a hand mill; one will be taken and the other left.
Mt24:42 "Therefore keep watch, because you do not know on what day your Lord will come.
Mt24:43 But understand this: If the owner of the house had known at what time of night the thief was coming, he would have kept watch and would not have let his house be broken into.
Mt24:44 So you also must be ready, because the Son of Man will come at an hour when you do not expect Him.
1Th5:2 for you know very well that the day of the Lord will come like a thief in the night.
1Th5:4 But you, brothers, are not in darkness so that this day should surprise you like a thief.
2Pe3:10 But the day of the Lord will come like a thief. The heavens will disappear with a roar; the elements will be destroyed by fire, and the earth and everything in it will be laid bare.

2) We do not know when (Mt 24:36, 25:13, Mk 13:22)[44)]
3) Place to come : from the Third Heaven into the air (1Th 4:16~17)[45)]
4) Method of coming : apart from awakened believers, coming like a thief to all other people without letting anyone know.
5) Purpose of the Second Coming in the air : to obtain a bride and to judge the believers in the air (Ro 14:10, 2Co 5:10, Rev 19:7~8)[46)]
6) Jesus Christ coming in the air is to reap the harvest (1Th 4:17, Mt 3:30, Rev 14:15~16)[47)].

---

44) Mt24:36 "No one knows about that day or hour, not even the angels in heaven, nor the Son, but only the Father.
Mt25:13 "Therefore keep watch, because you do not know the day or the hour.
Mk13:32 "No one knows about that day or hour, not even the angels in heaven, nor the Son, but only the Father.

45) 1Th4:16 For the Lord Himself will come down from heaven, with a loud command, with the voice of the archangel and with the trumpet call of God, and the dead in Christ will rise first.
1Th4:17 After that, we who are still alive and are left will be caught up together with them in the clouds to meet the Lord in the air. And so we will be with the Lord forever.

46) Ro14:10 You, then, why do you judge your brother? Or why do you look down on your brother? For we will all stand before God's judgment seat.
2Co5:10 For we must all appear before the judgment seat of Christ, that each one may receive what is due him for the things done while in the body, whether good or bad.
Rev19:7 Let us rejoice and be glad and give Him glory! For the wedding of the Lamb has come, and His bride has made herself ready.
Rev19:8 Fine linen, bright and clean, was given her to wear." (Fine linen stands for the righteous acts of the saints.)

47) 1Th4:17 After that, we who are still alive and are left will be caught up together with them in the clouds to meet the Lord in the air. And so we will be with the Lord forever.
Mt13:30 Let both grow together until the harvest. At that time I will

b. **<u>The Second coming on the earth</u>**

1) Time: After the Great Tribulation, He will come down from the air to the ground (Mt 24:29～31)[48].

2) Place: He will come down to the Mount of Olives and then head for Armageddon (Acts 1:11, Rev 1:7, Isa 63:1～2, Rev 19:11～16)[49].

---

tell the harvesters: First collect the weeds and tie them in bundles to be burned; then gather the wheat and bring it into My barn.'"

Rev14:15 Then another angel came out of the temple and called in a loud voice to Him who was sitting on the cloud, "Take Your sickle and reap, because the time to reap has come, for the harvest of the earth is ripe."

Rev14:16 So He who was seated on the cloud swung His sickle over the earth, and the earth was harvested.

48) Mt24:29 "Immediately after the distress of those days "'the sun will be darkened, and the moon will not give its light; the stars will fall from the sky, and the heavenly bodies will be shaken.'

Mt24:30 "At that time the sign of the Son of Man will appear in the sky, and all the nations of the earth will mourn. They will see the Son of Man coming on the clouds of the sky, with power and great glory.

Mt24:31 And He will send His angels with a loud trumpet call, and they will gather His elect from the four winds, from one end of the heavens to the other.

49) Ac1:11 "Men of Galilee," they said, "why do you stand here looking into the sky? This same Jesus, who has been taken from you into heaven, will come back in the same way you have seen Him go into heaven."

Rev1:7 Look, He is coming with the clouds, and every eye will see Him, even those who pierced Him; and all the peoples of the earth will mourn because of Him. So shall it be! Amen.

Isa63:1 Who is this coming from Edom, from Bozrah, with His garments stained crimson? Who is this, robed in splendor, striding forward in the greatness of His strength? "It is I, speaking in righteousness, mighty to save."

Isa63:2 Why are Your garments red, like those of one treading the winepress?

Rev19:11 I saw heaven standing open and there before me was a white horse, whose rider is called Faithful and True. With

3) Appearance: coming on the clouds (Ac 1:11, Mt 24:30)[50].
4) Method: coming publicly (Rev 1:7, Mt 24:30, 31)[51].
5) Status: coming as the King of kings and the Lord of lords.
6) Purpose :
a) To save the remnant in Israel (Ro 11:25～27)[52].

---

justice He judges and makes war.
Rev19:12 His eyes are like blazing fire, and on His head are many crowns. He has a name written on Him that no one knows but He Himself.
Rev19:13 He is dressed in a robe dipped in blood, and His name is the Word of God.
Rev19:14 The armies of heaven were following Him, riding on white horses and dressed in fine linen, white and clean.
Rev19:15 Out of His mouth comes a sharp sword with which to strike down the nations. "He will rule them with an iron scepter." He treads the winepress of the fury of the wrath of God Almighty.
Rev19:16 On His robe and on His thigh He has this name written: KING OF KINGS AND LORD OF LORDS.

50) Ac1:11 "Men of Galilee," they said, "why do you stand here looking into the sky? This same Jesus, who has been taken from you into heaven, will come back in the same way you have seen Him go into heaven."
Mt24:30 "At that time the sign of the Son of Man will appear in the sky, and all the nations of the earth will mourn. They will see the Son of Man coming on the clouds of the sky, with power and great glory.

51) Rev1:7 Look, He is coming with the clouds, and every eye will see Him, even those who pierced Him; and all the peoples of the earth will mourn because of Him. So shall it be! Amen.
Mt24:30 "At that time the sign of the Son of Man will appear in the sky, and all the nations of the earth will mourn. They will see the Son of Man coming on the clouds of the sky, with power and great glory.
Mt24:31 And He will send His angels with a loud trumpet call, and they will gather His elect from the four winds, from one end of the heavens to the other.

52) Ro11:25 I do not want you to be ignorant of this mystery, brothers,

b) To destroy the Antichrist and imprison Satan in the Abyss through the war of Armageddon (Rev 19:11～16, Isa 63:1～6)[53].

c). To judge the Nations (Mt 25:31～46, Joel 3:1～2, Mic 4:3～4)[54].

---

so that you may not be conceited: Israel has experienced a hardening in part until the full number of the Gentiles has come in.

Ro11:26 And so all Israel will be saved, as it is written: "The deliverer will come from Zion; He will turn godlessness away from Jacob.

Ro11:27 And this is My covenant with them when I take away their sins."

53) Rev19:11～16 ☞See footnote 49

Isa63:1 Who is this coming from Edom, from Bozrah, with His garments stained crimson? Who is this, robed in splendor, striding forward in the greatness of His strength? "It is I, speaking in righteousness, mighty to save."

Isa63:2 Why are Your garments red, like those of one treading the winepress?

Isa63:3 "I have trodden the winepress alone; from the nations no one was with Me. I trampled them in My anger and trod them down in My wrath; their blood spattered My garments, and I stained all My clothing.

Isa63:4 For the day of vengeance was in My heart, and the year of My redemption has come.

Isa63:5 I looked, but there was no one to help, I was appalled that no one gave support; so My own arm worked salvation for Me, and My own wrath sustained Me.

Isa63:6 I trampled the nations in My anger; in My wrath I made them drunk and poured their blood on the ground."

54) Mt25:31 "When the Son of Man comes in His glory, and all the angels with Him, He will sit on His throne in heavenly glory.

Mt25:32 All the nations will be gathered before Him, and He will separate the people one from another as a shepherd separates the sheep from the goats.

Mt25:33 He will put the sheep on His right and the goats on His left.

Mt25:34 "Then the King will say to those on His right, 'Come, you who are blessed by My Father; take your inheritance, the kingdom prepared for you since the creation of the world.

Mt25:35 For I was hungry and you gave Me something to eat, I was thirsty and you gave Me something to drink, I was a stranger and you invited Me in,
Mt25:36 I needed clothes and you clothed Me, I was sick and you looked after Me, I was in prison and you came to visit me.'
Mt25:37 "Then the righteous will answer Him, 'Lord, when did we see You hungry and feed You, or thirsty and give You something to drink?
Mt25:38 When did we see You a stranger and invite You in, or needing clothes and clothe You?
Mt25:39 When did we see You sick or in prison and go to visit You?'
Mt25:40 "The King will reply, 'I tell you the truth, whatever you did for one of the least of these brothers of Mine, you did for me.'
Mt25:41 "Then He will say to those on His left, 'Depart from Me, you who are cursed, into the eternal fire prepared for the devil and his angels.
Mt25:42 For I was hungry and you gave Me nothing to eat, I was thirsty and you gave Me nothing to drink,
Mt25:43 I was a stranger and you did not invite Me in, I needed clothes and you did not clothe Me, I was sick and in prison and you did not look after me.'
Mt25:44 "They also will answer, 'Lord, when did we see You hungry or thirsty or a stranger or needing clothes or sick or in prison, and did not help You?'
Mt25:45 "He will reply, 'I tell you the truth, whatever you did not do for one of the least of these, you did not do for me.'
Mt25:46 "Then they will go away to eternal punishment, but the righteous to eternal life."
Joel3:1 'In those days and at that time, when I restore the fortunes of Judah and Jerusalem,
Joel3:2 I will gather all nations and bring them down to the Valley of Jehoshaphat. There I will enter into judgment against them concerning My inheritance, My people Israel, for they scattered My people among the nations and divided up My land.
Mic4:3 He will judge between many peoples and will settle disputes for strong nations far and wide. They will beat their swords into plowshares and their spears into pruning hooks. Nation will not take up sword against nation, nor will they train for war anymore.
Mic4:4 Every man will sit under his own vine and under his own fig

d). To rule over all nations during the Millennial Kingdom (Rev 20:1～6)[55].

2. every eye will see Him
All who live on the earth will see the Lord

3. Even those who pierced Him will see Him
Those who are dead and trapped in Hades (everyone who pierced Jesus) will also see (Jn 19:32～34)[56].

4. all tribes of the earth will mourn on account of Him.
All tribes of the earth means all the tribes of Israel (Mt

---

tree, and no one will make them afraid, for the LORD Almighty has spoken.

55) Rev20:1 And I saw an angel coming down out of heaven, having the key to the Abyss and holding in his hand a great chain.
Rev20:2 He seized the dragon, that ancient serpent, who is the devil, or Satan, and bound him for a thousand years.
Rev20:3 He threw him into the Abyss, and locked and sealed it over him, to keep him from deceiving the nations anymore until the thousand years were ended. After that, he must be set free for a short time.
Rev20:4 I saw thrones on which were seated those who had been given authority to judge. And I saw the souls of those who had been beheaded because of their testimony for Jesus and because of the word of God. They had not worshiped the beast or his image and had not received his mark on their foreheads or their hands. They came to life and reigned with Christ a thousand years.
Rev20:5 (The rest of the dead did not come to life until the thousand years were ended.) This is the first resurrection.
Rev20:6 Blessed and holy are those who have part in the first resurrection. The second death has no power over them, but they will be priests of God and of Christ and will reign with Him for a thousand years.

56) Jn19:32 The soldiers therefore came and broke the legs of the first man who had been crucified with Jesus, and then those of the other.
Jn19:33 But when they came to Jesus and found that He was already dead, they did not break His legs.
Jn19:34 Instead, one of the soldiers pierced Jesus' side with a spear, bringing a sudden flow of blood and water.

24:30, Zec 12:10～14)[57].

Verse 8 "I am the Alpha and the Omega," says the Lord God, "who is, and who was, and who is to come, the Almighty."

1. "I am the Alpha and the Omega."
   It means He is the beginning and the end and also first and the last. God is the planner, supplier and fulfiller of all things. In Revelation, He completes the book that started in Genesis.
2. "who is, and who was, and who is to come, the Almighty."
   God is who exists now, has existed even before eternity and who is to come. God will not stay in the third heaven eternally but will come down to the new earth on the day when His plans are completed, to be with the believers forever. We should abandon the idea that we ascend into heaven and live there forever.

Verse 9 I, John, your brother and companion in the suffering and kingdom and patient endurance that are ours in

---

57) Mt24:30 "At that time the sign of the Son of Man will appear in the sky, and all the nations of the earth will mourn. They will see the Son of Man coming on the clouds of the sky, with power and great glory.
Zec12:10 "And I will pour out on the house of David and the inhabitants of Jerusalem a spirit of grace and supplication. They will look on Me, the One they have pierced, and they will mourn for Him as one mourns for an only child, and grieve bitterly for Him as one grieves for a firstborn son.
Zec12:11 On that day the weeping in Jerusalem will be great, like the weeping of Hadad Rimmon in the plain of Megiddo.
Zec12:12 The land will mourn, each clan by itself, with their wives by themselves: the clan of the house of David and their wives, the clan of the house of Nathan and their wives,
Zec12:13 the clan of the house of Levi and their wives, the clan of Shimei and their wives,
Zec12:14 and all the rest of the clans and their wives.

Jesus, was on the island of Patmos because of the word of God and the testimony of Jesus.

1. I, John, your brother
   John became a brother of Jesus Christ (Jn 20:17)[58]. In order to receive this word of God we should be able to become brother both to Jesus Christ and to John.
2. In the suffering of Jesus
   We can enjoy good things such as salvation, grace and power in Christ, but we have to participate in the tribulation in Jesus. We are in suffering and persecution in Jesus owing to our honesty and sincerity. It is because the world is wicked and dishonest.
3. Kingdom that are ours in Jesus
   When we are in Jesus, we also participate in the Kingdom of Jesus (Ro 14:17)[59].
   Today's church life is the life of the kingdom of Jesus. This means to be governed by the Kingdom of Heaven according to God's nature (Ac 14:22, Jn 16:33)[60].
   The kingdoms of today are not of glory, and a kingdom of glory is formed when Jesus Christ returns as king (Rev 19:1 ~6, 20:1~6)[61].

---

58) Jn20:17 Jesus said, "Do not hold on to Me, for I have not yet returned to the Father. Go instead to My brothers and tell them, 'I am returning to My Father and your Father, to My God and your God.'"

59) Ro14:17 For the kingdom of God is not a matter of eating and drinking, but of righteousness, peace and joy in the Holy Spirit,

60) Ac14:22 strengthening the disciples and encouraging them to remain true to the faith. "We must go through many hardships to enter the kingdom of God," they said.
Jn16:33 "I have told you these things, so that in Me you may have peace. In this world you will have trouble. But take heart! I have overcome the world."

61) Rev19:1 After this I heard what sounded like the roar of a great

4. Companion in the patient endurance that are ours in Jesus.
   Today, we must be companions in the patience of Jesus. It is because today's kingdom in Jesus is a kingdom of suffering. We are not in His sovereign kingdom yet, but a kingdom to receive suffering; we must go through much tribulation in order to enter the Kingdom of Christ (Lk 21:19, 2Ti 2:12, Ac 14:22)[62].
5. was on the island of Patmos because of the word of God and the testimony of Jesus.
   This means that apostle John had lived a life for the gospel and for the word of God and had been exiled to Patmos as a witness of Jesus Christ (circa 98CE).

Verse 10 On the Lord's Day I was in the Spirit, and I heard behind me a loud voice like a trumpet,

---

multitude in heaven shouting: "Hallelujah! Salvation and glory and power belong to our God,

Rev19:2 for true and just are His judgments. He has condemned the great prostitute who corrupted the earth by her adulteries. He has avenged on her the blood of His servants."

Rev19:3 And again they shouted: "Hallelujah! The smoke from her goes up for ever and ever."

Rev19:4 The twenty-four elders and the four living creatures fell down and worshiped God, who was seated on the throne. And they cried: "Amen, Hallelujah!"

Rev19:5 Then a voice came from the throne, saying: "Praise our God, all you His servants, you who fear Him, both small and great!"

Rev19:6 Then I heard what sounded like a great multitude, like the roar of rushing waters and like loud peals of thunder, shouting: "Hallelujah! For our Lord God Almighty reigns.

62) Lk21:19 By standing firm you will gain life.(Niv)
Lk21:19 In your patience possess ye your souls.(Kjv)
2Ti2:12 if we endure, we will also reign with Him. If we disown Him, He will also disown us;
Ac14:22 strengthening the disciples and encouraging them to remain true to the faith. "We must go through many hardships to enter the kingdom of God," they said.

1. <u>On the Lord's day</u>
   Lord's Day means the first day of the week, namely the day of the Lord's Resurrection (Jn 20:1, Ac 20:7, 1Co 16:2)[63]. From this time onwards, Christians started to have a worship service on the Lord's day (Sundays).
2. <u>was in the Spirit</u>
   It means to be inspired by the Holy Spirit, so that impressions from the Holy Spirit are transmitted to the heart, and one can hear, see, and speak in the spirit. We should be able to sense whether we are in the flesh or in the spirit (inner person).
3. <u>I heard behind me a loud voice like a trumpet</u>
   A loud voice like a trumpet sound means an obvious and loud voice. When we are inspired by the Holy Spirit, we can not only hear a loud voice like a trumpet sound but also can see all the visions of the Church (1Ki 19:12, Job 4:16)[64].
   ※ Among the believers of the Old Testament, even the prophets heard the Lord's small voice.

Verse 11 which said: "Write on a scroll what you see and send it to the seven churches: to Ephesus, Smyrna, Pergamum, Thyatira, Sardis, Philadelphia and Laodicea."

---

63) Jn20:1 Early on the first day of the week, while it was still dark, Mary Magdalene went to the tomb and saw that the stone had been removed from the entrance.
Ac20:7 On the first day of the week we came together to break bread. Paul spoke to the people and, because he intended to leave the next day, kept on talking until midnight.
1Co16:2 On the first day of every week, each one of you should set aside a sum of money in keeping with his income, saving it up, so that when I come no collections will have to be made.

64) 1Ki19:12 After the earthquake came a fire, but the LORD was not in the fire. And after the fire came a gentle whisper.
Job4:16 It stopped, but I could not tell what it was. A form stood before my eyes, and I heard a hushed voice:

1. Write on a scroll what you see

Chapters 2 and 3 are about the seven churches written by apostle John under the inspiration of the Holy Spirit.

2. send it to the seven churches: to Ephesus, Smyrna, Pergamum, Thyatira, Sardis, Philadelphia, and Laodicea.

These seven churches were in existence in Asia when John was alive. The reason why God shows us the condition of these seven churches is in order to show us the condition of all the churches in the world and the changing phases of the Church throughout history. That is, it is a record to show to us today the condition and circumstances and transitions of all the churches from the past until today and up to the second coming of the Lord.

Verse 12 I turned around to see the voice that was speaking to me. And when I turned I saw seven golden lampstands,

1. I turned around

It is necessary to turn (our body) when listening to the voice of the Lord.

Turning seems to be a small thing but often not easy to turn.

2. I saw **seven golden lampstands**

In the book of Revelation, churches appeared as lampstands (lighthouse). In the New Testament, the Church is the gathering of the believers, the body of Christ and the temple of God (Eph 2:21~22, 4:12, 5:23)[65].

---

65) Eph2:21 In Him the whole building is joined together and rises to become a holy temple in the Lord.
Eph2:22 And in Him you too are being built together to become a dwelling in which God lives by His Spirit.
Eph4:12 to prepare God's people for works of service, so that the body of Christ may be built up
Eph5:23 For the husband is the head of the wife as Christ is the head of the church, His body, of which He is the Savior.

Except the book of Revelation, there is no other place that describes the Church as a lampstand (Rev 1:20)[66].

The Church, the lampstands should be a place to shine through the darkness. In order for the Church to shine, there must be a life of Christ in them.

God is light, Christ is a lamp of shining light and the Church is a lampstand (lighthouse) to support the lamp.

The lampstands are made of gold and it means the Church is woven with the nature of God.

Verse 13 and among the lampstands was someone like a son of man, dressed in a robe reaching down to His feet and with a golden sash around His chest.

1. Someone "like a son of man"
   a. Whenever He is related to the Church revealed within the human nature. The very fact that He is still the Son of Man even after His ascension means He had not taken His human nature off (Rev 14:14, Da 10:16, 7:13)[67].
   b. As a high priest in the Heavenly temple, He is looking after the churches in His nature (Heb 5:5～6, 7:26～28)[68].

---

66) Rev1:20 The mystery of the seven stars that you saw in My right hand and of the seven golden lampstands is this: The seven stars are the angels of the seven churches, and the seven lampstands are the seven churches.

67) Rev14:14 I looked, and there before me was a white cloud, and seated on the cloud was one "like a son of man" with a crown of gold on His head and a sharp sickle in His hand.
Da10:16 Then one who looked like a man touched my lips, and I opened my mouth and began to speak. I said to the one standing before me, "I am overcome with anguish because of the vision, my lord, and I am helpless.
Da7:13 "In my vision at night I looked, and there before me was one like a son of man, coming with the clouds of heaven. He approached the Ancient of Days and was led into His presence.

68) Heb5:5 So Christ also did not take upon Himself the glory of

2. clothed with a garment down to the feet and girded about the chest with a golden band
   Gold symbolizes God's nature. A garment down to the feet belongs to the priest and priests in the Old Testament girded a band around the waist while conducting their priest's duties.
   But a high priest who looks after the Church girds a band of love in His chest while looking after the Church.

Verse 14 : The hair on His head was white like wool, as white as snow, and His eyes were like blazing fire.

1. His head and hair were white like wool.
   White head hair symbolizes His holiness and purity and old age and ancient times (Da 7:9, Job 15:10)[69].
2. His eyes were like a blazing fire
   a. In the book of Song of Solomon 5:12 describes His sweet love and the eyes of Christ as the eyes of a dove.
   b. Eyes like a flame of fire expresses the minute (= refined) eyes of judgment and observation (Heb 12:29, Ro 14:10)[70].

---

becoming a high priest. But God said to Him, "You are My Son; today I have become Your Father."

Heb5:6 And He says in another place, "You are a priest forever, in the order of Melchizedek."

Heb7:26 Such a high priest meets our need—one who is holy, blameless, pure, set apart from sinners, exalted above the heavens.

Heb7:27 Unlike the other high priests, He does not need to offer sacrifices day after day, first for His own sins, and then for the sins of the people. He sacrificed for their sins once for all when He offered Himself.

Heb7:28 For the law appoints as high priests men who are weak; but the oath, which came after the law, appointed the Son, who has been made perfect forever.

69) Da7:9 "As I looked, "thrones were set in place, and the Ancient of Days took His seat. His clothing was as white as snow; the hair of His head was white like wool. His throne was flaming with fire, and its wheels were all ablaze.

70) Hev12:29 for our "God is a consuming fire."

Verse 15 His feet were like bronze glowing in a furnace, and His voice was like the sound of rushing waters.

1. His feet were like bronze glowing in a furnace
   a. His feet were like fine brass symbolizes His perfect and shining footsteps giving Him the qualification to execute the holy judgment (Da 10:6, Rev 10:1, Eze 1:7)[71].
   ※ Footsteps means His life behaviour.
   b. refined in a furnace means His behaviour has been burned, tested and made perfect and complete (Heb 5:8-9)[72].
2. His voice was like the sound of rushing waters.
   a. When He came as the Lord of salvation, His voice was gentle and tender (Jn 20:16)[73].
   b. When He comes as the Lord of judgment, His voice will sound grave and solemn like thunder and the roar of rushing water (Eze 1:24, 43:2, Rev 19:6)[74].

Ro14:10 You, then, why do you judge your brother? Or why do you look down on your brother? For we will all stand before God's judgment seat.

71) Da10:6 His body was like chrysolite, His face like lightning, His eyes like flaming torches, His arms and legs like the gleam of burnished bronze, and His voice like the sound of a multitude.
Rev10:1 Then I saw another mighty angel coming down from heaven. He was robed in a cloud, with a rainbow above His head; His face was like the sun, and His legs were like fiery pillars.
Eze1:7 Their legs were straight; their feet were like those of a calf and gleamed like burnished bronze.

72) Hev8:9 It will not be like the covenant I made with their forefathers when I took them by the hand to lead them out of Egypt, because they did not remain faithful to My covenant, and I turned away from them, declares the Lord.
73) Jn20:16 Jesus said to her, "Mary." She turned toward Him and cried out in Aramaic, "Rabboni!" (which means Teacher).
74) Eze1:24 When the creatures moved, I heard the sound of their wings, like the roar of rushing waters, like the voice of the Almighty, like the tumult of an army. When they stood still,

Verse 16 In His right hand He held seven stars, and coming out of His mouth was a sharp, double-edged sword. His face was like the sun shining in all its brilliance.

1. In His right hand He held seven stars
   Seven stars are the seven churches' messengers shining like stars. As Christ walks in the midst, He is holding the angels of seven churches with His right hand (Rev 1:20)[75].
2. And out of His mouth came a sharp double-edged sword.
   a. A sharp two-edged sword is the sword of the word of God (Heb 4:12, Eph 6:17, Rev 19:15)[76].
   b. The book of the Song of Solomon 5:16[77], says that His mouth is very sweet and Luke 4:22[78], says that "gracious

---

they lowered their wings.

Eze43:2 and I saw the glory of the God of Israel coming from the east. His voice was like the roar of rushing waters, and the land was radiant with His glory.

Rev19:6 Then I heard what sounded like a great multitude, like the roar of rushing waters and like loud peals of thunder, shouting: "Hallelujah! For our Lord God Almighty reigns.

75) Rev1:20 The mystery of the seven stars that you saw in My right hand and of the seven golden lampstands is this: The seven stars are the angels of the seven churches, and the seven lampstands are the seven churches.

76) Hev4:12 For the word of God is living and active. Sharper than any double-edged sword, it penetrates even to dividing soul and spirit, joints and marrow; it judges the thoughts and attitudes of the heart.

Eph6:17 Take the helmet of salvation and the sword of the Spirit, which is the word of God.

Rev19:15 Out of His mouth comes a sharp sword with which to strike down the nations. "He will rule them with an iron scepter." He treads the winepress of the fury of the wrath of God Almighty.

77) SS5:16 His mouth is sweetness itself; he is altogether lovely. This is my lover, this my friend, O daughters of Jerusalem.

78) Lk4:22 All spoke well of Him and were amazed at the gracious words that came from His lips. "Isn't this Joseph's son?" they asked.

words proceeded out of His mouth." However, 'out of His mouth went a sharp two-edged sword' means His sword of words which discerns and judges and kills.

3. His face was like the sun shining in all its brilliance.

In 2 Corinthians 4:16[79], He shines the light of the knowledge of the glory of God in order to give life to believers, but here the sun shining in its strength means the light of judgment which uncovers and reveals all things (Eze 43:2, Da 10:6, Rev 10:1)[80].

But here, the sun shining in all its brilliance means the light of judgment, which reveals all things with nothing to be hidden (Rev 10:1)[81].

Verse 17 When I saw Him, I fell at His feet as though dead. Then He placed His right hand on me and said: "Do not be afraid. I am the First and the Last.

1. I fell at His feet as though dead

When John was reclining in the bosom of 'Lamb of God'

---

79) 2Co4:16 Therefore we do not lose heart. Though outwardly we are wasting away, yet inwardly we are being renewed day by day.

80) Eze43:2 and I saw the glory of the God of Israel coming from the east. His voice was like the roar of rushing waters, and the land was radiant with His glory.

Da10:6 His body was like chrysolite, His face like lightning, His eyes like flaming torches, His arms and legs like the gleam of burnished bronze, and His voice like the sound of a multitude.

Rev10:1 Then I saw another mighty angel coming down from heaven. He was robed in a cloud, with a rainbow above His head; His face was like the sun, and His legs were like fiery pillars.

81) Rev10:1 ☞See footnote 80) on the previous page

Jesus at the last supper, Jesus was soft and tender, but when John saw the face of the Lord of judgment he became, through fear, like a dead man (Heb 10:30~31, Da 10:7~9, Rev 19:15~16)[82]

2. <u>Then he placed His right hand on me and said: "do not be afraid</u>" (Da 8:15~19)[83]

   The Lord, the Lord of judgment, lays His right hand on John and comforts him, John, who had shared in the tribulation and kingdom and patience of Jesus.

---

82) Hev10:30 For we know Him who said, "It is Mine to avenge; I will repay," and again, "The Lord will judge His people."
Hev10:31 It is a dreadful thing to fall into the hands of the living God.
Da10:7 I, Daniel, was the only one who saw the vision; the men with me did not see it, but such terror overwhelmed them that they fled and hid themselves.
Da10:8 So I was left alone, gazing at this great vision; I had no strength left, my face turned deathly pale and I was helpless.
Da10:9 Then I heard Him speaking, and as I listened to Him, I fell into a deep sleep, my face to the ground.
Rev19:15 Out of His mouth comes a sharp sword with which to strike down the nations. "He will rule them with an iron scepter." He treads the winepress of the fury of the wrath of God Almighty.
Rev19:16 On His robe and on His thigh he has this name written: KING OF KINGS AND LORD OF LORDS.

83) Da8:15 While I, Daniel, was watching the vision and trying to understand it, there before me stood one who looked like a man.
Da8:16 And I heard a man's voice from the Ulai calling, "Gabriel, tell this man the meaning of the vision."
Da8:17 As he came near the place where I was standing, I was terrified and fell prostrate. "Son of man," he said to me, "understand that the vision concerns the time of the end."
Da8:18 While he was speaking to me, I was in a deep sleep, with my face to the ground. Then he touched me and raised me to my feet.
Da8:19 He said: "I am going to tell you what will happen later in the time of wrath, because the vision concerns the appointed time of the end.

3. I am the first and the last

   Expresses the fact that Jesus is the beginning and the end.

Verse 18 I am the Living One; I was dead, and now look, I am alive for ever and ever! And I hold the keys of death and Hades.

1. I am the Living One; I was dead

   This speaks of the resurrection from the dead. This resurrection life is eternal and cannot be killed.

2. And I hold the keys of death and Hades

   Christ destroyed death on the cross and conquered Hades in the resurrection (Ac 2:23~27, Ro 6:9)[84].

   Because of man's fall and sin, death entered the earth. All sinful people die, and Hades is collecting dead souls (Rev 6:8)[85].

   The resurrected sovereign Lord has the keys to this death and Hades.

---

84) Ac2:23 This man was handed over to you by God's set purpose and foreknowledge; and you, with the help of wicked men, put Him to death by nailing Him to the cross.
Ac2:24 But God raised Him from the dead, freeing Him from the agony of death, because it was impossible for death to keep its hold on Him.
Ac2:25 David said about Him: "'I saw the Lord always before me. Because He is at my right hand, I will not be shaken.
Ac2:26 Therefore my heart is glad and my tongue rejoices; my body also will live in hope,
Ac2:27 because You will not abandon me to the grave, nor will You let Your Holy One see decay.

85) Rev6:8 I looked, and there before me was a pale horse! Its rider was named Death, and Hades was following close behind him. They were given power over a fourth of the earth to kill by sword, famine and plague, and by the wild beasts of the earth.

Verse 19 "Write, therefore, what you have seen, what is now and what will take place later.

1. What you have seen (Rev 1:1~20)
2. what is now (Rev 2:1~3:22)
3. what will take place later (Rev 4:1~22:5)

[the seven stars]

Verse 20 The mystery of the seven stars that you saw in My right hand and of the seven golden lampstands is this: The seven stars are the angels of the seven churches, and the seven lampstands are the seven churches.

1. Of the numerous churches scattered at the time of the apostle John (which reached 63 after Pentecost), choosing only these seven churches means that every church (from the Ascension to the Second Coming) can be divided into seven parts.
2. The Lord sovereignly prepared all church history through seven churches in Asia Minor.
3. The seven churches are the record of the seven ways in which Satan infiltrates and attacks the church. We must be able to cope with this.

Chapter 2

Introduction

[The seven churches]

1. The letters to the seven churches in chapters 2 and 3 are a record of the current state of the seven churches at the time of writing.
2. However, the content regarding these seven churches is also of prophetic nature (a prophetic symbol of the progress of the church).
   a. The church of Ephesus (the Church immediately following the early Church)
   A picture of the Church during the latter half of the first century.
   b. The church of Smyrna (the Church until Constantine the Great in 313 AD)
   From the late first century, the church was under persecution until the Christianity of Constantine the Great.
   c. The church of Pergamos (the Church from 313 AD to 590 AD)
   From the time of Constantine to the establishment of the papacy in the late 6th century, the Church is compromised by the world.
   d. The church of Thyatira (the Church from 590 AD until the Second Coming)
   From the proclamation of the papacy in the late 6th century to the time of the Second Coming, this is a Church that is apostate to the end.
   e. The church of Sardis (from the beginning of the 16th century until the Second Coming)
   Represents Protestantism from the Reformation of the early 16th century until the Second Coming of Christ.
   f. The church of Philadelphia (early 19th century to the Second Coming)
   The Church of brotherly love from the early 19th century until the Second Coming of the Lord, the recovery of

proper church life.

g. The church of Laodicea (late 19th century to the Second Coming)
 A picture of a fallen church from the late 19th century until the Second Coming of the Lord where brotherly love has grown luke warm.

[To the Church in Ephesus]
(After the Early Church to the late first century)

Verse 1: "To the angel of the church in Ephesus write: These are the words of Him who holds the seven stars in His right hand and walks among the seven golden lampstands.

▣Meaning of 'Ephesus' in Greek: 'Desirable'

1. Him who holds the **seven stars** in His right hand
The Lord is the One who holds the messengers of the seven churches in His right hand.
2. and walks among the **seven golden lampstands**
The Lord is the One who is always looking out for and taking care of the churches. The Lord reveals Himself to the church in Ephesus by showing them that it is He who holds the seven stars in His right hand, and it is He who comes and goes among the churches as their caretaker.

Verse 2: I know your deeds, your hard work and your perseverance. I know that you cannot tolerate wicked people, that you have tested those who claim to be apostles but are not, and have found them false.

1. I know your deeds, your hard work, and your perseverance, I know that you cannot tolerate wicked men,
The church in Ephesus was a church of good behaviour, hard work and endurance.
The Church should accept repentant sinners, but must not tolerate wicked men (2Ti 3:5, 1Co 5:9～13)[86].

2. that you have tested those who claim to be apostles but are not, and have found them false.
   a. After the early church, there were many people who were not apostles, though claiming to be such, who were confusing the church (Gal 1:6~9)[87].
   b. In order to expose these people, you must:
      1) test their spirits (1Jn 4:1)[88]
      2) examine their teaching (1Ti 4:1)[89]

---

86) 2Ti3:5 having a form of godliness but denying its power. Have nothing to do with them.
1Co5:9 I have written you in my letter not to associate with sexually immoral people--
1Co5:10 not at all meaning the people of this world who are immoral, or the greedy and swindlers, or idolaters. In that case you would have to leave this world.
1Co5:11 But now I am writing you that you must not associate with anyone who calls himself a brother but is sexually immoral or greedy, an idolater or a slanderer, a drunkard or a swindler. With such a man do not even eat.
1Co5:12 What business is it of mine to judge those outside the church? Are you not to judge those inside?
1Co5:13 God will judge those outside. "Expel the wicked man from among you."

87) Gal 1:6 I am astonished that you are so quickly deserting the One who called you by the grace of Christ and are turning to a different gospel--
Gal 1:7 which is really no gospel at all. Evidently some people are throwing you into confusion and are trying to pervert the gospel of Christ.
Gal 1:8 But even if we or an angel from heaven should preach a gospel other than the one we preached to you, let him be eternally condemned!
Gal 1:9 As we have already said, so now I say again: If anybody is preaching to you a gospel other than what you accepted, let him be eternally condemned!

88) 1Jn4:1 Dear friends, do not believe every spirit, but test the spirits to see whether they are from God, because many false prophets have gone out into the world.

89) 1Ti4:1 The Spirit clearly says that in later times some will abandon the faith and follow deceiving spirits and things taught by demons.

3) recognize them by their fruit (Mt 7:15~18)[90]

Verse 3 You have persevered and have endured hardships for My name, and have not grown weary.

1. For the name of the Lord, we should persevere and endure, and serve the Lord with diligence.
2. The church in Ephesus had persevered and endured hardships for the name of the Lord and served the Lord diligently.

Verse 4 Yet I hold this against you: You have forsaken the love you had at first.

1. <u>Yet I hold this against you</u>
   a. whether an individual or a church, there are many things that can be reproved, but it is difficult to do so. In this day and age, we must be able to distinguish faults and rebuke with love (2Ti 3:16, Heb 12:5~8)[91].
   b. rebuke = by God's word (Ps 119:9)[92].

---

90) Mt7:15 "Watch out for false prophets. They come to you in sheep's clothing, but inwardly they are ferocious wolves.
Mt7:16 By their fruit you will recognize them. Do people pick grapes from thornbushes, or figs from thistles?
Mt7:17 Likewise every good tree bears good fruit, but a bad tree bears bad fruit.
Mt7:18 A good tree cannot bear bad fruit, and a bad tree cannot bear good fruit.

91) 2Ti3:16 All Scripture is God-breathed and is useful for teaching, rebuking, correcting and training in righteousness,
Hev12:5 And you have forgotten that word of encouragement that addresses you as sons: "My son, do not make light of the Lord's discipline, and do not lose heart when He rebukes you,
Hev12:6 because the Lord disciplines those He loves, and He punishes everyone He accepts as a son."
Hev12:7 Endure hardship as discipline; God is treating you as sons. For what son is not disciplined by his father?
Hev12:8 If you are not disciplined (and everyone undergoes discipline), then you are illegitimate children and not true sons.

92) Ps119:9 How can a young man keep his way pure? By living according to Your word.

advise as a brother (Mt 18:15)[93]
tell it to the church (Mt 18:17)[94]
God rebukes with discipline (Ps 119:67, 71, Heb 12:5~11)[95]

2. You have forsaken your first love
   a. first love (Greek): we can see it as the first and greatest love (Mt 22:37, Jn 21:15~17)[96].

---

93) Mt18:15 "If your brother sins against you, go and show him his fault, just between the two of you. If he listens to you, you have won your brother over.

94) Mt18:17 If he refuses to listen to them, tell it to the church; and if he refuses to listen even to the church, treat him as you would a pagan or a tax collector.

95) Ps119:67 Before I was afflicted I went astray, but now I obey Your word.
Ps119:71 It was good for me to be afflicted so that I might learn Your decrees.
Hev12:5 And you have forgotten that word of encouragement that addresses you as sons: "My son, do not make light of the Lord's discipline, and do not lose heart when He rebukes you,
Hev12:6 because the Lord disciplines those He loves, and He punishes everyone He accepts as a son."
Hev12:7 Endure hardship as discipline; God is treating you as sons. For what son is not disciplined by his father?
Hev12:8 If you are not disciplined (and everyone undergoes discipline), then you are illegitimate children and not true sons.
Hev12:9 Moreover, we have all had human fathers who disciplined us and we respected them for it. How much more should we submit to the Father of our spirits and live!
Hev12:10 Our fathers disciplined us for a little while as they thought best; but God disciplines us for our good, that we may share in His holiness.
Hev12:11 No discipline seems pleasant at the time, but painful. Later on, however, it produces a harvest of righteousness and peace for those who have been trained by it.

96) Mt22:37 Jesus replied: "'Love the Lord your God with all your heart and with all your soul and with all your mind.'
Jn21:15 When they had finished eating, Jesus said to Simon Peter,

b. shows that the corruption of the church begins with forsaking the first love for the Lord.
c. even though a church may have many other good characteristics, such as hard work, perseverance, diligence, and so on, forsaking your first love is the root of all corruption of a church and its development.
d. even though the church in Ephesus had worked hard and there were a lot of good things, their love had decreased compared to the beginning (had grown cold).
e. whatever we do, it must come from our love for the Lord. Love provides the motivation for everything we do for the Lord.
f. everything we do should just be an expression of our love for Him.

Verse 5 Consider how far you have fallen! Repent and do the things you did at first. If you do not repent, I will come to you and remove your lampstand from its place.

1. Remember the height from which you have fallen!
   It is important to think about the height from which our first love has fallen. And once we have determined that, we must repent, and turn, and recover the first love.
2. Repent and do the things you did at first
   a. To repent and do the things we did at first, and to recover the first love means to recover the first love through a life of inner fullness.

"Simon son of John, do you truly love Me more than these?" "Yes, Lord," he said, "you know that I love you." Jesus said, "Feed My lambs."

Jn21:16 Again Jesus said, "Simon son of John, do you truly love me?" He answered, "Yes, Lord, You know that I love you." Jesus said, "Take care of My sheep."

Jn21:17 The third time He said to him, "Simon son of John, do you love me?" Peter was hurt because Jesus asked him the third time, "Do you love me?" He said, "Lord, You know all things; You know that I love you." Jesus said, "Feed My sheep.

b. Forsaken first love is love that has grown cold. This is because the outward fullness of the Holy Spirit gradually became cold.

c. When we are filled with the inner Holy Spirit, the fullness of our outward Holy Spirit will be made up, then our inward love can never go cold.

3. remove your lampstand from its place.

a. If we don't recover our first love, the Lord said that He will remove our lampstand from its place.

b. If the lampstand is removed, then the light will disappear and only the darkness will remain. That is, the living testimony of the church will perish.

Verse 6 But you have this in your favor: You hate the practices of the Nicolaitans, which I also hate.

▣**Nicolaitans** ⇒ (Greek) Νικολαϊτῶν, Nikolaitōn

Composed of two greek words: niko + laos

niko: Conquer another person (rule over)

laos: ordinary people, ordinary church members

※Nicolaitans think of themselves as higher than any other members in the church (denoting a class system among the members of the church).

Verse 7 Whoever has ears, let them hear what the Spirit says to the churches. To the one who is victorious, I will give the right to eat from the tree of life, which is in the paradise of God.

1. He who has an ear

Even though everyone has an ear in the flesh, if we want to hear what the Spirit says to the churches, our ears have to be circumcised. (Jer 6:10, Ac 7:51)[97]

---

97) Jer6:10 To whom can I speak and give warning? Who will listen to me? Their ears are closed so they cannot hear. The word of the LORD is offensive to them; they find no pleasure in it.

Ac7:51 "You stiff-necked people, with uncircumcised hearts and

2. what the Spirit says to the churches
   a. It is the Lord who speaks at the opening of each of the seven letters, but it is the Spirit who speaks at the ending of each letter. This means that the speaking Christ is the Holy Spirit, and that Christ also speaks by the Holy Spirit.
   b. Although this letter has been sent to the messenger of the church in Ephesus, it speaks for all churches even in today's day and age, and the Holy Spirit is the One who speaks in the letter.
3. let him hear. (Jer 6:10, Ac 7:51, Ro 11:8)[98]
   a. John heard the voice of the Lord first, (Rev 1:10)[99] and then saw the vision (Rev 1:12)[100]. If we cannot hear because our ears are numb, then we also cannot see (Isa 6:9～10)[101].
   b. The Jews were not willing to hear the word of God at all, therefore, they couldn't see the Lord nor the Lord's work (A numb ear must be circumcised) (Lev 14:17, 28)[102].

---

ears! You are just like your fathers: You always resist the Holy Spirit!

98) Jer6:10, Ac7:51 ☝ See footnote 97
Ro11:8 as it is written: "God gave them a spirit of stupor, eyes so that they could not see and ears so that they could not hear, to this very day."

99) Rev1:10 On the Lord's Day I was in the Spirit, and I heard behind me a loud voice like a trumpet,

100)Rev1:12 I turned around to see the voice that was speaking to me. And when I turned I saw seven golden lampstands,

101)Isa6:9 He said, "Go and tell this people: "'Be ever hearing, but never understanding; be ever seeing, but never perceiving.'
Isa6:10 Make the heart of this people calloused; make their ears dull and close their eyes. Otherwise they might see with their eyes, hear with their ears, understand with their hearts, and turn and be healed."

102)Lev14:17 The priest is to put some of the oil remaining in his palm

4. which is in the paradise of God.
   a. The paradise of God is pointing to the New Jerusalem (Rev 22:1～2)[103].
   b. The tree of life was originally in the garden of Eden. By eating this, man could have lived with God, but Man became corrupted by the serpent's temptation so he couldn't eat it (Ge 2:16～17, 3:1～7)[104].

---

on the lobe of the right ear of the one to be cleansed, on the thumb of his right hand and on the big toe of his right foot, on top of the blood of the guilt offering.

Lev14:28 Some of the oil in his palm he is to put on the same places he put the blood of the guilt offering—on the lobe of the right ear of the one to be cleansed, on the thumb of his right hand and on the big toe of his right foot.

103)Rev22:1 Then the angel showed me the river of the water of life, as clear as crystal, flowing from the throne of God and of the Lamb

Rev22:2 down the middle of the great street of the city. On each side of the river stood the tree of life, bearing twelve crops of fruit, yielding its fruit every month. And the leaves of the tree are for the healing of the nations.

104)Ge2:16 And the LORD God commanded the man, "You are free to eat from any tree in the garden;

Ge2:17 but you must not eat from the tree of the knowledge of good and evil, for when you eat of it you will surely die."

Ge3:1 Now the serpent was more crafty than any of the wild animals the LORD God had made. He said to the woman, "Did God really say, 'You must not eat from any tree in the garden'?"

Ge3:2 The woman said to the serpent, "We may eat fruit from the trees in the garden,

Ge3:3 but God did say, 'You must not eat fruit from the tree that is in the middle of the garden, and you must not touch it, or you will die.'"

Ge3:4 "You will not surely die," the serpent said to the woman.

Ge3:5 "For God knows that when you eat of it your eyes will be opened, and you will be like God, knowing good and evil."

Ge3:6 When the woman saw that the fruit of the tree was good for food and pleasing to the eye, and also desirable for gaining wisdom, she took some and ate it. She also gave some to her husband, who was with her, and he ate it.

5. I will give the right to eat fruit from the tree of life (In the Korean Bible). ⇒ I will give you **the tree of life** to eat (correct translation).
   a. In the life of the church today, by eating the tree of life that is Christ, we can live like Christ and receive the life of Christ, and we can be changed (Jn 6:35, 51, 53~58)[105].
      1) The tree of life is Christ
      2) The fruits of the tree of life are miraculous signs, powers, healing, a life devoted to the Word, etc.
      3) The tree of life and the tree of knowledge of good and evil (Ge 2:9, 2:16~17, 3:1, 3:11~12, 3:22, Rev 2:7)[106].

Ge3:7 Then the eyes of both of them were opened, and they realized they were naked; so they sewed fig leaves together and made coverings for themselves.

105)Jn6:35 Then Jesus declared, "I am the bread of life. He who comes to Me will never go hungry, and he who believes in Me will never be thirsty.
Jn6:51 I am the living bread that came down from heaven. If anyone eats of this bread, he will live forever. This bread is My flesh, which I will give for the life of the world."
Jn6:53 Jesus said to them, "I tell you the truth, unless you eat the flesh of the Son of Man and drink His blood, you have no life in you.
Jn6:54 Whoever eats My flesh and drinks My blood has eternal life, and I will raise him up at the last day.
Jn6:55 For My flesh is real food and My blood is real drink.
Jn6:56 Whoever eats My flesh and drinks My blood remains in Me, and I in him.
Jn6:57 Just as the living Father sent Me and I live because of the Father, so the one who feeds on Me will live because of Me.
Jn6:58 This is the bread that came down from heaven. Your forefathers ate manna and died, but he who feeds on this bread will live forever."
106)Ge2:9 And the LORD God made all kinds of trees grow out of the ground--trees that were pleasing to the eye and good for food. In the middle of the garden were the tree of life and the tree of the knowledge of good and evil.
Ge2:16 And the LORD God commanded the man, "You are free to eat from any tree in the garden;
Ge2:17 but you must not eat from the tree of the knowledge of good

※ The fruits of the tree of life is the wrong translation. The right translation is the tree of life.

4) The fruit of the tree of knowledge of good and evil (Ge 3:2~3, 6)[107].

※ The word fruit in Genesis 3:2~3, 6 was inserted by Eve in her thoughts.

b. We must recover our first love for Christ, if we want to rejoice in Christ, who is the tree of life, and be supplied with life, and be changed.

c. The corruption of the church has been attributed to replacing the eating of Christ as our food with the consumption of the teaching of the church for knowledge.

d. In Genesis chapters 2 and 3, there is the tree of life, but there is no fruit of the tree of life. All the fruits are the fruits of the tree of knowledge of good and evil. The

---

and evil, for when you eat of it you will surely die."

Ge3:1 Now the serpent was more crafty than any of the wild animals the LORD God had made. He said to the woman, "Did God really say, 'You must not eat from any tree in the garden'?"

Ge3:11 And He said, "Who told you that you were naked? Have you eaten from the tree that I commanded you not to eat from?"

Ge3:12 The man said, "The woman You put here with me—she gave me some fruit from the tree, and I ate it."

Ge3:22 And the LORD God said, "The man has now become like one of us, knowing good and evil. He must not be allowed to reach out his hand and take also from the tree of life and eat, and live forever."

Rev2:7 He who has an ear, let him hear what the Spirit says to the churches. To him who overcomes, I will give the right to eat from the tree of life, which is in the paradise of God.

107)Ge3:2 The woman said to the serpent, "We may eat fruit from the trees in the garden,

Ge3:3 but God did say, 'You must not eat fruit from the tree that is in the middle of the garden, and you must not touch it, or you will die.'"

Ge3:6 When the woman saw that the fruit of the tree was good for food and pleasing to the eye, and also desirable for gaining wisdom, she took some and ate it. She also gave some to her husband, who was with her, and he ate it.

fruits of the tree of life will eventually be eaten in the New Jerusalem as it says in Revelation chapter 22.

[The church in Smyrna] (Late 1st century ~ early 4th century, the church that had suffered)

Verse 8 "To the angel of the church in Smyrna write: These are the words of Him who is the First and the Last, who died and came to life again.

▣Smyrna ⇒ (Greek) means myrrh: This is the incense that symbolizes suffering.

1. These are the words of Him who is the First and the Last, who died and came to life again.
   a. Whatever kinds of suffering the Church faces, she must not be broken and discouraged. The Church must pass through all the tribulations and reach the end. This is because Christ, who is the life and the head of the Church, is the First and the Last, the Beginning and the End. No matter how much persecution there is, the Church is as alive as ever. This is because Christ, the resurrection life, has triumphed over the power of death.
   b. The most that suffering and persecution can do is kill us. After death due to persecution, there will be a resurrection for the one who overcomes. Death is not the end. It is the gateway to resurrection. When I step into death, I enter into resurrection. We should be able to rejoice when we reach death through suffering and persecution because we will obtain authority to reign as kings in the Millennial Kingdom (Rev 20:4)[108].

---

108)Rev20:4 I saw thrones on which were seated those who had been given authority to judge. And I saw the souls of those who had been beheaded because of their testimony for Jesus and because of the word of God. They had not worshiped the beast or his image and had not received his mark on their foreheads or their hands. They came to life and reigned with

Verse 9 I know your afflictions and your poverty--yet you are rich! I know about the slander of those who say they are Jews and are not, but are a synagogue of Satan.

1. I know your afflictions and your poverty- yet you are rich!
   a. The Lord was personally acquainted with all the afflictions and poverty of the church in Smyrna and was watching over them.
   b. Tribulation is a test of life for the church. The extent to which the church experiences and enjoys the resurrection life of Christ is verified only by tribulation, and tribulation is the medium that brings the abundance of the resurrection life of Christ.
   c. The church in Smyrna was a church that was suffering hardship and materially poor, but this church was spiritually rich.
   d. Though in worldly things it was poor, in all heavenly things it prospered.
2. I know the slander of those who say they are Jews and are not, but are **a synagogue of Satan**.
   a. The Jews were Jews in the flesh, but they were not Jews in spirit. Instead, they were a group controlled by Satan (Ac 17:5~7, 13)[109].
   b. Outwardly, the synagogue had existed for God and His word, but internally it had opposed Jesus and persecuted the apostles and churches (Ac 6:9~15)[110].

Christ a thousand years.

109)Ac17:5 But the Jews were jealous; so they rounded up some bad characters from the marketplace, formed a mob and started a riot in the city. They rushed to Jason's house in search of Paul and Silas in order to bring them out to the crowd.

Ac17:6 But when they did not find them, they dragged Jason and some other brothers before the city officials, shouting: "These men who have caused trouble all over the world have now come here,

Ac17:7 and Jason has welcomed them into his house. They are all defying Caesar's decrees, saying that there is another king, one called Jesus."

c. On the surface, they were worshipping and sacrificing to God, but in reality they were opposing Him.
d. They had persecuted those who believed in the Lord Jesus, all the while thinking that they were offering a service to God (Jn 16:2, Ac 8:1~3)[111].

Verse 10 Do not be afraid of what you are about to suffer. I tell you, the devil will put some of you in prison to test

---

110)Ac6:9 Opposition arose, however, from members of the Synagogue of the Freedmen (as it was called)--Jews of Cyrene and Alexandria as well as the provinces of Cilicia and Asia. These men began to argue with Stephen,
Ac6:10 but they could not stand up against his wisdom or the Spirit by whom he spoke.
Ac6:11 Then they secretly persuaded some men to say, "We have heard Stephen speak words of blasphemy against Moses and against God."
Ac6:12 So they stirred up the people and the elders and the teachers of the law. They seized Stephen and brought him before the Sanhedrin.
Ac6:13 They produced false witnesses, who testified, "This fellow never stops speaking against this holy place and against the law.
Ac6:14 For we have heard him say that this Jesus of Nazareth will destroy this place and change the customs Moses handed down to us."
Ac6:15 All who were sitting in the Sanhedrin looked intently at Stephen, and they saw that his face was like the face of an angel.

111)Jn16:2 They will put you out of the synagogue; in fact, a time is coming when anyone who kills you will think he is offering a service to God.
Ac8:1 And Saul was there, giving approval to his death. On that day a great persecution broke out against the church at Jerusalem, and all except the apostles were scattered throughout Judea and Samaria.
Ac8:2 Godly men buried Stephen and mourned deeply for him.
Ac8:3 But Saul began to destroy the church. Going from house to house, he dragged off men and women and put them in prison.

you, and you will suffer persecution for ten days. Be faithful, even to the point of death, and I will give you life as your victor's crown.

1. Do not be afraid of what you are about to suffer.
   a. Suffering was waiting for the church in Smyrna, which had been in affliction and poverty. The reason why God allowed the church in Smyrna to suffer was not only to demonstrate that the Lord's resurrection life defeats and overcomes death, but also so that the church could enjoy the abundance of His life.
   b. Only this church, which has overcome suffering and poverty, can overcome the suffering which brings spiritual prosperity. And so, The Lord had allowed additional suffering onto the church in Smyrna.
2. I tell you, the devil will put some of you in prison to test you
   a. The devil: (Greek) accuser, slanderer (Job 1:9～11)[112].
   b. The devil can test the members of the church by throwing them into prison. Of course, there must be permission from the Lord (Lk 22:31～32, Job 1:12, Mt 4:1～3)[113].
3. you will suffer persecution for ten days.
   a. Ten is the number of completion or fulfillment (ten commandments, tithe, etc.).
   b. Ten days is the full number to receive the life of God and ten days of tribulation means the complete or full schedule of tribulation.

---

112)Job1:9 "Does Job fear God for nothing?" Satan replied.
Job1:10 "Have You not put a hedge around him and his household and everything he has? You have blessed the work of his hands, so that his flocks and herds are spread throughout the land.
Job1:11 But stretch out Your hand and strike everything he has, and he will surely curse You to Your face."

113)Lk22:31 "Simon, Simon, Satan has asked to sift you as wheat.
Lk22:32 But I have prayed for you, Simon, that your faith may not fail. And when you have turned back, strengthen your brothers."

c. The suffering church has to undergo the ten-day ordeal.
d. Ten days is a sign of prophetic reference to the ten persecutions of the Church under the Roman emperors, from Caesar Nero at the end of the first century to the official recognition of Christianity as the state religion by Constantine at the beginning of the fourth century.

4. Be faithful, even to the point of death, and I will give you **the crown of life**.
   a. Churches can face suffering, even to the point of death. Because we have Christ, the life of resurrection, we can become triumphant martyrs.
   b. Externally, even though there is no affliction, the Christian life is one of self-denial and dying on the cross. Through this one can receive resurrection life.
   c. The saints who can pass through the ten-day ordeal will be able to receive the crown of life.
   Ultimately, the reason for allowing the ten-day ordeal is to give us the crown of life (Jas 1:12)[114].
   d. If we overcome affliction, poverty, and the ten-day ordeal we will receive the crown of life when we appear before the judgment seat of Christ and nothing will harm us (1Co 3:12~15, 2Co 5:10, Lk 12:47~48)[115].

---

114)Jas1:12 Blessed is the man who perseveres under trial, because when he has stood the test, he will receive the crown of life that God has promised to those who love Him.

115)1Co3:12 If any man builds on this foundation using gold, silver, costly stones, wood, hay or straw,
1Co3:13 his work will be shown for what it is, because the Day will bring it to light. It will be revealed with fire, and the fire will test the quality of each man's work.
1Co3:14 If what he has built survives, he will receive his reward.
1Co3:15 If it is burned up, he will suffer loss; he himself will be saved, but only as one escaping through the flames.
2Co5:10 For we must all appear before the judgment seat of Christ, that each one may receive what is due him for the things done while in the body, whether good or bad.
Lk12:47 "That servant who knows his master's will and does not get

e. Types of crown
 1) The crown of life : (Jas 1:12, Rev 2:10)[116] overcoming trials
 2) The crown of glory: (1Pe 5:4)[117] becoming examples to the flock
 3) The crown of righteousness: (2Ti 4:8)[118] fighting the good fight, keeping the faith
 4) The crown that will never fade: (1Co 9:25)[119] competing in the race

Verse 11 Whoever has ears, let them hear what the Spirit says to the churches. The one who is victorious will not be hurt at all by the second death.

1. These words are what the Lord said to the messenger of the church in Smyrna. In today's day and age, we must be able

---

ready or does not do what his master wants will be beaten with many blows.

Lk12:48 But the one who does not know and does things deserving punishment will be beaten with few blows. From everyone who has been given much, much will be demanded; and from the one who has been entrusted with much, much more will be asked.

116)Jas1:12 Blessed is the man who perseveres under trial, because when he has stood the test, he will receive the crown of life that God has promised to those who love Him.

Rev2:10 Do not be afraid of what you are about to suffer. I tell you, the devil will put some of you in prison to test you, and you will suffer persecution for ten days. Be faithful, even to the point of death, and I will give you the crown of life.

117)1Pe5:4 And when the Chief Shepherd appears, you will receive the crown of glory that will never fade away.

118)2Ti4:8 Now there is in store for me the crown of righteousness, which the Lord, the righteous Judge, will award to me on that day--and not only to me, but also to all who have longed for His appearing.

119)1Co9:25 Everyone who competes in the games goes into strict training. They do it to get a crown that will not last; but we do it to get a crown that will last forever.

to receive the words spoken through the Holy Spirit.

2. The Second death is a lake of fire (Rev 20:11～15)[120].

※ The lake of fire :

a. the fiery lake of burning sulfur (Rev 19:20)[121]

b. the lake of burning sulfur (Rev 20:10)[122]

c. the fiery lake of burning sulfur (Rev 21:8)[123]

d. the eternal fire (Mt 25:41)[124]: prepared for the devil

---

120)Rev20:11 Then I saw a great white throne and Him who was seated on it. Earth and sky fled from His presence, and there was no place for them.

Rev20:12 And I saw the dead, great and small, standing before the throne, and books were opened. Another book was opened, which is the book of life. The dead were judged according to what they had done as recorded in the books.

Rev20:13 The sea gave up the dead that were in it, and death and Hades gave up the dead that were in them, and each person was judged according to what he had done.

Rev20:14 Then death and Hades were thrown into the lake of fire. The lake of fire is the second death.

Rev20:15 If anyone's name was not found written in the book of life, he was thrown into the lake of fire.

121)Rev19:20 But the beast was captured, and with him the false prophet who had performed the miraculous signs on his behalf. With these signs he had deluded those who had received the mark of the beast and worshiped his image. The two of them were thrown alive into the fiery lake of burning sulfur.

122)Rev20:10 And the devil, who deceived them, was thrown into the lake of burning sulfur, where the beast and the false prophet had been thrown. They will be tormented day and night for ever and ever.

123)Rev21:8 But the cowardly, the unbelieving, the vile, the murderers, the sexually immoral, those who practice magic arts, the idolaters and all liars--their place will be in the fiery lake of burning sulfur. This is the second death."

124)Mt25:41 "Then He will say to those on His left, 'Depart from Me, you who are cursed, into the eternal fire prepared for the devil and his angels.

and his angels

3. **"hurt by the Second death"** means to suffer excruciating hurt like a second death.
   ※ hurt by the Second death: If anyone worships the beast and his image and receives his mark on the forehead or on the hand, he too will drink of the wine of God's fury, which has been poured full strength into the cup of His wrath. He will be tormented with burning sulfur in the presence of the holy angels and of the Lamb. And the smoke of their torment rises for ever and ever (In Greek, it doesn't mean eternal but a temporary period) (Rev 14:9 ~11).
4. If we are faithful even to the point of death, we will receive the crown of life and not be hurt at all by the second death (Rev 2:10~11).

[To the Church in Pergamum] A.D. 313 ~ A.D. 590

Verse 12: "To the angel of the church in Pergamum write: These are the words of Him who has the sharp, double-edged sword.

1. Pergamum Περιγαμος → Περι(peri)+γαμος(gamos)
   ↓ ↓
   (dual) (wedding)
   a. The church in Pergamum means the marriage between Christ and the world.
   b. As a chaste bride (2Co 11:2)[125], the church must become the bride of Christ, but the church that has united with the world is considered to have committed spiritual adultery in the eyes of God.
2. These are the words of Him who has the sharp, double

125)2Co11:2 I am jealous for you with a godly jealousy. I promised you to one husband, to Christ, so that I might present you as a pure virgin to Him.

-edged sword.

a. The church is a company of people called out of the world and separated unto God. Nevertheless, in the early 4th century, after Constantine the Great established Christianity as a national religion, the church became worldly, even plunging into a state of marriage with the world.
b. The church in Pergamum that has married with Christ and the world at the same time is to be divided by a double-edged sword with regard to what is truth and what is of this world.

Verse 13 I know where you live--where Satan has his throne. Yet you remain true to My name. You did not renounce your faith in Me, not even in the days of Antipas, My faithful witness, who was put to death in your city--where Satan lives.

1. I know where you live - **[where Satan has his throne]**.
Satan's throne is the world. Because the church has entered the world and has become worldly, it is dwelling in the world where Satan dwells.
2. Yet you remain true to My name.
The church in Pergamum had remained true to the Lord's name, the reality of the Lord's character. Therefore, the church did not renounce their faith in the Lord, even in the days of being slain.
3. Even in the days of **Antipas, My faithful witness**, who was put to death in your city - where Satan lives.
   a. Antipas: (Greek) to go against everything (of this world)
   b. Antipas went against everything the worldy churches had done, and because of that, he was put to death. (Eph 6:12, 1Jn 2:15)[126]

126)Eph6:12 For our struggle is not against flesh and blood, but against the rulers, against the authorities, against the powers of this dark world and against the spiritual forces of evil in the heavenly realms.

c. To testify against the churches of the world, we need the spirit of the Martyr. Until we are put to death, we must go against the church becoming worldly and we must remain faithful to the Lord's witness. In Greek, the word "martyr" is the same as "witness".

Verse 14 Nevertheless, I have a few things against you: There are some among you who hold to the teaching of Balaam, who taught Balak to entice the Israelites to sin so that they ate food sacrificed to idols and committed sexual immorality.

1. You have people there who hold to **the teaching of Balaam**.
   a. Balaam brought sexual immorality and idol worship to the people of God for profit (Nu 25:1～3, 31:16)[127].
   b. In worldly churches some have been taught to love such worldly things and things of the world (2Pe 2:15, Jude 1:11)[128].
2. Balaam, who taught Balak to entice the Israelites to sin by eating **food sacrificed to idols** and by committing sexual immorality.
   a. Balaam made Balak build the altar for his gods in front of the Israelites, and when the women sacrificed to their gods, they invited the Israelites, which was a trap. Because

---

1Jn2:15 Do not love the world or anything in the world. If anyone loves the world, the love of the Father is not in him.

127)Nu25:1 While Israel was staying in Shittim, the men began to indulge in sexual immorality with Moabite women, ☞next page

Nu25:2 who invited them to the sacrifices to their gods. The people ate and bowed down before these gods.

Nu25:3 So Israel joined in worshiping the Baal of Peor. And the LORD'S anger burned against them.

128)2Pe2:15 They have left the straight way and wandered off to follow the way of Balaam son of Beor, who loved the wages of wickedness.

Jude1:11 Woe to them! They have taken the way of Cain; they have rushed for profit into Balaam's error; they have been destroyed in Korah's rebellion.

of this, the Israelites ate the food sacrificed to idols and began to fornicate with the women (Nu 25:1～3)[129].

b. Idolatry always leads to sexual immorality (Ac 15:29)[130].
c. Christ is to be the only husband of the church and the only bridegroom to all the Saints. But many churches today, through various teachings, teach people to accept demonic and worldly things.

Verse 15 Likewise you also have those who hold to the teaching of the Nicolaitans.

1. Decadent worldly churches not only hold to the teaching of Balaam but also to the teaching of the Nicolaitans.
2. The teaching of Balaam leads Christians to put off Christ's character and go into idolatry, from enjoying Christ to committing spiritual adultery. Also, [the teaching of the Nicolaitans] destroys the function of believers, members of the body of Christ, rendering the Lord's body powerless to express Him.
3. The former teaching ignores the head and the latter teaching destroys the body. The class system of the Nicolaitans kills the functions of the branches of the body and the Lord hates this because they build up organization instead of living organism.
   a. The church in Ephesus: Nicolaitan behaviour was present
   b. The church in Pergamum: Because the **teachings of the Nicolaitans** were present, behaviour developed into teaching.

---

129)Nu25:1 While Israel was staying in Shittim, the men began to indulge in sexual immorality with Moabite women,
Nu25:2 who invited them to the sacrifices to their gods. The people ate and bowed down before these gods.
Nu25:3 So Israel joined in worshiping the Baal of Peor. And the LORD'S anger burned against them.

130)Ac15:29 You are to abstain from food sacrificed to idols, from blood, from the meat of strangled animals and from sexual immorality. You will do well to avoid these things. Farewell.

Verse 16 Repent therefore! Otherwise, I will soon come to you and will fight against them with the sword of My mouth.

1. Repent therefore!
   a. On the surface, the teaching of Balaam seems to make people follow the word of God, but on the inside, led by greed, it makes them eat food sacrificed to idols and commit sexual immorality. We must repent of it.
   b. People who follow the teaching of the Nicolaitans must destroy the class system in the church and must repent and turn away from it in order to build the body of Christ.
   c. The church cannot build the body of Christ through organization. The church must become a living organism and be built through fellowship and sharing of life.
2. Otherwise, I will soon come to you and will fight against them with the sword of My mouth.
   a. Unless the Church abandons the teachings of Balaam and the teachings of the Nicolaitans, they are bound to be enemies of Christ.
   b. If the church does not repent and turn, it will become an enemy of Christ, and Christ will fight against them with the sword of the word.
   c. The Lord does not have a bow (Rev 6:2)[131]; He fights with the sword of the word (Rev 19:15, 2Th 2:8, Rev 1:16, 2:12)[132].

---

131)Rev6:2 I looked, and there before me was a white horse! Its rider held a bow, and he was given a crown, and he rode out as a conqueror bent on conquest.

132)Rev19:15 Out of His mouth comes a sharp sword with which to strike down the nations. "He will rule them with an iron scepter." He treads the winepress of the fury of the wrath of God Almighty.
2Th2:8 And then the lawless one will be revealed, whom the Lord Jesus will overthrow with the breath of His mouth and destroy by the splendor of His coming.
Rev1:16 In His right hand He held seven stars, and out of His

Verse 17 Whoever has ears, let them hear what the Spirit says to the churches. To the one who is victorious, I will give some of the hidden manna. I will also give that person a white stone with a new name written on it, known only to the one who receives it.

1. To him who overcomes, I will give some of **the hidden manna**.
   a. 'him who overcomes' in the church of Pergamum refers to the person who does not follow the unity of the church and the world, idolatry, or the teachings of Balaam and the Nicolaitans.
   b. Unhidden manna was for the Lord's people who lived in the desert to enjoy openly. Hidden manna is the manna in the gold jar in the ark of the Most Holy Place. It represents the deep mystery of Christ and is a special portion for those who overcome the corruption of the worldly churches.
   c. The manna in the gold jar represents Christ hidden in the divine nature of God.
   d. The hidden manna is for those who are familiar with the Lord, who have forsaken the world and all the barriers that were between them and God.
   e. In order to eat the hidden manna while the worldly church is falling into decadence, we must escape from Egypt into the desert, from the desert enter into the land of Canaan, from the land of Canaan into the temple courtyard, from the courtyard into the Holy Place, from the Holy Place into the Most Holy Place, open the Ark of the Covenant and touch the gold jar. There, we can enjoy Christ, the hidden manna.
   f. To enjoy Christ, the hidden manna, we must enter the deep presence of God.

---

mouth came a sharp double-edged sword. His face was like the sun shining in all its brilliance.

Rev2:12 "To the angel of the church in Pergamum write: These are the words of Him who has the sharp, double-edged sword.

2. I will also give him **a white stone** with a new name written on it, known only to him who receives it.
   a. In the Old Testament, stone is used to build God's temple, and in the New Testament, stone refers to believers (Mt 16:18)[133].
   b. Man was originally formed from the dust of the earth (Ge 2:7)[134], and by eating manna Man has been born again by faith and become stone.
   c. The church is made up of this stone, which starts from Christ - who is the headstone and the cornerstone – and is joined together and built with Him.
   d. With the refinement of the Spirit, the stone is transformed into a white stone (jade) (Eph 2:20~22)[135] and the white stone is converted into a jewel during the Millennial Kingdom and used to build the New Jerusalem (Rev 21:18~20)[136].
   e. The new name represents a person who has been refined by the Holy Spirit (a saint whose soul has been reborn).
   Saul → Paul (Ac 13:9)[137], Simon → Peter (Mk 3:16)[138]

---

133)Mt16:18 And I tell you that you are Peter, and on this rock I will build My church, and the gates of Hades will not overcome it.

134)Ge2:7 the LORD God formed the man from the dust of the ground and breathed into his nostrils the breath of life, and the man became a living being.

135)Eph2:20 built on the foundation of the apostles and prophets, with Christ Jesus Himself as the chief cornerstone.
Eph2:21 In Him the whole building is joined together and rises to become a holy temple in the Lord.
Eph2:22 And in Him you too are being built together to become a dwelling in which God lives by His Spirit.

136)Rev21:18 The wall was made of jasper, and the city of pure gold, as pure as glass.
Rev21:19 The foundations of the city walls were decorated with every kind of precious stone. The first foundation was jasper, the second sapphire, the third chalcedony, the fourth emerald,
Rev21:20 the fifth sardonyx, the sixth carnelian, the seventh chrysolite, the eighth beryl, the ninth topaz, the tenth chrysoprase, the eleventh jacinth, and the twelfth amethyst.

Abram → Abraham (Ge 17:5)[139)]
Jacob → Israel (Ge 32:28)[140)] Sarai → Sarah (Ge 17:15)[141)]
James and John, the sons of Zebedee → Boanerges, sons of Thunder (Mk 3:17)[142)]

f. If man eats the manna, he becomes stone, and when the saint eats the hidden manna, he becomes white stone, and only the transformed man himself can know how much he has changed.

[The church in Thyatira] (A.D. 590 – The second coming)

Verse 18 "To the angel of the church in Thyatira write: These are the words of the Son of God, whose eyes are like blazing fire and whose feet are like burnished bronze.

1. To the angel in Thyatira write:
   a. Thyatira → (Greek) fragrant offerings, unceasing offerings
   b. Foreshadows the Roman Catholic Church as an apostate church with an established papal system (late 6th century).
2. whose eyes are like blazing fire and whose feet are like burnished bronze.
   a. The Church of Pergamum, having married the world, followed

---

137)Ac13:9 Then Saul, who was also called Paul, filled with the Holy Spirit, looked straight at Elymas and said,

138)Mk3:16 These are the twelve He appointed: Simon (to whom He gave the name Peter);

139)Ge17:5 No longer will you be called Abram; your name will be Abraham, for I have made you a father of many nations.

140)Ge32:28 Then the man said, "Your name will no longer be Jacob, but Israel, because you have struggled with God and with men and have overcome."

141)Ge17:15 God also said to Abraham, "As for Sarai your wife, you are no longer to call her Sarai; her name will be Sarah.

142)Mk3:17 James son of Zebedee and his brother John (to them He gave the name Boanerges, which means Sons of Thunder);

the teachings of Balaam and the teachings of the Nicolaitans, resulting in a church full of corruption through idolatry and the establishment of class systems.

b. The Roman Church fell to the point of no return due to the fact that the church was literally packed with idols. Statues of Mary, Paul, Peter, countless saints, etc. were made and erected to be worshipped.

c. The Roman Church does not consist of only the Pope but Cardinals too, as the whole church is full of hierarchy.

d. In the apostate church of Thyatira, a keen searching eye like blazing fire is needed (Rev 1:14, Heb 12:29)[143].

e. Feet like burnished bronze represents life and conduct refined in blazing hot fire. It means that Christ is qualified to have authority to judge.

f. **[The history of the Catholic Church]**

A.D 607: Boniface the third, the first pope is established
709: The first occurrence of a saint kissing the Pope's feet.
786: Worshipped icons and relics.
850: Begins using Holy Water.
995: Started keeping records of dead Saints in the roll of Saints.
1079: Celibacy of the Priesthood.
1090: Rosary used in prayer.
1184: Religious trials.
1190: Sale of indulgences.
1215: Transubstantiation.
1229: Reading the Bible for ordinary believers is forbidden.
1439: The ordinance of Purgatory is declared.
1508: The Ave Maria (Hail Mary) prayer is officially recognized.
1545: Tradition is accorded the same authority as the Bible.

---

143)Rev1:14 His head and hair were white like wool, as white as snow, and His eyes were like blazing fire.
Heb12:29 for our "God is a consuming fire."

1546: The Apocrypha are included in the Bible
1854: The Immaculate Conception of the Virgin Mary.
1864: List of sins proclaimed.
1870: Papal infallibility declared
1905: Mary recognized as the mother of the church.
1950: The Assumption of Mary

3. These are the words of the Son of God.
   In the Catholic church, they emphasize that Jesus is the son of Mary, but this verse strongly emphasizes Christ as the Son of God.

Verse 19 I know your deeds, your love and faith, your service and perseverance, and that you are now doing more than you did at first.

1. The apostate Catholic church has been doing more deeds and service than in the past.
2. They do many good deeds, work, and service, and more later than at first.

Verse 20 Nevertheless, I have this against you: You tolerate that woman Jezebel, who calls herself a prophet. By her teaching she misleads My servants into sexual immorality and the eating of food sacrificed to idols.

1. You tolerate **the woman Jezebel**, who calls herself a prophetess.
   a. As the wife of Ahab, Jezebel is the antitype of the pagan apostate church (1Ki 16:31, 2Ki 9:7)[144].
   b. Genesis → Woman (Eve) is the model of the church

144)1Ki16:31 He not only considered it trivial to commit the sins of Jeroboam son of Nebat, but he also married Jezebel daughter of Ethbaal king of the Sidonians, and began to serve Baal and worship him.
2Ki9:7 You are to destroy the house of Ahab your master, and I will avenge the blood of My servants the prophets and the blood of all the LORD'S servants shed by Jezebel.

The Old Testament → The Israelites are portrayed as woman, daughter, wife, etc. (Jer 3:20, 8:19)[145]
The New Testament → Virgin, (Mt 25:1)[146] bride, wife (Rev 19:7)[147]
↘
The apostate church : is called a prostitute or woman. (Rev 17:1, 3～6)[148]

c. Female Jezebel symbolizes evil, heresy and paganism (Mt 13:33)[149].

---

145)Jer3:20 But like a woman unfaithful to her husband, so you have been unfaithful to Me, O house of Israel," declares the LORD.
Jer8:19 Listen to the cry of My people from a land far away: "Is the LORD not in Zion? Is her King no longer there?" "Why have they provoked Me to anger with their images, with their worthless foreign idols?"

146)Mt25:1 "At that time the kingdom of heaven will be like ten virgins who took their lamps and went out to meet the bridegroom.

147)Rev19:7 Let us rejoice and be glad and give Him glory! For the wedding of the Lamb has come, and His bride has made herself ready.

148)Rev17:1 One of the seven angels who had the seven bowls came and said to me, "Come, I will show you the punishment of the great prostitute, who sits on many waters.
Rev17:3 Then the angel carried me away in the Spirit into a desert. There I saw a woman sitting on a scarlet beast that was covered with blasphemous names and had seven heads and ten horns.
Rev17:4 The woman was dressed in purple and scarlet, and was glittering with gold, precious stones and pearls. She held a golden cup in her hand, filled with abominable things and the filth of her adulteries.
Rev17:5 This title was written on her forehead: MYSTERY BABYLON THE GREAT THE MOTHER OF PROSTITUTES AND OF THE ABOMINATIONS OF THE EARTH.
Rev17:6 I saw that the woman was drunk with the blood of the saints, the blood of those who bore testimony to Jesus. When I saw her, I was greatly astonished.

149)Mt13:33 He told them still another parable: "The kingdom of heaven is like yeast that a woman took and mixed into a large amount of flour until it worked all through the dough."

[The food sacrificed to idols]

2. By her teaching she misleads my servants into sexual immorality and the eating of **food sacrificed to idols**.
   a. The apostate church is full of every kind of sexual immorality and idolatry, spiritually and physically.
   b. They act as self-proclaimed prophets themselves, and the pope pretends to be authorized by God and, what is worse, to even be above God (Papal Infallibility places the pope's word above the authority of the Bible).
   c. Idolatry is adultery against God, and everything offered for idol worship is an idol offering. That is, in an idol worshipping church, the use of all offerings and sacrifices is ultimately equivalent to eating food sacrificed to idols.

Verse 21 I have given her time to repent of her immorality, but she is unwilling

1. When the church goes down the wrong path, the Lord always gives an opportunity to repent. We must immediately repent when that opportunity comes.
2. Immorality represents spiritual adultery. In other words, it means to worship idols and have greed for worldly desires (Eph 5:5, Col 3:5, 1Jn 2:15,16)[150].

Verse 22 So I will cast her on a bed of suffering, and I will make those who commit adultery with her suffer

---

150)Eph5:5 For of this you can be sure: No immoral, impure or greedy person--such a man is an idolater--has any inheritance in the kingdom of Christ and of God.

Col3:5 Put to death, therefore, whatever belongs to your earthly nature: sexual immorality, impurity, lust, evil desires and greed, which is idolatry.

1Jn2:15 Do not love the world or anything in the world. If anyone loves the world, the love of the Father is not in him.

1Jn2:16 For everything in the world—the cravings of sinful man, the lust of his eyes and the boasting of what he has and does—comes not from the Father but from the world.

intensely, unless they repent of her ways.

1. I will cast her on a bed
   a. "cast her on a bed" means that she will be bedridden; the apostate church is sick with a terminal illness and will be left like that until the judgment.
   b. They are not healthy spiritually. Some things belong to heaven while others belong to the earth. Some things are holy, but others are very worldly.
2. and I will make those who commit adultery with her suffer intensely, unless they repent of her ways.
   'Those who commit adultery with her' represents Catholics and they will suffer great distress due to the Antichrist (Rev 17:16~18)[151].

Verse 23 I will strike her children dead. Then all the churches will know that I am He who searches hearts and minds, and I will repay each of you according to your deeds.

1. 'Her children' refers to the adherents of the Catholic church. In the last days, they will be killed first (Rev 17:16~17)[152].
2. We must think twice, turn and repent because the Lord is the One who searches hearts and minds. Otherwise we will reap what we have sown.

[The death]

3. And I will kill her children with **death**; and all the churches shall know that I am He which searcheth the reins and hearts: and I will give unto every one of you according to your works. [KJV]-Rev2:23

---

151)Rev17:16 The beast and the ten horns you saw will hate the prostitute. They will bring her to ruin and leave her naked; they will eat her flesh and burn her with fire.
Rev17:17 For God has put it into their hearts to accomplish His purpose by agreeing to give the beast their power to rule, until God's words are fulfilled.
Rev17:18 The woman you saw is the great city that rules over the kings of the earth."

152) Rev17:16~17 ☞See footnote 151)

Verse 24 Now I say to the rest of you in Thyatira, to you who do not hold to her teaching and have not learned Satan's so-called deep secrets, 'I will not impose any other burden on you,

1. The Catholic church holds many secrets and deep doctrines
   a. The suffering church in Smyrna
      ⇒ There was the synagogue of Satan (Rev 2:9)[153].
   b. The worldly church in Pergamum
      ⇒ There was the throne of Satan (Rev 2:13)[154].
   [Satan's deep secrets]
   c. The betrayed church in Thyatira
      ⇒ There was the so-called **deep secrets of Satan** (Rev 2:24)[155]
2. The church in Ephesus became decadent when they had forsaken their first love, and in the suffering church in Smyrna, persecution entered through the synagogue of Satan; after that, the church was secularized and became the worldly church in Pergamum, and the church was built right on top of Satan's throne. After that, because the church becomes apostate, Satan's so-called deep secrets infiltrate with an appearance of beauty, resulting in total corruption. Today, Satan is building up the church, adding to it many elements of leaven and corruption (The Virgin Mary, Blessing, Christmas, Torch, etc.).

---

153)Rev2:9 I know your afflictions and your poverty--yet you are rich! I know the slander of those who say they are Jews and are not, but are a synagogue of Satan.

154)Rev2:13 I know where you live--where Satan has his throne. Yet you remain true to My name. You did not renounce your faith in Me, even in the days of Antipas, My faithful witness, who was put to death in your city--where Satan lives.

155)Rev2:24 Now I say to the rest of you in Thyatira, to you who do not hold to her teaching and have not learned Satan's so-called deep secrets (I will not impose any other burden on you):

Verse 25 except to hold on to what you have until I come.'

▣ The Lord says to strongly hold on to the things that remain in the Catholic church, which are business, love, faith, service, and perseverance.

Verse 26 To the one who is victorious and does My will to the end, I will give authority over the nations--

1. To him who overcomes and does My will to the end,
   a. He who overcomes in the church in Thyatira does not accept Jezebel who calls herself a prophetess (Rev 2:24).
   b. The overcomers are those who break free from Jezebel's enticement, sexual immorality and eating food sacrificed to idols, and repent of sexual immorality, and refuse to eat food sacrificed to idols, and forsake the greed of the world, and depart from idolatry.
   c. The overcomers are those who hold on to the Lord's testimony and obey the Lord's work until His coming. (The life of the cross, the life of resurrection, the works of the Lord).
   d. Ultimately, to overcome is to break away from Roman Catholicism and the apostate Church.
2. I will give **authority over the nations**
   a. The authority to rule over the nations means to reign with Christ over the nations during the Millennial Kingdom (1Pe 2:9, Rev 20:4~6)[156].
   b. Those among the corrupted Christians (Catholic church included)

---

156)1Pe2:9 But you are a chosen people, a royal priesthood, a holy nation, a people belonging to God, that you may declare the praises of Him who called you out of darkness into His wonderful light.

Rev20:4 I saw thrones on which were seated those who had been given authority to judge. And I saw the souls of those who had been beheaded because of their testimony for Jesus and because of the word of God. They had not worshiped the beast or his image and had not received his mark on their foreheads or their hands. They came to life and reigned with Christ a thousand years.

who are not able to overcome will not be able to take part in reigning over the nations in the Millennial Kingdom.

c. When the doors to the eternal state are opened, the overcomers will become the principal figures in the New Jerusalem, and they will reign for ever and ever (Rev 22:5)[157].

Verse 27 that one 'will rule them with an iron scepter and will dash them to pieces like pottery' --just as I have received authority from My Father.

1. In the Church age, Christ is gentle, humble, forgives seventy-seven times, and waits like a Father for the return of the prodigal son.

[Dash them to pieces like pottery]

2. But after the Lord's second coming, when He reigns during the Millennial Kingdom, He will strike down the nations with the sword from His mouth and rule them with an iron scepter, and dash those who rebel against Him **to pieces like pottery** (Ps 2:7～9, Rev 19:25)[158]. The overcomers, the kings, namely those who will receive the authority to rule over the nations, will be able to reign with Christ with an iron scepter.

Verse 28 I will also give that one the morning star.

1. The **morning star** is the inheritance that the Lord gives to the

---

157)Rev22:5 There will be no more night. They will not need the light of a lamp or the light of the sun, for the Lord God will give them light. And they will reign for ever and ever.

158)Ps2:7 I will proclaim the decree of the LORD: He said to Me, "You are My Son; today I have become Your Father.

Ps2:8 Ask of Me, and I will make the nations Your inheritance, the ends of the earth Your possession.

Ps2:9 You will rule them with an iron scepter; You will dash them to pieces like pottery."

Rev19:15 Out of His mouth comes a sharp sword with which to strike down the nations. "He will rule them with an iron scepter." He treads the winepress of the fury of the wrath of God Almighty.

overcomers (Rev 22:16, 2Pe 1:19)[159].

2. The others (those who are not overcomers) in the end will get to see Christ, the sun of righteousness (Mal 4:2, Lk 1:78, Mt 4:16)[160].

Verse 29 Whoever has ears, let them hear what the Spirit says to the churches.

1. This scripture was sent to the messenger in the church in Thyatira and although it is a rebuke towards the church in Thyatira (Catholic), today the churches that bear a resemblance to the church in Thyatira must listen to what the Holy Spirit says.
2. The word of rebuke towards the church in Thyatira applies to us today.

---

159)Rev22:16 "I, Jesus, have sent My angel to give you this testimony for the churches. I am the Root and the Offspring of David, and the bright Morning Star."

2Pe1:19 And we have the word of the prophets made more certain, and you will do well to pay attention to it, as to a light shining in a dark place, until the day dawns and the morning star rises in your hearts.

160)Mal4:2 But for you who revere My name, the sun of righteousness will rise with healing in its wings. And you will go out and leap like calves released from the stall.

Lk1:78 because of the tender mercy of our God, by which the rising sun will come to us from heaven

Mt4:16 the people living in darkness have seen a great light; on those living in the land of the shadow of death a light has dawned."

Chapter 3

[The church in Sardis]
- (early 16th century - the Second Coming of Christ)

1. Sardis ⇒ (Greek) the things that remain (the remnant) has the meaning of restoration.
2. The church in Sardis represents the Protestant church from the early 16th century, the Reformation period to the second coming of Christ.
3. The Reformation is the reformation of the corrupt church in Thyatira (Catholic church), it represents the recovery of faith by achieving reformation for the few who believe in the Lord (the remnant).

Verse 1 "To the angels of the church in Sardis write: These are the words of Him who holds the seven spirits of God and the seven stars. I know your deeds: you have a reputation of being alive, but you are dead.

1. These are the words of Him who holds **the seven spirits** of God and **the seven stars**.
   a. The church in Ephesus: The Lord reveals Himself as the One who holds the seven stars and walks among the seven golden lampstands. The early Church needed the care of Christ and its leaders.
   b. The church in Smyrna: The Lord reveals Himself as the One who died and came to life again, and with His resurrection life He was a nurturing figure to the suffering church which needed His care.
   c. The church in Pergamum: The Lord reveals Himself as the One who has the sharp double-edged sword and the One who distinguishes between the world, the spirit, the soul, and the body for the churches that have become worldly.
   d. The church in Thyatira: The Lord reveals Himself as the

One whose eyes are like blazing fire and whose feet are like burnished bronze. He is revealed as the One who searches the apostate church with eyes like a blazing fire and the One who has the feet of judgment.

e. The church in Sardis: The Lord reveals Himself as He who holds the seven spirits of God and the seven stars. And He says the dead reformed church needs the complete work of the Spirit and bright leaders who shine like the seven stars.

2. I know your deeds; you have a reputation of being alive, but you are dead.
   a. The Lord is the One who inspects our hearts and watches over and knows our lives.
   b. According to the doctrine of salvation by faith, our spirits may be saved but our works remain imperfect. Our spirits are alive but our deeds before God are dead.
   c. Nothing that began with the Reformation is perfect. Therefore, until the church, born again in faith, is perfected by the Word and the Holy Spirit, we are to be tried and trained in the seven Spirits, and for this we need leaders who shine like stars.

Verse 2 Wake up! Strengthen what remains and is about to die, for I have not found your deeds complete in the sight of My God.

1. To strengthen what remains and is about to die is to become righteous by faith and strengthen what has been restored by the Reformation.
2. Although our spirits are saved by becoming righteous through faith, the Lord deplores that our deeds are not sound at all. The only possible way for our deeds to be sound is for us to be filled with inner life.

Verse 3 Remember, therefore, what you have received and heard; hold it fast, and repent. But if you do not wake

up, I will come like a thief, and you will not know at what time I will come to you.

1. The Reformation was achieved through much blood, suffering, and sacrifice. The Lord says that we must obey and repent by thinking of how we have been blessed by God's help and have heard the words of truth.
2. To obey and repent means to convert those unsound deeds to sound deeds by the word heard through grace.
3. We can distinguish between those who are awakened and those who are not by whether their deeds are sound or not.
4. To the saints that are not awake, The Lord will come like a thief and they will not be able to face the Lord (Mt 24:42, 43, 1Th 5:1～6)[161].
5. But to those saints that are awake, the Lord will not come like a thief. Because the awakened saints live in the light, when the Lord comes like a thief, they will be able to recognize it (Mt 25:1～13)[162].

---

161)Mt24:42 "Therefore keep watch, because you do not know on what day your Lord will come.
Mt24:43 But understand this: If the owner of the house had known at what time of night the thief was coming, he would have kept watch and would not have let his house be broken into.
1Th5:1 Now, brothers, about times and dates we do not need to write to you,
1Th5:2 for you know very well that the day of the Lord will come like a thief in the night.
1Th5:3 While people are saying, "Peace and safety," destruction will come on them suddenly, as labor pains on a pregnant woman, and they will not escape.
1Th5:4 But you, brothers, are not in darkness so that this day should surprise you like a thief.
1Th5:5 You are all sons of the light and sons of the day. We do not belong to the night or to the darkness.
1Th5:6 So then, let us not be like others, who are asleep, but let us be alert and self-controlled.

162)Mt25:1 "At that time the kingdom of heaven will be like ten virgins who took their lamps and went out to meet the bridegroom.
Mt25:2 Five of them were foolish and five were wise.
Mt25:3 The foolish ones took their lamps but did not take any oil

Verse 4 Yet you have a few people in Sardis who have not soiled their clothes. They will walk with Me dressed in white, for they are worthy.

1. In the Bible, clothes represent how we act and live. Clothes that have been soiled means that our actions have been tainted. In other words, it represents death. The dirtiness of the church in Sardis is not the dirtiness of sin, but of death. Death is dirtier than sin (Rev 19:7~8, Lev 11:24~25, Nu 6:7~9)[163].

---

with them.

Mt25:4 The wise, however, took oil in jars along with their lamps.
Mt25:5 The bridegroom was a long time in coming, and they all became drowsy and fell asleep.
Mt25:6 "At midnight the cry rang out: 'Here's the bridegroom! Come out to meet him!'
Mt25:7 "Then all the virgins woke up and trimmed their lamps.
Mt25:8 The foolish ones said to the wise, 'Give us some of your oil; our lamps are going out.'
Mt25:9 "'No,' they replied, 'there may not be enough for both us and you. Instead, go to those who sell oil and buy some for yourselves.'
Mt25:10 "But while they were on their way to buy the oil, the bridegroom arrived. The virgins who were ready went in with him to the wedding banquet. And the door was shut.
Mt25:11 "Later the others also came. 'Sir! Sir!' they said. 'Open the door for us!'
Mt25:12 "But he replied, 'I tell you the truth, I don't know you.'
Mt25:13 "Therefore keep watch, because you do not know the day or the hour.

163)Rev19:7 Let us rejoice and be glad and give Him glory! For the wedding of the Lamb has come, and His bride has made herself ready.
Rev19:8 Fine linen, bright and clean, was given her to wear." (Fine linen stands for the righteous acts of the saints.)
Lev11:24 "'You will make yourselves unclean by these; whoever touches their carcasses will be unclean till evening.
Lev11:25 Whoever picks up one of their carcasses must wash his clothes, and he will be unclean till evening.
Nu6:7 Even if his own father or mother or brother or sister dies, he must not make himself ceremonially unclean on account of them, because the symbol of his separation to God is on his head.

2. In the Old Testament, someone who committed a sin was forgiven through a simple sin offering (Lev 4:27~31)[164], but someone who has touched a corpse (death) must wait 7 days to be cleansed (Nu 6:6~9, 19:11~13)[165].

Nu6:9 "'If someone dies suddenly in his presence, thus defiling the hair he has dedicated, he must shave his head on the day of his cleansing—the seventh day.

164)Lev4:27 "'If a member of the community sins unintentionally and does what is forbidden in any of the LORD'S commands, he is guilty.
Lev4:28 When he is made aware of the sin he committed, he must bring as his offering for the sin he committed a female goat without defect.
Lev4:29 He is to lay his hand on the head of the sin offering and slaughter it at the place of the burnt offering.
Lev4:30 Then the priest is to take some of the blood with his finger and put it on the horns of the altar of burnt offering and pour out the rest of the blood at the base of the altar.
Lev4:31 He shall remove all the fat, just as the fat is removed from the fellowship offering, and the priest shall burn it on the altar as an aroma pleasing to the LORD. In this way the priest will make atonement for him, and he will be forgiven.

165)Nu6:6 Throughout the period of his separation to the LORD he must not go near a dead body.
Nu6:7 Even if his own father or mother or brother or sister dies, he must not make himself ceremonially unclean on account of them, because the symbol of his separation to God is on his head.
Nu6:8 Throughout the period of his separation he is consecrated to the LORD.
Nu6:9 "'If someone dies suddenly in his presence, thus defiling the hair he has dedicated, he must shave his head on the day of his cleansing—the seventh day.
Nu19:11 "Whoever touches the dead body of anyone will be unclean for seven days.
Nu19:12 He must purify himself with the water on the third day and on the seventh day; then he will be clean. But if he does not purify himself on the third and seventh days, he will not be clean.
Nu19:13 Whoever touches the dead body of anyone and fails to purify himself defiles the LORD'S tabernacle. That person must be cut off from Israel. Because the water of cleansing has not been sprinkled on him, he is unclean; his

[White clothes]

3. The color white symbolizes purity and acceptance. White clothes represent a life and deeds not spoiled by sin or death and recognized by the Lord. Having **white clothes** is the condition of eligibility to walk alongside the Lord not only during the church age, but also in the kingdom age that is to come.

Verse 5 The one who is victorious will, like them, be dressed in white. I will never blot out the name of that person from the book of life, but will acknowledge that name before My Father and His angels.

1. The fulfillment of the promise for the overcomers of the church is talking about kingdom destiny. The overcomers, dressed in white, will rejoice with Christ during the Millennial Kingdom.
2. Also, the white garments worn by those who overcome will be a reward, for those who overcome, in the Millennial Kingdom. How they act in this age (the church age) will be rewarded in the coming kingdom age (Rev 6:11)[166].
3. There are two kinds of garment in Christianity.
   a. The garment of salvation: a garment worn by the faith of Christ (Ge 3:21, garments of skin) (Isa 61:10, Ge 3:21)[167].
   b. The garment of righteousness: a garment received by virtue

---

uncleanness remains on him.

166)Rev6:11 Then each of them was given a white robe, and they were told to wait a little longer, until the number of their fellow servants and brothers who were to be killed as they had been was completed.

167)Isa61:10 I delight greatly in the LORD; my soul rejoices in my God. For He has clothed me with garments of salvation and arrayed me in a robe of righteousness, as a bridegroom adorns his head like a priest, and as a bride adorns herself with her jewels.

Ge3:21 The LORD God made garments of skin for Adam and his wife and clothed them.

of the believer's righteous living (Rev 19:8, Lk 15:22, Col 3:12, Eph 4:24)[168].

4. <u>He who overcomes will, like them, be dressed in white. I will never blot out his name from the **book of life**</u>.
   This means that they have lived by the life of God and by the life-giving Spirit (Jn 6:63)[169] and have walked by the Holy Spirit (Gal 5:16, Mt 25:21, 23)[170].
5. If we do not become overcomers, our names can be erased from the book of life, and we will not be able to live kingdom lives in the Kingdom (Mt 18:31～35, 22:11～14, 25:30)[171].

---

168)Rev19:8 Fine linen, bright and clean, was given her to wear." (Fine linen stands for the righteous acts of the saints.)
Lk15:22 "But the father said to his servants, 'Quick! Bring the best robe and put it on him. Put a ring on his finger and sandals on his feet.
Col3:12 Therefore, as God's chosen people, holy and dearly loved, clothe yourselves with compassion, kindness, humility, gentleness and patience.
Eph4:24 and to put on the new self, created to be like God in true righteousness and holiness.

169)Jn6:63 The Spirit gives life; the flesh counts for nothing. The words I have spoken to you are spirit and they are life.

170)Gal5:16 So I say, live by the Spirit, and you will not gratify the desires of the sinful nature.
Mt25:21 "His master replied, 'Well done, good and faithful servant! You have been faithful with a few things; I will put you in charge of many things. Come and share your master's happiness!'
Mt25:23 "His master replied, 'Well done, good and faithful servant! You have been faithful with a few things; I will put you in charge of many things. Come and share your master's happiness!'
171)Mt18:31 When the other servants saw what had happened, they were greatly distressed and went and told their master everything that had happened.
Mt18:32 "Then the master called the servant in. 'You wicked servant,' he said, 'I canceled all that debt of yours because

Verse 6 Whoever has ears, let them hear what the Spirit says to the churches.

■The dead church in Sardis needs the words of the life- giving living Spirit. To hear the Spirit's voice, our spiritual ears must be opened. The letter kills (2Co 3:6)[172], but the Spirit gives life (Jn 6:63)[173].

[The church in Philadelphia]

⇒ (Early 19th century - Till the Lord's Second coming)

1. Philadelphia ⇒ (Greek) Brotherly love
2. Represents the church in the early 19th century which had deep brotherly love, from the restoration of proper church life to the Second Coming.
3. The response of the Catholic Church, exemplified by the church of Thyatira, is the church of Sardis (Protestant Reformed

---

you begged me to.

Mt18:33 Shouldn't you have had mercy on your fellow servant just as I had on you?'

Mt18:34 In anger his master turned him over to the jailers to be tortured, until he should pay back all he owed.

Mt18:35 "This is how My heavenly Father will treat each of you unless you forgive your brother from your heart."

Mt22:11 "But when the king came in to see the guests, he noticed a man there who was not wearing wedding clothes.

Mt22:12 'Friend,' he asked, 'how did you get in here without wedding clothes?' The man was speechless.

Mt22:13 "Then the king told the attendants, 'Tie him hand and foot, and throw him outside, into the darkness, where there will be weeping and gnashing of teeth.'

Mt22:14 "For many are invited, but few are chosen."

Mt25:30 And throw that worthless servant outside, into the darkness, where there will be weeping and gnashing of teeth.'

172)2Co3:6 He has made us competent as ministers of a new covenant--not of the letter but of the Spirit; for the letter kills, but the Spirit gives life.

173)Jn6:63 The Spirit gives life; the flesh counts for nothing. The words I have spoken to you are spirit and they are life.

Church). Reformation was accomplished, but their deeds were dead, and the response was the church of brotherly love, the church of Philadelphia.

Verse 7 "To the angel of the church in Philadelphia write: These are the words of Him who is holy and true, who holds the key of David. What He opens no one can shut, and what He shuts no one can open.

1. The Lord reveals Himself as holy and true and speaks to the church in Philadelphia which loves its brothers.
2. **The key of David** is the key of God's sovereignty. This sovereignty refers to the sovereignty of Israel, God's primary kingdom, and David represented God in establishing God's kingdom on earth. He was a man who had waged war for the kingdom and made perfect preparations for the building of the temple (Lk 1:31~33, Mt 16:19)[174].
3. The Lord opens and shuts the gate of Heaven and only the Lord can open the gate of Heaven; if He closes it, there is no one else who can open it (Mt 25:10~12, Lk 13:25, 28)[175]

---

174)Lk1:31 You will be with child and give birth to a son, and you are to give Him the name Jesus.
Lk1:32 He will be great and will be called the Son of the Most High. The Lord God will give Him the throne of His father David,
Lk1:33 and He will reign over the house of Jacob forever; His kingdom will never end."
Mt16:19 I will give you the keys of the kingdom of heaven; whatever you bind on earth will be bound in heaven, and whatever you loose on earth will be loosed in heaven."

175)Mt25:10 "But while they were on their way to buy the oil, the bridegroom arrived. The virgins who were ready went in with him to the wedding banquet. And the door was shut.
Mt25:11 "Later the others also came. 'Sir! Sir!' they said. 'Open the door for us!'
Mt25:12 "But he replied, 'I tell you the truth, I don't know you.'
Lk13:25 Once the owner of the house gets up and closes the door, you will stand outside knocking and pleading, 'Sir, open the door for us.' "But he will answer, 'I don't know you or where you come from.'
Lk13:28 "There will be weeping there, and gnashing of teeth, when

Verse 8 I know your deeds. See, I have placed before you an open door that no one can shut. I know that you have little strength, yet you have kept My word and have not denied My name.

1. Before the church in Philadelphia, an open door of Heaven has been placed that no one can shut. Loving a brother in Christ is a sufficient condition to enter into Heaven.
2. The church in Philadelphia had little strength. It is not our strength (great ability) that pleases the Lord, but rather doing our best to obey the word of God in our present condition, with the little strength that we have; the Lord gives grace and life to such people.
3. Possessing great ability is not necessary in order to keep the word of the Lord, but prayerfully doing our best with little strength, the word can be kept.

Verse 9 I will make those who are of the synagogue of Satan, who claim to be Jews though they are not, but are liars —I will make them come and fall down at your feet and acknowledge that I have loved you.

[Those who claim to be Jews]

1. These are Jews in the flesh only, not in the spirit; because of their traditional religious concepts they did not know God's will. They opposed God's will and hindered His purpose. Their synagogue became the synagogue of Satan. Even today, there are many who call themselves Christians but oppose God's will.
2. From **the groups belonging to Satan**, the Lord will convert some people and, through their conversion, will show that He loves restored churches.

Verse 10 Since you have kept My command to endure

you see Abraham, Isaac and Jacob and all the prophets in the kingdom of God, but you yourselves thrown out.

patiently, I will also keep you from the hour of trial that is going to come on the whole world to test the inhabitants of the earth.

1. All the Lord's words are words of endurance, because to obey the word, perseverance is needed. It is because the word brings suffering to us. We must be able to share in the Lord's suffering, kingdom, and patience (endurance) (Rev 1:9)[176].
2. If we are to keep the Lord's word of endurance, we must go through rejection and persecution (Ac 14:22, Heb 5:8~9, Jn 16:33)[177].
3. **The hour of trial** means the great tribulation from the first trumpet, and it will be all over the world just before the Lord's coming (Mt 24:15~24)[178].

---

176)Rev1:9 I, John, your brother and companion in the suffering and kingdom and patient endurance that are ours in Jesus, was on the island of Patmos because of the word of God and the testimony of Jesus.

177)Ac14:22 strengthening the disciples and encouraging them to remain true to the faith. "We must go through many hardships to enter the kingdom of God," they said.
Heb5:8 Although He was a son, He learned obedience from what He suffered
Heb5:9 and, once made perfect, He became the source of eternal salvation for all who obey Him

178)Mt24:15 "So when you see standing in the holy place 'the abomination that causes desolation,' spoken of through the prophet Daniel--let the reader understand--
Mt24:16 then let those who are in Judea flee to the mountains.
Mt24:17 Let no one on the roof of his house go down to take anything out of the house.
Mt24:18 Let no one in the field go back to get his cloak.
Mt24:19 How dreadful it will be in those days for pregnant women and nursing mothers!
Mt24:20 Pray that your flight will not take place in winter or on the Sabbath.
Mt24:21 For then there will be great distress, unequaled from the beginning of the world until now—and never to be equaled again.
Mt24:22 If those days had not been cut short, no one would survive,

4. The Lord will keep us from the hour of trial when we have kept His word of endurance. The reason being that through obeying the word of endurance, we have already paid the price of suffering and remained obedient (Lk 21:34～36)[179].
5. When we do not keep the word of endurance, we are left to tribulation. Whether or not we pass through tribulation will be determined by our church life now.

Verse 11 I am coming soon. Hold on to what you have, so that no one will take your crown.

1. To the saints that love and work hard to keep the word, the Lord will come to them soon. But, to those who don't love the word and have no regard to obey the word, the Lord is far from coming. To them, the Lord will come like a trap.
2. The restored church has already obtained a crown. We must hold on firmly until the Lord comes, because Satan will constantly tempt us in order to take the crowns away. Satan the devil desperately tries to prevent us from obtaining crowns and becoming overcomers.
3. To the suffering church in Smyrna, the crown of life is promised to them when they are faithful to the point of death. As for the church of brotherly love, the church in Philadelphia, they have already received the crown of life.

---

but for the sake of the elect those days will be shortened.

Mt24:23 At that time if anyone says to you, 'Look, here is the Christ!' or, 'There He is!' do not believe it.

Mt24:24 For false Christs and false prophets will appear and perform great signs and miracles to deceive even the elect—if that were possible.

179)Lk21:34 "Be careful, or your hearts will be weighed down with dissipation, drunkenness and the anxieties of life, and that day will close on you unexpectedly like a trap.

Lk21:35 For it will come upon all those who live on the face of the whole earth.

Lk21:36 Be always on the watch, and pray that you may be able to escape all that is about to happen, and that you may be able to stand before the Son of Man."

Verse 12 The one who is victorious I will make a pillar in the temple of My God. Never again will they leave it. I will write on them the name of My God and the name of the city of My God, the new Jerusalem, which is coming down out of heaven from My God; and I will also write on them My new name.

1. He who overcomes in the church in Pergamum becomes a white stone and becomes a stone that can be built into the temple. He who overcomes in the church in Philadelphia becomes a pillar for the temple and is built within the temple. As he is built as a pillar, he will never leave the temple again. Some people remain for a little while, a couple of months and then leave. But if they are built as pillars of the temple, they cannot leave.
2. Those who overcome in the church in Philadelphia do not gain anything, but they keep what they have already gained.
3. The Lord writes God's name on the overcomer. The name is one of many signs. Your name shows who you are. This means that God works through us and we become one with Him. Also, God's name being written on the overcomer means that he has been drenched in Him.
4. The name of the New Jerusalem being written on the overcomer means that he becomes a part of the New Jerusalem. This means that the coming New Jerusalem was to be worked in His presence. The name always corresponds with the identity (we do not call a sheep a cat nor a lion a monkey).
5. Also, the Lord says He will write on him his new name. The new name is written according to our experience. If we experience God, He is incarnated in us to the extent that we experience Him.
6. The name of God, the name of the New Jerusalem, and the new name of the Lord, written on the overcomer, means that the overcomer is owned by God and by the New Jerusalem and by the Lord. It also means being one with God, the New

Jerusalem, and the Lord. For God's name means God, the name of the New Jerusalem means the city itself, and the new name of the Lord means the Lord Himself forever.

Verse 13 Whoever has ears, let them hear what the Spirit says to the churches.

▣ This scripture was spoken by the Lord at that time to the church in Philadelphia. On this day, He speaks to the churches and also to us through the Spirit. Only those who have an ear can hear.

[The church in Laodicea]

⇒ (Late 19th century ~ the Lord's second coming)

1. Laodicea ⇒ (Greek) The opinion and decision of the people.
2. Laodicea portrays a church whose brotherly love has become cold and has fallen, representing the Church from the late 19th century to the Lord's second coming.

Verse 14 "To the angel of the church in Laodicea write: These are the words of the Amen, the faithful and true witness, the ruler of God's creation.

1. Amen ⇒ (Greek) that is absolutely right. I hope so.
   means fastened, unwavering, believable.
2. The Lord speaks to the church in Laodicea as an unwavering, fastened, believable, faithful, and true witness, because the church is not unwavering and true as a witness of the Lord.
3. Speaking as the ruler of God's creation is emphasizing the fact that the creator fulfills the purpose of creation and that the end is imminent.

Verse 15 I know your deeds, that you are neither cold nor hot. I wish you were either one or the other!

1. The church in Laodicea's acts of faith were neither cold nor hot.

Our acts of faith should be burning hot, but since theirs were not, the Lord had rebuked them.

2. If our deeds of faith are neither cold nor hot, then it is hard to determine our state of faith. If our deeds of faith were cold, it would be easy to realize what we are lacking and return to the Lord.
3. Our deeds of faith must be hot, otherwise if our state of faith is lukewarm, the Lord will spit us out of His mouth.

Verse 16 So, because you are lukewarm—neither hot nor cold — I am about to spit you out of My mouth.

1. If the church (individual) whose faith has been restored is corrupt, it becomes lukewarm.
2. To be spat out of the Lord's mouth is to be rejected by the Lord.

Verse 17 You say, 'I am rich; I have acquired wealth and do not need a thing.' But you do not realize that you are wretched, pitiful, poor, blind and naked.

1. If the church becomes corrupt (lukewarm), it will begin to think of itself as rich. But they are actually only rich in the knowledge of dogma.
2. If our faith becomes lukewarm, we fail to realize that we are wretched in life, are blind to what is right under our nose, and cannot see that what we do is shameful. The most remarkable sign of a corrupt congregation is its pride. They think that they know everything. Although they have a lot of knowledge concerning doctrine, it is only knowledge. But when it comes to life, they are blind and poor. Their actions are naked, their spiritual eyes are blind, and they are pitiful because they are full of shame and darkness.
3. They are poor in their experience with Jesus Christ and the spiritual reality of God. They are blind to spiritual things and lacking when it comes to spiritual insight, so that although they have knowledge they cannot see.

4. The corrupt church (the lukewarm church whose faith has gone cold) is not in a place where the believers are in pursuit of gaining rich experience of the Lord, so if they do not repent to be hot again (fix their actions), that church will be spat out of the Lord's mouth. This means that they will lose the ability to enjoy God's grace and life.

[white clothes]

Verse 18 I counsel you to buy from Me gold refined in the fire, so you can become rich; and white clothes to wear, so you can cover your shameful nakedness; and salve to put on your eyes, so you can see.

1. Buying means to pay the price. The corrupt (lukewarm) church must pay the price in order to get what is desperately needed: gold, white clothes, and eye medicine. Even when we are awakened to the truth, in order to experience the abundance of Christ we must pay the price.
2. In the Bible, gold is likened to faith, and the divine nature of God, which speaks of the divinity of Christ, is also typified by gold (1Pe 1:7, Job 23:10)[180]. We participate in God's divine nature as gold faith. The church must pay the price of fiery hot trials in order to participate in pure gold. The church thus becomes the pure gold lampstand for the construction of the gold New Jerusalem (Rev 1:20)[181].
3. We are to buy **white clothes**, which represent our works (Rev

---

180)1Pe1:7 These have come so that your faith--of greater worth than gold, which perishes even though refined by fire--may be proved genuine and may result in praise, glory and honor when Jesus Christ is revealed.
Job23:10 But He knows the way that I take; when He has tested me, I will come forth as gold.

181)Rev1:20 The mystery of the seven stars that you saw in My right hand and of the seven golden lampstands is this: The seven stars are the angels of the seven churches, and the seven lampstands are the seven churches.

19:8, Isa 61:10)[182]. The white clothes represent deeds which are acceptable to the Lord and are the living expression of the Lord Himself and a call to cover the nakedness of the fallen church. In other words, everything that expresses Christ in our lives is white clothes (Col 3:12~14)[183].

4. When we have a living faith and participate in the divine nature of God, this divine nature will eventually proceed from us and become our life. This life is Christ alive in our being, the second garment that gives us status and qualification to be recognized by the Lord (Isa 61:10)[184]. This garment will cover our nakedness.
5. The '**[salve]** to put on your eyes' refers to the anointing spirit and the Lord Himself as the life-giving Spirit (1Co 15:45)[185]. Spiritual insight is always related to the Spirit. What we need is not more knowledge and doctrine, but for the Lord's Spirit to anoint our eyes and the depths of our inner beings so that we can see spiritual things.

---

182)Rev19:8 Fine linen, bright and clean, was given her to wear." (Fine linen stands for the righteous acts of the saints.)
Isa61:10 I delight greatly in the LORD; my soul rejoices in my God. For He has clothed me with garments of salvation and arrayed me in a robe of righteousness, as a bridegroom adorns his head like a priest, and as a bride adorns herself with her jewels.

183)Col3:12 Therefore, as God's chosen people, holy and dearly loved, clothe yourselves with compassion, kindness, humility, gentleness and patience.
Col3:13 Bear with each other and forgive whatever grievances you may have against one another. Forgive as the Lord forgave you.
Col3:14 And over all these virtues put on love, which binds them all together in perfect unity.

184) Isa61:10 ☝ See footnote 182)

185)1Co15:45 So it is written: "The first man Adam became a living being"; the last Adam, a life-giving spirit.

※ We do not begrudge paying a lot for jewellery, but we are unwilling to pay the price to get the things within Christ. This is because we do not realize how noble and precious Christ is. In our eyes, we view things of flesh and things that are pleasurable to the flesh - gold, silver, and precious stones - as more valuable than Christ. When the salve is applied to our eyes so that we have spiritual insight, we will realize that no matter the price we pay for Christ, it is the most noble and valuable deed.

※ Gold, white clothes, and eye salve is Christ who works in us and brings change in us as much as we have been anointed.

Verse 19 Those whom I love I rebuke and discipline. So be earnest and repent.

1. The Lord rebukes and disciplines the lukewarm church. If the church willingly accepts the rebuke, through the Lord's rebuke the corrupt church will be able to open their eyes (Heb 12:5~11)[186]. If we are proud, we cannot accept reproof and we must seek His mercy so that we can accept it.

---

186)Heb12:5 And you have forgotten that word of encouragement that addresses you as sons: "My son, do not make light of the Lord's discipline, and do not lose heart when He rebukes you,
Heb12:6 because the Lord disciplines those He loves, and He punishes everyone He accepts as a son."
Heb12:7 Endure hardship as discipline; God is treating you as sons. For what son is not disciplined by his father?
Heb12:8 If you are not disciplined (and everyone undergoes discipline), then you are illegitimate children and not true sons.
Heb12:9 Moreover, we have all had human fathers who disciplined us and we respected them for it. How much more should we submit to the Father of our spirits and live!
Heb12:10 Our fathers disciplined us for a little while as they thought best; but God disciplines us for our good, that we may share in His holiness.
Heb12:11 No discipline seems pleasant at the time, but painful. Later on, however, it produces a harvest of righteousness and peace for those who have been trained by it.

2. Discipline is a step beyond rebuke. If the church accepts the rebuke willingly, the Lord will not discipline the church.
3. Dead knowledge and doctrines make the corrupt church lukewarm. As the church throws out the dead knowledge which makes the church lukewarm, it should burn with passion and break free from the bondage of religious dogma.
4. No matter the cost the lukewarm church pays, it must burn hot with passion. The corrupt church must repent of its lukewarmness and must not boast about its knowledge.
5. When the church is lukewarm, it must be zealous and pay any price until its deeds become hot. The Lord will speak to us to repent. We are to repent and turn after the Holy Spirit.

Verse 20 Here I am! I stand at the door and knock. If anyone hears My voice and opens the door, I will come in and eat with that person, and they with Me.

1. In lukewarm and arrogant churches which only have knowledge and doctrines and think of themselves as rich, the Lord's presence is absent. Rather, Christ who is the head is outside knocking on the corrupt church's door.
2. The opening of the door means that it has been opened by each believer in the church. To open the door takes passion and repentance. If we hear the Lord's voice and open the door to Him, He will come inside and we will be able to feel His presence.
3. And then, we will eat and drink with the Lord and He will eat and drink with us. This will become a Supper which we eat and drink with the Lord (Jn 6:35, 48~51, Mt 26:26~30)[187] and through this we will grow spiritually.

---

187)Jn6:35 Then Jesus declared, "I am the bread of life. He who comes to Me will never go hungry, and he who believes in Me will never be thirsty.
Jn6:48 I am the bread of life.
Jn6:49 Your forefathers ate the manna in the desert, yet they died.
Jn6:50 But here is the bread that comes down from heaven, which a

4. The Lord implies that to those who overcome in the church in Ephesus, the Lord will let them eat the tree of life, and will let the church in Pergamum eat the hidden manna, and will let those who show passion and repent in the church in Laodicea enjoy the word of God as the bread of life.

Verse 21 To the one who is victorious, I will give the right to sit with Me on My throne, just as I was victorious and sat down with My Father on His throne.

1. In the letters to the seven churches, to overcome means to overcome the fallen abnormal conditions of the churches, rather than to overcome our weaknesses and the sin which so easily ensnares us.
2. To overcome in the church in Laodicea is to overcome the pride and lukewarmness of the corrupt church. In order to do this, we have to be earnest and repent as we pay the price and be restored. In other words, the door has to be opened so that the Lord may come into our hearts.
3. The Lord will let those who overcome sit with Him on the throne and it will be a reward during the Millennial Kingdom to share in the authority of the Lord.
4. All the promises in the 7 letters are about the coming kingdom.

---

man may eat and not die.

Jn6:51 I am the living bread that came down from heaven. If anyone eats of this bread, he will live forever. This bread is My flesh, which I will give for the life of the world."

Mt26:26 While they were eating, Jesus took bread, gave thanks and broke it, and gave it to His disciples, saying, "Take and eat; this is My body."

Mt26:27 Then He took the cup, gave thanks and offered it to them, saying, "Drink from it, all of you.

Mt26:28 This is My blood of the covenant, which is poured out for many for the forgiveness of sins.

Mt26:29 I tell you, I will not drink of this fruit of the vine from now on until that day when I drink it anew with you in My Father's kingdom."

Mt26:30 When they had sung a hymn, they went out to the Mount of Olives.

What this is saying is that everything that brings suffering and hurt will be what happens in the Millennial Kingdom. Everything we were promised that we would obtain and enjoy is our special inheritance which is Christ during the Millennial Kingdom.

5. <u>But these promises apply even today, and through obedience in the church age, we can enjoy a foretaste of everything that we will enjoy during the Millennial Kingdom.</u> So today, through church life, let us give thanks for the privilege of this foretaste of the coming kingdom. Hallelujah!

Verse 22 Whoever has ears, let them hear what the Spirit says to the churches."

▣ Only those who have spiritual ears (ears of inner being) can hear these words. Today the Holy Spirit is constantly speaking to us and to the churches. Those who can hear these words and who are able to say "Amen" from their hearts are those who are specially blessed by God and are walking down the path of the overcomer. Hallelujah!

Chapter 4 [The Throne in Heaven]

Verse 1 After this I looked, and there before me was a door standing open in heaven. And the voice I had first heard speaking to me like a trumpet said, "Come up here, and I will show you what must take place after this."

1. <u>When God gains a man after His own heart on earth, Heaven will open up to the man</u>. To Jacob (Ge 28:12~17)[188], to Ezekiel (Eze 1:1)[189], to Stephen (Ac 7:56)[190], to Peter (Ac 10:11)[191], to John (Rev 4:1, 19:11)[192], and to all the

---

188)Ge28:12 He had a dream in which he saw a stairway resting on the earth, with its top reaching to heaven, and the angels of God were ascending and descending on it.
Ge28:13 There above it stood the LORD, and He said: "I am the LORD, the God of your father Abraham and the God of Isaac. I will give you and your descendants the land on which you are lying.
Ge28:14 Your descendants will be like the dust of the earth, and you will spread out to the west and to the east, to the north and to the south. All peoples on earth will be blessed through you and your offspring.
Ge28:15 I am with you and will watch over you wherever you go, and I will bring you back to this land. I will not leave you until I have done what I have promised you."
Ge28:16 When Jacob awoke from his sleep, he thought, "Surely the LORD is in this place, and I was not aware of it."
Ge28:17 He was afraid and said, "How awesome is this place! This is none other than the house of God; this is the gate of heaven."

189)Eze1:1 In the thirtieth year, in the fourth month on the fifth day, while I was among the exiles by the Kebar River, the heavens were opened and I saw visions of God.

190)Ac7:56 "Look," he said, "I see heaven open and the Son of Man standing at the right hand of God."

191)Ac10:11 He saw heaven opened and something like a large sheet being let down to earth by its four corners.

true Saints in spirit (Jn 1:51)[193].

2. <u>**A voice like a trumpet**</u> (Rev 1:10, Ex 19:19～20)[194]
<u>**a gentle whisper**</u> (1Ki 19:12, Job 4:16)[195]
3. <u>After hearing "come up here", he was caught up to be shown what must take place after this (after the church age).</u> During this encounter, the body of John was in the flesh on the island of Patmos while his spirit had gone up to Heaven (Rev 11:12, 2Co 12:1～4)[196].

---

192)Rev4:1 After this I looked, and there before me was a door standing open in heaven. And the voice I had first heard speaking to me like a trumpet said, "Come up here, and I will show you what must take place after this."
Rev19:11 I saw heaven standing open and there before me was a white horse, whose rider is called Faithful and True. With justice He judges and makes war.

193)Jn1:51 He then added, "I tell you the truth, you shall see heaven open, and the angels of God ascending and descending on the Son of Man."

194)Rev1:10 On the Lord's Day I was in the Spirit, and I heard behind me a loud voice like a trumpet,
Ex19:19 and the sound of the trumpet grew louder and louder. Then Moses spoke and the voice of God answered him.
Ex19:20 The LORD descended to the top of Mount Sinai and called Moses to the top of the mountain. So Moses went up

195)1Ki19:12 After the earthquake came a fire, but the LORD was not in the fire. And after the fire came a gentle whisper.
Job4:16 It stopped, but I could not tell what it was. A form stood before my eyes, and I heard a hushed voice:

196)Rev11:12 Then they heard a loud voice from heaven saying to them, "Come up here." And they went up to heaven in a cloud, while their enemies looked on.
2Co12:1 I must go on boasting. Although there is nothing to be gained, I will go on to visions and revelations from the Lord.
2Co12:2 I know a man in Christ who fourteen years ago was caught up to the third heaven. Whether it was in the body or out of the body I do not know—God knows.
2Co12:3 And I know that this man—whether in the body or apart from the body I do not know, but God knows--

Verse 2 At once I was in the Spirit, and there before me was a throne in heaven with someone sitting on it.

1. I was in the Spirit
2. When we are in our reborn spirit, we can be *in the Spirit*. John got to see the throne in Heaven and God's appearance sitting on the throne while in the reborn spirit.
3. The throne in the letters represents the throne of the church age and the throne of grace (Heb 4:16)[197]. From that throne we will receive compassion and grace. But the throne in this verse is the throne of judgment and the world will be judged before this throne. In the end, after all the judgments have been carried out by God, His throne will be the everlasting throne of life. The water of life will flow out from this throne (Rev 22:1～2)[198].

Verse 3 And the One who sat there had the appearance of jasper and ruby. A rainbow that shone like an emerald encircled the throne.

1. It is God who sits on the throne (Rev 3:11), and His appearance is like jasper (green ⇒ life) and carnelian (red ⇒ symbolizes redemption). It shows that God is the God of life and the God of redemption.
2. In the Old Testament, there were 12 kinds of precious

2Co12:4 was caught up to paradise. He heard inexpressible things, things that man is not permitted to tell.

197)Heb4:16 Let us then approach the throne of grace with confidence, so that we may receive mercy and find grace to help us in our time of need.

198)Rev22:1 Then the angel showed me the river of the water of life, as clear as crystal, flowing from the throne of God and of the Lamb

Rev22:2 down the middle of the great street of the city. On each side of the river stood the tree of life, bearing twelve crops of fruit, yielding its fruit every month. And the leaves of the tree are for the healing of the nations.

stones that were on the breast piece of the chief priest. The first was ruby (Ex 28:17)[199] and the last was jasper (Ex 28:20)[200]. What this means is that God is the One that redeems His people and ultimately perfects them with the glory of life.

3. The rainbow is a sign of the covenant that God made with all the people and living things, that He will not destroy them again with a flood (Ge 9:8～17)[201].
4. The emerald represents life on the earth and means that when God had passed judgment on the earth with water,

---

199)Ex28:17 Then mount four rows of precious stones on it. In the first row there shall be a ruby, a topaz and a beryl;

200)Ex28:20 in the fourth row a chrysolite, an onyx and a jasper. Mount them in gold filigree settings.

201)Ge9:8 Then God said to Noah and to his sons with him:
Ge9:9 "I now establish My covenant with you and with your descendants after you
Ge9:10 and with every living creature that was with you—the birds, the livestock and all the wild animals, all those that came out of the ark with you—every living creature on earth.
Ge9:11 I establish My covenant with you: Never again will all life be cut off by the waters of a flood; never again will there be a flood to destroy the earth."
Ge9:12 And God said, "This is the sign of the covenant I am making between Me and you and every living creature with you, a covenant for all generations to come:
Ge9:13 I have set My rainbow in the clouds, and it will be the sign of the covenant between Me and the earth.
Ge9:14 Whenever I bring clouds over the earth and the rainbow appears in the clouds,
Ge9:15 I will remember My covenant between Me and you and all living creatures of every kind. Never again will the waters become a flood to destroy all life.
Ge9:16 Whenever the rainbow appears in the clouds, I will see it and remember the everlasting covenant between God and all living creatures of every kind on the earth."
Ge9:17 So God said to Noah, "This is the sign of the covenant I have established between Me and all life on the earth."

He remembered His covenant (of creation; Genesis 1:26～28) and did not destroy all living creatures.

Verse 4 Surrounding the throne were twenty-four other thrones, and seated on them were twenty-four elders. They were dressed in white and had crowns of gold on their heads.

1. **Twenty four** is a factor of twelve, which is the perfect number of the fulfilment of God's dispensation. So twenty four symbolizes the double strength of God's absolute administration. David divided the priests and Levites into twenty-four groups to perform God's administrative service.
2. **The twenty-four elders** are not of the church (2Jn 1:1, 3 Jn 1:1, 1Pe 5:1)[202] but of the angels, because they were already sitting on the throne even before Christ came (the Lord's second coming). After the Lord's second coming, the disciples will also sit on twelve thrones, judging the twelve tribes of Israel (Mt 19:28)[203]. The overcomers among the Saints will judge and reign over the nations (Rev 20:4)[204].
3. The angelic elders being dressed in white means they have

---

202)2Jn1:1 The elder, To the chosen lady and her children, whom I love in the truth--and not I only, but also all who know the truth--
3Jn1:1 The elder, To my dear friend Gaius, whom I love in the truth.
1Pe5:1 To the elders among you, I appeal as a fellow elder, a witness of Christ's sufferings and one who also will share in the glory to be revealed:

203)Mt19:28 Jesus said to them, "I tell you the truth, at the renewal of all things, when the Son of Man sits on His glorious throne, you who have followed Me will also sit on twelve thrones, judging the twelve tribes of Israel.

204)Rev20:4 I saw thrones on which were seated those who had been given authority to judge. And I saw the souls of those who had been beheaded because of their testimony for Jesus and because of the word of God. They had not worshiped the beast or his image and had not received his mark on their foreheads or their hands. They came to life and reigned with Christ a thousand years.

bodies (Gen 18), and since their deeds have been good they have been dressed in white.

4. The angelic elders sitting and having **crowns of gold** (Stefanos; Greek) (Php 4:1, 1Th 2:19, Rev 2:10)[205] on their heads represents the fact that they rule and reign over the universe until the Lord comes.
   ※ diadema (Greek) crown (Rev 12:3, 19:12, 13:1)[206]

Verse 5 From the throne came flashes of lightning, rumblings and peals of thunder. In front of the throne, seven lamps were blazing. These are the seven spirits of God.

1. "From the throne came flashes of lightning, rumblings and peals of thunder" is seen as a warning to the sinning world. The throne is the throne of judgment (Rev 8:5, 11:19, 16:18)[207].

---

205)Php4:1 Therefore, my brothers, you whom I love and long for, my joy and crown, that is how you should stand firm in the Lord, dear friends!
1Th2:19 For what is our hope, our joy, or the crown in which we will glory in the presence of our Lord Jesus when He comes? Is it not you?
Rev2:10 Do not be afraid of what you are about to suffer. I tell you, the devil will put some of you in prison to test you, and you will suffer persecution for ten days. Be faithful, even to the point of death, and I will give you the crown of life.

206)Rev12:3 Then another sign appeared in heaven: an enormous red dragon with seven heads and ten horns and seven crowns on his heads.
Rev19:12 His eyes are like blazing fire, and on His head are many crowns. He has a name written on Him that no one knows but He Himself.
Rev13:1 And the dragon stood on the shore of the sea. And I saw a beast coming out of the sea. He had ten horns and seven heads, with ten crowns on his horns, and on each head a blasphemous name.

207)Rev8:5 Then the angel took the censer, filled it with fire from the altar, and hurled it on the earth; and there came peals of thunder, rumblings, flashes of lightning and an earthquake.
Rev11:19 Then God's temple in heaven was opened, and within His

2. "seven lamps were blazing" shows that in enhanced light, seven times as bright as before, God's judgment will be without a speck of doubt, a perfect judgment (Zec 4:2)[208].
3. The work of light blazing through the seven lamps is also the work of the Spirit of God.

[The working of the seven spirits]

a. Ministry aspect: [fire (Ac 2:3), living water (Jn 7:38), dove (Jn 1:32), wind (Jn 3:8), oil (Jas 5:14, 1Jn 2:20), light (Jn 1:5, 9) cloud (Dt 1:33)][209].

b. Essential aspect : [the Spirit of truth (Jn 14:16~17), the

---

temple was seen the ark of His covenant. And there came flashes of lightning, rumblings, peals of thunder, an earthquake and a great hailstorm.

Rev16:18 Then there came flashes of lightning, rumblings, peals of thunder and a severe earthquake. No earthquake like it has ever occurred since man has been on earth, so tremendous was the quake.

208)Zec4:2 He asked me, "What do you see?" I answered, "I see a solid gold lampstand with a bowl at the top and seven lights on it, with seven channels to the lights.

209)Ac2:3 They saw what seemed to be **tongues of fire** that separated and came to rest on each of them.

Jn7:38 Whoever believes in Me, as the Scripture has said, streams of **living water** will flow from within him."

Jn1:32 Then John gave this testimony: "I saw the Spirit come down from heaven as a **dove** and remain on Him.

Jn3:8 The **wind** blows wherever it pleases. You hear its sound, but you cannot tell where it comes from or where it is going. So it is with everyone born of the Spirit."

Jas5:14 Is any one of you sick? He should call the elders of the church to pray over him and anoint him with **oil** in the name of the Lord.

1Jn2:20 But you have an **anointing** from the Holy One, and all of you know the truth.

Jn1:5 The **light** shines in the darkness, but the darkness has not understood it.

Jn1:9 The true **light** that gives **light** to every man was coming into the world.

Spirit of life (Ro 8:2), the Spirit of power (Lk 24:49), the Spirit of God (Ro 8:9), the Spirit of Christ (Ro 8:9), the Spirit of Jesus (Ac 16:7), the Spirit of Jesus Christ (Php 1:19)][210]

c. Functional aspect : (Isa 11:2)[211]: The Spirit of the Lord, the Spirit of Wisdom, the Spirit of understanding, the Spirit of counsel, the Spirit of power, the Spirit of knowledge, the Spirit of the fear of the Lord.

Verse 6 Also in front of the throne there was what looked like a sea of glass, clear as crystal. In the center, around the throne, were four living creatures, and they were covered with eyes, in front and in back.

[A sea of glass as clear as crystal]

1. The **sea of glass as clear as crystal** before the throne is the sea for judgment. When we pass this sea of glass, because all the

---

210)Jn14:16 And I will ask the Father, and He will give you another Counselor to be with you forever--

Jn14:17 the **Spirit of truth**. The world cannot accept Him, because it neither sees Him nor knows Him. But you know Him, for He lives with you and will be in you.

Ro8:2 because through Christ Jesus the law of the **Spirit of life** set me free from the law of sin and death.

Lk24:49 I am going to send you what My Father has promised; but stay in the city **until you have been clothed with power** from on high."

Ro8:9 You, however, are controlled not by the sinful nature but by the Spirit, if the **Spirit of God** lives in you. And if anyone does not have the **Spirit of Christ**, he does not belong to Christ.

Ac16:7 When they came to the border of Mysia, they tried to enter Bithynia, but the **Spirit of Jesus** would not allow them to.

Php1:19 for I know that through your prayers and the help given by the **Spirit of Jesus Christ**, what has happened to me will turn out for my deliverance.

211)Isa11:2 The **Spirit of the LORD** will rest on him--the **Spirit of wisdom and of understanding**, the **Spirit of counsel and of power**, the **Spirit of knowledge and of the fear of the LORD**--

things (sins) will be revealed in the shining light, anyone who carries sins will not be able to pass.

2. After this, this sea will become the sea of fire (Rev 15:2)[212], and those who were not able to pass through the sea of glass as clear as crystal must pass this sea of fire in order to reach the throne.
3. After the flood of Noah, God made a covenant to never again judge the world with water (Ge 9:11~16)[213]. Since then, God has been judging the world with fire (Ge 19:24, Lev 10:2, Nu 16:35, Rev 14:10, 19:20)[214].

---

212)Rev15:2 And I saw what looked like a sea of glass mixed with fire and, standing beside the sea, those who had been victorious over the beast and his image and over the number of his name. They held harps given them by God

213)Ge9:11 I establish My covenant with you: Never again will all life be cut off by the waters of a flood; never again will there be a flood to destroy the earth."
Ge9:12 And God said, "This is the sign of the covenant I am making between Me and you and every living creature with you, a covenant for all generations to come:
Ge9:13 I have set My rainbow in the clouds, and it will be the sign of the covenant between Me and the earth.
Ge9:14 Whenever I bring clouds over the earth and the rainbow appears in the clouds,
Ge9:15 I will remember My covenant between Me and you and all living creatures of every kind. Never again will the waters become a flood to destroy all life.
Ge9:16 Whenever the rainbow appears in the clouds, I will see it and remember the everlasting covenant between God and all living creatures of every kind on the earth."

214)Ge19:24 Then the LORD rained down **burning sulfur** on Sodom and Gomorrah--from the LORD out of the heavens.
Lev10:2 So **fire** came out from the presence of the LORD and consumed them, and they died before the LORD.
Nu16:35 And **fire** came out from the LORD and consumed the 250 men who were offering the incense.
Rev14:10 he, too, will drink of the wine of God's fury, which has been poured full strength into the cup of His wrath. He will be tormented with burning sulfur in the presence of the holy angels and of the Lamb.

4. In the end, the sea of glass turns into the lake of fire. (Rev 20:14)[215)]
5. To the four living creatures covered with eyes in front and back, there is nothing that can be hidden from them, and from their view everything is seen as clear as crystal.

Verse 7 The first living creature was like a lion, the second was like an ox, the third had a face like a man, the fourth was like a flying eagle.

1. **The four living creatures** represent all the living creatures (living creatures among all creation).
   a. The first living creature ⇒ a lion : represents wild animals
   b. The second living creature ⇒ an ox : represents domesticated animals
   c. The third living creature ⇒ man : represents humanity
   d. The fourth living creature ⇒ eagle : represents birds

※ The redemption of Christ will not only affect man but all creation as well (Col 1:20, Ro 8:19～22).[216)]

Rev19:20 But the beast was captured, and with him the false prophet who had performed the miraculous signs on his behalf. With these signs he had deluded those who had received the mark of the beast and worshiped his image. The two of them were thrown alive into the fiery lake of burning sulfur.

215)Rev20:14 Then death and Hades were thrown into the **lake of fire**. The lake of fire is the second death.

216)Col1:20 and through Him to reconcile to Himself all things, whether things on earth or things in heaven, by making peace through His blood, shed on the cross.
Ro8:19 The creation waits in eager expectation for the sons of God to be revealed.
Ro8:20 For the creation was subjected to frustration, not by its own choice, but by the will of the One who subjected it, in hope
Ro8:21 that the creation itself will be liberated from its bondage to decay and brought into the glorious freedom of the children of God.
Ro8:22 We know that the whole creation has been groaning as in the pains of childbirth right up to the present time.

Verse 8 Each of the four living creatures had six wings and was covered with eyes all around, even under its wings. Day and night they never stop saying: " 'Holy, holy, holy is the Lord God Almighty,' who was, and is, and is to come."

1. Each of the four living creatures that have six wings is similar to the cherubim of Ezekiel (Eze 1:5~10, 10:14, 15)[217] and the seraphs of Isaiah (Isa 6:2)[218]. The cherubim have two wings (Ex 25:20, 1Ki 6:27)[219], and in Ezekiel 1:6 the cherubim have 4 wings. Therefore, the four creatures are

---

217)Eze1:5 and in the fire was what looked like four living creatures. In appearance their form was that of a man,
Eze1:6 but each of them had four faces and four wings.
Eze1:7 Their legs were straight; their feet were like those of a calf and gleamed like burnished bronze.
Eze1:8 Under their wings on their four sides they had the hands of a man. All four of them had faces and wings,
Eze1:9 and their wings touched one another. Each one went straight ahead; they did not turn as they moved.
Eze1:10 Their faces looked like this: Each of the four had the face of a man, and on the right side each had the face of a lion, and on the left the face of an ox; each also had the face of an eagle.
Eze10:14 Each of the cherubim had four faces: One face was that of a cherub, the second the face of a man, the third the face of a lion, and the fourth the face of an eagle.
Eze10:15 Then the cherubim rose upward. These were the living creatures I had seen by the Kebar River.

218)Isa6:2 Above Him were **seraphs, each with six wings**: With two wings they covered their faces, with two they covered their feet, and with two they were flying.

219)Ex25:20 The cherubim are to have their wings spread upward, overshadowing the cover with them. The cherubim are to face each other, looking toward the cover.
1Ki6:27 He placed the cherubim inside the innermost room of the temple, with their wings spread out. The wing of one cherub touched one wall, while the wing of the other touched the other wall, and their wings touched each other in the middle of the room.

compelling evidence that they are a combination of the cherubim and the seraphs.

2. The seraphs exist for the holiness of God (Ps 6:3)[220] while the cherubim exist for the glory of God (Eze 10:18~19, Heb 9:5)[221]. With that said, they exist for the purpose of revealing the reality of God's holiness and for the glory of God's appearance.
3. The four living creatures saying "holy" three times reveals God's trinity.
4. The Lord God almighty, who was, who is, and is to come is emphasized. In the end, God will come down on to the New Earth with the New Jerusalem and be with us forever.

Verse 9 Whenever the living creatures give glory, honor and thanks to Him who sits on the throne and who lives for ever and ever,

▣ The four creatures give glory, honour, and thanks to God because they give God glory, honour, and thanksgiving for the joy of salvation (The twenty-four elders praise God for glory, honor, and power).

Verse 10 the twenty-four elders fall down before Him who sits on the throne and worship Him who lives for ever and ever. They lay their crowns before the throne and say:

1. The twenty-four elders lay (return) their crowns before the

---

220)Ps6:3 My soul is in anguish. How long, O LORD, how long?

221)Eze10:18 Then the glory of the LORD departed from over the threshold of the temple and stopped above the **cherubim**.

Eze10:19 While I watched, the **cherubim spread their wings** and rose from the ground, and as they went, the wheels went with them. They stopped at the entrance to the east gate of the LORD'S house, and the glory of the God of Israel was above them.

Heb9:5 Above the ark were the **cherubim of the Glory**, overshadowing the atonement cover. But we cannot discuss these things in detail now.

throne, and praise God. This means that they had authority to reign for a time until Christ came.

2. Their laying down of their crowns before the throne of God means that they give back to God the offices that have governed the universe so far, because their offices are to be delegated to those who overcome with Christ (Rev 20:4~6)[222].

Verse 11 "You are worthy, our Lord and God, to receive glory and honor and power, for You created all things, and by Your will they were created and have their being."

▣ The twenty-four elders praise the Lord with glory, honour and power. That is, they do not give thanks for the grace of redemption, but because they have enjoyed the power of God and have ruled and reigned over the universe. Also, they praise Him for creating all things in the universe, and for the power by which He created all things according to His will.

※ The praise of the twenty-four elders (5 times)

a. (Rev 4:10~11)[223] ⇒ Praising God's power to create.

---

222)Rev20:4 I saw thrones on which were seated those who had been given authority to judge. And I saw the souls of those who had been beheaded because of their testimony for Jesus and because of the word of God. They had not worshiped the beast or his image and had not received his mark on their foreheads or their hands. They came to life and reigned with Christ a thousand years.

Rev20:5 (The rest of the dead did not come to life until the thousand years were ended.) This is the first resurrection.

Rev20:6 Blessed and holy are those who have part in the first resurrection. The second death has no power over them, but they will be priests of God and of Christ and will reign with Him for a thousand years.

223)Rev4:10 the twenty-four elders fall down before Him who sits on the throne, and worship Him who lives for ever and ever. They lay their crowns before the throne and say:

Rev4:11 "You are worthy, our Lord and God, to receive glory and honor and power, for You created all things, and by Your will they were created and have their being."

b. (Rev 5:8~9)[224] ⇒ Praising the Lamb who is worthy to take the scroll from God's right hand and open its seal.
c. (Rev 7:11~12)[225] Praising those 144,000 from the 12 tribes of Israel who were sealed, and the salvation of Gentiles who are clothed in white and holding palm branches in their hands.
d. (Rev 11:16~18)[226] ⇒ Praise that this land is the kingdom of Christ, and He will reign forever.
e. (Rev 19:4~5)[227] Praise for the judgment and the fall of Babylon with Amen, Hallelujah!

---

224)Rev5:8 And when He had taken it, the four living creatures and the twenty-four elders fell down before the Lamb. Each one had a harp and they were holding golden bowls full of incense, which are the prayers of the saints.
Rev5:9 And they sang a new song: "You are worthy to take the scroll and to open its seals, because You were slain, and with Your blood You purchased men for God from every tribe and language and people and nation.

225)Rev7:11 All the angels were standing around the throne and around the elders and the four living creatures. They fell down on their faces before the throne and worshiped God,
Rev7:12 saying: "Amen! Praise and glory and wisdom and thanks and honor and power and strength be to our God for ever and ever. Amen!"

226)Rev11:16 And the twenty-four elders, who were seated on their thrones before God, fell on their faces and worshiped God,
Rev11:17 saying: "We give thanks to You, Lord God Almighty, the One who is and who was, because You have taken Your great power and have begun to reign.
Rev11:18 The nations were angry; and Your wrath has come. The time has come for judging the dead, and for rewarding Your servants the prophets and Your saints and those who reverence Your name, both small and great--and for destroying those who destroy the earth."

227)Rev19:4 The twenty-four elders and the four living creatures fell down and worshiped God, who was seated on the throne. And they cried: "Amen, Hallelujah!"
Rev19:5 Then a voice came from the throne, saying: "Praise our God, all you His servants, you who fear Him, both small and great!"

Chapter 5

Verse 1 Then I saw in the right hand of Him who sat on the throne a scroll with writing on both sides and sealed with seven seals.

1. The One who sits on the throne is God and He is holding in His right hand a scroll sealed with seven seals.
2. This secret scroll sealed with seven seals is about the fate of the universe, and the God of life and redemption holds these secrets and mysteries of the universe.
3. The scroll sealed with seven seals means that the secrets and mysteries of the universe are not shown to Man and are hidden (Isa 29:11～12, Da 12:4, 9).[228]

Verse 2-3 And I saw a mighty angel proclaiming in a loud voice, "Who is worthy to break the seals and open the scroll?" But no one in heaven or on earth or under the earth could open the scroll or even look inside it.

1. No angel in Heaven, or person living on earth, or dead person under the earth was able to open the scroll which was sealed with 7 seals, and none was worthy to break the seals.
2. As we now read the book of Revelation, the contents of a scroll that was opened by Christ at the right hand of the throne are being unfolded.

---

228)Isa29:11 For you this whole vision is nothing but words sealed in a scroll. And if you give the scroll to someone who can read, and say to him, "Read this, please," he will answer, "I can't; it is sealed."

Isa29:12 Or if you give the scroll to someone who cannot read, and say, "Read this, please," he will answer, "I don't know how to read."

Da12:4 But you, Daniel, close up and seal the words of the scroll until the time of the end. Many will go here and there to increase knowledge."

Da12:9 He replied, "Go your way, Daniel, because the words are closed up and sealed until the time of the end.

3. Other revelations can be understood and be known by those moved by the Spirit, but since this Revelation sealed with the seven seals is opened and shown to us, and the contents of Revelation are being progressed by Christ, only those in Christ can understand.

Verse 4-5 I wept and wept because no one was found who was worthy to open the scroll or look inside. Then one of the elders said to me, "Do not weep! See, the Lion of the tribe of Judah, the Root of David, has triumphed. He is able to open the scroll and its seven seals."

1. John knew that this scroll must be opened for the secrets of the universe to be made public, but he wept and wept as no one was found who was able to open the scroll.
2. Christ is the Lion who fights and wins and triumphs (Ge 49:8～9)[229]. He has won the fight. So, because of His triumph He has become worthy to break the seals of this scroll.
3. David is the servant of God who has fought God's battles and triumphed. Christ is indeed the root of David (Mt 22:42～45)[230].
4. Christ has triumphed over Satan, the hinderer, and is therefore worthy to break the seven seals.

---

229)Ge49:8 "Judah, your brothers will praise you; your hand will be on the neck of your enemies; your father's sons will bow down to you.
Ge49:9 You are a lion's cub, O Judah; you return from the prey, my son. Like a lion he crouches and lies down, like a lioness--who dares to rouse him?

230)Mt22:42 "What do you think about the Christ? Whose son is he?" "The son of David," they replied.
Mt22:43 He said to them, "How is it then that David, speaking by the Spirit, calls Him 'Lord'? For he says,
Mt22:44 "'The Lord said to my Lord: "Sit at My right hand until I put Your enemies under Your feet." '
Mt22:45 If then David calls Him 'Lord,' how can He be his son?"

Verse 6 Then I saw a Lamb, looking as if it had been slain, standing at the center of the throne, encircled by the four living creatures and the elders. The Lamb had seven horns and seven eyes, which are the seven spirits aof God sent out into all the earth.

1. In the universe, there are two problems: Satan and sin. As a lion, Christ has defeated Satan, and as a lamb Christ has removed our sins.
   He is the Lion-**Lamb** of victory and redemption.
2. The angelic elder saw Christ as the Lion, but John saw Christ as the Lamb.
3. Looking as if it had been slain means Christ, the Lamb who is standing encircled by the four living creatures and the elders, is about to take the scroll from God's right hand and break the seals. Therefore Christ, the Lamb, is portrayed as being slain in the past.
4. He dealt with the serpent by dying on the cross and dealt with sins with the blood He shed when He died.
5. Christ has fighting horns (**seven horns)** in other words, He achieves absolute victory in battle.
6. **The seven eyes** penetrate even to dividing a person's soul and spirit, joints and marrow, and seven eyes means perfect sight.
7. Finally, the seven eyes are the Holy Spirit, **the seven spirits of God.**
   ※ The seven spirits :
   Rev 1:4 the seven spirits[231].
   Rev 3:1 the seven spirits of God[232].
   Rev 4:5 the seven lamps are the seven spirits[233].

---

231)Rev1:4 John, To the seven churches in the province of Asia: Grace and peace to you from Him who is, and who was, and who is to come, and from the seven spirits before His throne,

232)Rev3:1 "To the angel of the church in Sardis write: These are the words of Him who holds the seven spirits of God and the seven stars. I know your deeds; you have a reputation of being alive, but you are dead.

233)Rev4:5 From the throne came flashes of lightning, rumblings and

Rev 5:6 the seven eyes are the seven spirits of God[234].

Verse 7 He went and took the scroll from the right hand of Him who sat on the throne.

▣In verse 7, The Lamb who takes the scroll is the Lion of the tribe of Judah, the root of David, the One who dealt with Satan and sins by dying on the cross, possessing seven horns and seven eyes, He is the seven spirits who fights and searches, Christ. Therefore, He is the One worthy to take the scroll.

Verse 8 And when He had taken it, the four living creatures and the twenty-four elders fell down before the Lamb. Each one had a harp and they were holding golden bowls full of incense, which are the prayers of God's people.

1. By taking the scroll, the four living creatures and the twenty-four elders in heaven praise Him with new songs and they give glory to God.
2. When the Lamb takes the scroll, no ascended saints can be seen in heaven, only angels (Verse 11), the four living creatures, and the elders (Verse 8) (the saints are praying under the altar) (Rev 6:9～11)[235].

---

peals of thunder. Before the throne, seven lamps were blazing. These are the seven spirits of God.

234)Rev5:6 Then I saw a Lamb, looking as if it had been slain, standing in the center of the throne, encircled by the four living creatures and the elders. He had seven horns and seven eyes, which are the seven spirits of God sent out into all the earth.

235)Rev6:9 When He opened the fifth seal, I saw under the altar the souls of those who had been slain because of the word of God and the testimony they had maintained.

Rev6:10 They called out in a loud voice, "How long, Sovereign Lord, holy and true, until You judge the inhabitants of the earth and avenge our blood?"

Rev6:11 Then each of them was given a white robe, and they were told to wait a little longer, until the number of their fellow servants and brothers who were to be killed as they had been

3. The four living creatures sing with harps and the twenty -four elders praise and give glory to God and the Lamb with golden bowls full of incense.
   a. The four living creatures: give glory to God with praise (Rev 4:9)[236]
   b. The twenty-four elders: serve God with golden bowls

Verse 9 And they sang a new song, saying: "You are worthy to take the scroll and to open its seals, because You were slain, and with Your blood You purchased for God persons from every tribe and language and people and nation.

1. A new song praises the worthiness of the Lamb, and the new song is the heavenly praise of those who overcome (Rev 14:3, Isa 42:10~12, Ps 33:3).[237]
2. The overcomers sang a new song that they will reign forever on the earth because through His death, Christ purchased men with His blood and gave them before God and made them kings and priests.

---

was completed.

236)Rev4:9 Whenever the living creatures give glory, honor and thanks to Him who sits on the throne and who lives for ever and ever,

237)Rev14:3 And they sang a new song before the throne and before the four living creatures and the elders. No one could learn the song except the 144,000 who had been redeemed from the earth.
Isa42:10 Sing to the LORD a new song, His praise from the ends of the earth, you who go down to the sea, and all that is in it, you islands, and all who live in them.
Isa42:11 Let the desert and its towns raise their voices; let the settlements where Kedar lives rejoice. Let the people of Sela sing for joy; let them shout from the mountaintops.
Isa42:12 Let them give glory to the LORD and proclaim His praise in the islands.
Ps33:3 Sing to Him a new song; play skillfully, and shout for joy.

Verse 10 You have made them to be a kingdom and priests to serve our God, and they will reign on the earth."

1. It is low-level thinking for us to think that believing in the death of the Lamb only leads to us being saved and becoming God's people. We must see that those who receive salvation will ultimately become kings and priests and reign in the kingdom of God, receiving forever the inheritance of God's kingdom.
   ※ Kingdom and priests ⇒ It should be translated as "**Kings and priests**".
2. The Kingdom is for the office of kings exercising God's authority, and the priests are the priesthood for sacred service to God (Rev 20:4～6, 7:15).[238]

Verse 11 Then I heard the voice of many angels, numbering thousands upon thousands, and ten thousand times ten thousand. They encircled the throne and the living creatures and the elders.

▣The twenty-four elders represent the many angels. Many angels follow the elders to praise the Lamb.

Verse 12 In a loud voice they were saying: "Worthy is the Lamb, who was slain, to receive power and wealth and wisdom and strength and honor and glory and praise!"

---

238)Rev20:4 I saw thrones on which were seated those who had been given authority to judge. And I saw the souls of those who had been beheaded because of their testimony for Jesus and because of the word of God. They had not worshiped the beast or his image and had not received his mark on their foreheads or their hands. They came to life and reigned with Christ a thousand years.
Rev20:5 (The rest of the dead did not come to life until the thousand years were ended.) This is the first resurrection.
Rev20:6 Blessed and holy are those who have part in the first resurrection. The second death has no power over them, but they will be priests of God and of Christ and will reign with Him for a thousand years.

1. The praise of the many angels is praise to the Lamb who was slain.
2. Through His death, He has become worthy of receiving power and wealth and wisdom, and strength and honour and glory and praise.
3. We must realize how great and honourable it is to live the life of the cross in Christ. Amen!

Verse 13-14 Then I heard every creature in heaven and on earth and under the earth and on the sea, and all that is in them, saying: "To Him who sits on the throne and to the Lamb be praise and honor and glory and power, for ever and ever!" The four living creatures said, "Amen," and the elders fell down and worshiped.

▣As all the creations give God and the Lamb continuous universal praise, the four living creatures respond with "Amen", and the twenty-four elders fall down to worship, so they may give glory and honor to God and the Lamb.

Chapter 6 (The first seal ~ the sixth seal)

Verse 1 I watched as the Lamb opened the first of the seven seals. Then I heard one of the four living creatures say in a voice like thunder, "Come!"

[The first seal]

1. The time of the Lamb opening the first of the seven seals is when God's throne of judgment in heaven has taken place and Christ has broken the seal right after He has received the scroll in His right hand. Therefore, it means that God's judgment is being progressed.
2. Because God's work for all of creation is in this scroll sealed with the seven seals, the four living creatures order the rider of the horse to come when the seal is opened

Verse 2 I looked, and there before me was a white horse! Its rider held a bow, and he was given a crown, and he rode out as a conqueror bent on conquest.

1. The rider of the white horse represents the Antichrist. At first, the Antichrist appears as a bright angel. (Mt 24:4~8)[239]. Revelation was written in order to warn and prepare the saints for the second coming of Christ. So, with that said, Revelation begins with the appearance of Antichrist.
2. When Jesus comes, He comes riding on a white horse (Rev 19:11)[240]. And when the Antichrist comes, he appears also

---

239)Mt24:4 Jesus answered: "Watch out that no one deceives you.
Mt24:5 For many will come in My name, claiming, 'I am the Christ,' and will deceive many.
Mt24:6 You will hear of wars and rumors of wars, but see to it that you are not alarmed. Such things must happen, but the end is still to come.
Mt24:7 Nation will rise against nation, and kingdom against kingdom. There will be famines and earthquakes in various places.
Mt24:8 All these are the beginning of birth pains.

240)Rev19:11 I saw heaven standing open and there before me was a

on a white horse, emulating Christ.

3. The Antichrist appears holding a bow. The bow is a necessary weapon when fighting the opponent, and the Antichrist fights with a bow. Christ does not fight with the bow, but instead fights with the sword of the word (Rev 19:15, 21, 1:16)[241].
4. By the countries of the ten horns, under the threat of the Antichrist, a 7-year treaty is confirmed (Da 9:27)[242]. The Antichrist is acknowledged as the one able to deliver world peace and obtains a crown (Stephanos). Later, his crown becomes a royal diadem (διαδήμα) and he will rule over the whole world (Rev 13:1~8)[243].

---

white horse, whose rider is called Faithful and True. With justice He judges and makes war.

241)Rev19:15 Out of His mouth comes a sharp sword with which to strike down the nations. "He will rule them with an iron scepter." He treads the winepress of the fury of the wrath of God Almighty.

Rev19:21 The rest of them were killed with the sword that came out of the mouth of the rider on the horse, and all the birds gorged themselves on their flesh.

Rev1:16 In His right hand He held seven stars, and out of His mouth came a sharp double-edged sword. His face was like the sun shining in all its brilliance.

242)Da9:27 He will confirm a covenant with many for one 'seven.' In the middle of the 'seven' he will put an end to sacrifice and offering. And on a wing of the temple he will set up an abomination that causes desolation, until the end that is decreed is poured out on him."

243)Rev13:1 And the dragon stood on the shore of the sea. And I saw a beast coming out of the sea. He had ten horns and seven heads, with ten crowns on his horns, and on each head a blasphemous name.

Rev13:2 The beast I saw resembled a leopard, but had feet like those of a bear and a mouth like that of a lion. The dragon gave the beast his power and his throne and great authority.

Rev13:3 One of the heads of the beast seemed to have had a fatal wound, but the fatal wound had been healed. The whole world was astonished and followed the beast.

Rev13:4 Men worshiped the dragon because he had given authority

5. 'He rode out as a conqueror' means that when he first appears, he wages war against the three horns which come before him (Da 7:20, 24)[244] and the saints and defeats them (Da 7:21, 12:7, Rev 12:17, 13:6~7)[245].

---

to the beast, and they also worshiped the beast and asked, "Who is like the beast? Who can make war against him?"

Rev13:5 The beast was given a mouth to utter proud words and blasphemies and to exercise his authority for forty-two months.

Rev13:6 He opened his mouth to blaspheme God, and to slander His name and His dwelling place and those who live in heaven.

Rev13:7 He was given power to make war against the saints and to conquer them. And he was given authority over every tribe, people, language and nation.

Rev13:8 All inhabitants of the earth will worship the beast--all whose names have not been written in the book of life belonging to the Lamb that was slain from the creation of the world.

244)Da7:20 I also wanted to know about the ten horns on its head and about the other horn that came up, before which three of them fell--the horn that looked more imposing than the others and that had eyes and a mouth that spoke boastfully.

Da7:24 The ten horns are ten kings who will come from this kingdom. After them another king will arise, different from the earlier ones; he will subdue three kings.

245)Da7:21 As I watched, this horn was waging war against the saints and defeating them,

Da12:7 The man clothed in linen, who was above the waters of the river, lifted his right hand and his left hand toward heaven, and I heard him swear by Him who lives forever, saying, "It will be for a time, times and half a time. When the power of the holy people has been finally broken, all these things will be completed."

Rev12:17 Then the dragon was enraged at the woman and went off to make war against the rest of her offspring--those who obey God's commandments and hold to the testimony of Jesus.

Rev13:6 He opened his mouth to blaspheme God, and to slander His name and His dwelling place and those who live in heaven.

Rev13:7 He was given power to make war against the saints and to

Verse 3-4 When the Lamb opened the second seal, I heard the second living creature say, "Come!" Then another horse came out, a fiery red one. Its rider was given power to take peace from the earth and to make people kill each other. To him was given a large sword.

1. The colour red represents bloodshed. The red horse represents the bloodshed of a fiery war.
2. 'Its rider was given power' means that it is God who has rule over all events and works of the universe. So, the rider on the red horse who was given power to take peace from the earth, takes peace and breaks down harmony from the earth, and all the world is dragged into the whirlpool of war.
3. 'To him was given a large sword' will probably mean there will be a great war, as great as World War 3.

Verse 5-6 When the Lamb opened the third seal, I heard the third living creature say, "Come!" I looked, and there before me was a black horse! Its rider was holding a pair of scales in his hand. Then I heard what sounded like a voice among the four living creatures, saying, "Two pounds aof wheat for a day's wages, band six pounds cof barley for a day's wages, dand do not damage the oil and the wine!"

1. The colour black represents famine, the colour of those faces in famine is black. The black horse means the spreading of famine which is followed by black faces (La 4:8~9, 5:9~10)[246].

---

conquer them. And he was given authority over every tribe, people, language and nation.

246)La4:8 But now they are blacker than soot; they are not recognized in the streets. Their skin has shriveled on their bones; it has become as dry as a stick.

La4:9 Those killed by the sword are better off than those who die of famine; racked with hunger, they waste away for lack of food

2. 1 denarius is a day's wages. That is, only being able to buy a quart of wheat or three quarts of barley for a day's wages show how serious the famine is.
3. The olive oil and wine represents the grace and joy of the Holy Spirit. Even in serious war and famine, the saints can live with the grace of the Spirit.

Verse 7-8 When the Lamb opened the fourth seal, I heard the voice of the fourth living creature say, "Come!" I looked, and there before me was a pale horse! Its rider was named Death, and Hades was following close behind him. They were given power over a fourth of the earth to kill by sword, famine and plague, and by the wild beasts of the earth.

1. The pale horse symbolizes death which brings about a pale appearance.
2. Hades
   a. The waiting place for dead souls in the underworld (until the Lord's Second Coming) (1Th 4:16, 1Co 15:51～52)[247].
   b. Hades is divided into paradise, where Abraham is (the place of rest), and hell where the rich are (the place of punishment) (Lk 16:23, Mt 12:40)[248].

---

from the field.
La5:9 We get our bread at the risk of our lives because of the sword in the desert.
La5:10 Our skin is hot as an oven, feverish from hunger.

247)1Th4:16 For the Lord Himself will come down from heaven, with a loud command, with the voice of the archangel and with the trumpet call of God, and the dead in Christ will rise first.
1Co15:51 Listen, I tell you a mystery: We will not all sleep, but we will all be changed--
1Co15:52 in a flash, in the twinkling of an eye, at the last trumpet. For the trumpet will sound, the dead will be raised imperishable, and we will be changed.
248)Lk16:23 In hell, where he was in torment, he looked up and saw Abraham far away, with Lazarus by his side.

3. As many people die, Hades, the collector of dead spirits, follows close behind them and swallows their dead spirits.
4. A fourth of the earth is destroyed and killed by the rider on the pale horse. Of around 7 billion people, 1 billion 750 million people are killed by war, famine, death, and by the beast, the Antichrist.

Verse 9-10 When He opened the fifth seal, I saw under the altar the souls of those who had been slain because of the word of God and the testimony they had maintained. They called out in a loud voice, "How long, Sovereign Lord, holy and true, until You judge the inhabitants of the earth and avenge our blood?"

1. The souls of those who had been slain calling out in a loud voice refers to the saints that were slain from the blood of Abel to the time the fifth seal is opened.
2. Their souls were slain because of God's word and the testimony they had maintained.
3. The fact that they are still under the altar means that, because the altar is in the courtyard, they are in the underworld. The place they are in is the paradise portion within the underworld (Mt 12:40, Lk 16:23, 23:43, 1Pe 3:18~19, 4:6, 1Th 4:16, 1Co 15:51~52)[249].

Mt12:40 For as Jonah was three days and three nights in the belly of a huge fish, so the Son of Man will be three days and three nights in the heart of the earth.

249)Mt12:40 For as Jonah was three days and three nights in the belly of a huge fish, so the Son of Man will be three days and three nights **in the heart of the earth.**

Lk16:23 In hell, where he was in torment, he looked up and saw Abraham far away, with Lazarus by his side.

Lk23:43 Jesus answered him, "I tell you the truth, today you will be with Me in paradise."

1Pe3:18 For Christ died for sins once for all, the righteous for the unrighteous, to bring you to God. He was put to death in the body but made alive by the Spirit,

1Pe3:19 through whom also He went and preached to the spirits in

4. That the souls of slain martyrs are under the altar means that God sees them as offerings on the altar, and that they are under the earth.
5. The fact that the souls are calling out (praying) to God about their unjust death means that they have not yet been taken in by God and are in a waiting state.

Verse 11 Then each of them was given a white robe, and they were told to wait a little longer, until the full number of their fellow servants, their brothers and sisters, were killed just as they had been.

1. Martyrs were given a white robe (stolay = στολή) means that their murder is acknowledged by God. (stolay = στολή is the robe worn by martyrs and those who have lived like martyrs).
2. 'they were told to wait a little longer' means they must wait until their fellow servants and brothers have been slain and their full number is reached. They represent the saints that are to be slain during the first three and a half years of the tribulation (Rev 20:4)[250].

---

prison

1Pe4:6 For this is the reason the gospel was preached even to those who are now dead, so that they might be judged according to men in regard to the body, but live according to God in regard to the spirit.

1Th4:16 For the Lord Himself will come down from heaven, with a loud command, with the voice of the archangel and with the trumpet call of God, and the dead in Christ will rise first.

1Co15:51 Listen, I tell you a mystery: We will not all sleep, but we will all be changed--

1Co15:52 in a flash, in the twinkling of an eye, at the last trumpet. For the trumpet will sound, the dead will be raised imperishable, and we will be changed.

250)Rev20:4 I saw thrones on which were seated those who had been given authority to judge. And I saw the souls of those who had been beheaded because of their testimony for Jesus and because of the word of God. They had not worshiped the

3. The slain martyrs' spiritual number must be reached in order for them to be taken in by God (Rev 12:2, 5)[251].

Verse 12-13 I watched as He opened the sixth seal. There was a great earthquake. The sun turned black like sackcloth made of goat hair, the whole moon turned blood red, and the stars in the sky fell to earth, as figs drop from a fig tree when shaken by a strong wind.

1. As He opens the sixth seal, supernatural disaster on the earth will begin. This will be God answering the call of the martyrs when the fifth seal was opened.
2. The supernatural disaster of the celestial bodies will be a clear warning to the inhabitants of the earth that the end of the world is near. This will bring about an immense urge among the people to repent in order to return to God.

Verse 14-15 The heavens receded like a scroll being rolled up, and every mountain and island was removed from its place. Then the kings of the earth, the princes, the generals, the rich, the mighty, and everyone else, both slave and free, hid in caves and among the rocks of the mountains.

1. "every mountain and island was removed from its place' is to notify us beforehand of the crustal movements that will sink every mountain, and every island will cease to exist by a great earthquake and tsunami.
2. There will be distortion of the celestial bodies in the universe, and all the peoples of the earth will hide in caves and

---

beast or his image and had not received his mark on their foreheads or their hands. They came to life and reigned with Christ a thousand years.

251)Rev12:2 She was pregnant and cried out in pain as she was about to give birth.

Rev12:5 She gave birth to a son, a male child, who will rule all the nations with an iron scepter. And her child was snatched up to God and to His throne.

among the rocks of the mountains, and they will call to hide them from the face of God and from the wrath of the Lamb.

3. The sixth seal does not yet express God's wrath, but it is meant as a warning and a call to the people to repent. This will be the introduction to God's wrath and the prelude of the Great Tribulation.

Verse 16-17 They called to the mountains and the rocks, "Fall on us and hide us from the face of Him who sits on the throne and from the wrath of the Lamb! For the great day of their wrath has come, and who can withstand it?"

1. When great disaster is brought upon the people, they still will not seek God, but rather call to the mountains and the rocks (Lk 23:30, Hos 10:8)[252].
2. The celestial bodies and the earth will be shaken and changed twice.
   a. The first disaster occurs before the Day of the Lord (the Great Tribulation). This will be the warning of the Great Tribulation and will mark its beginning (Joel 2:30~31, Lk 21:11, Rev 6:12～14)[253].

---

252)Lk23:30 Then "'they will say to the mountains, "Fall on us!" and to the hills, "Cover us!" '

Hos10:8 The high places of wickedness will be destroyed--it is the sin of Israel. Thorns and thistles will grow up and cover their altars. Then they will say to the mountains, "Cover us!" and to the hills, "Fall on us!"

253)Joel2:30 I will show wonders in the heavens and on the earth, blood and fire and billows of smoke.

Joel2:31 The sun will be turned to darkness and the moon to blood before the coming of the great and dreadful day of the LORD.

Lk21:11 There will be great earthquakes, famines and pestilences in various places, and fearful events and great signs from heaven.

Rev6:12 I watched as He opened the sixth seal. There was a great earthquake. The sun turned black like sackcloth made of goat hair, the whole moon turned blood red,

b. <u>The second disaster will occur after the Great Tribulation</u>. This will be a warning of the coming of the Lord and will happen just before the Second Coming (Joel 3:11~16, Mt 24:29~31, Lk 21:25~28, Rev 16:18~21)[254].

Rev6:13 and the stars in the sky fell to earth, as late figs drop from a fig tree when shaken by a strong wind.
Rev6:14 The sky receded like a scroll, rolling up, and every mountain and island was removed from its place.

254)Joel3:11 Come quickly, all you nations from every side, and assemble there. Bring down Your warriors, O LORD!
Joel3:12 'Let the nations be roused; let them advance into the Valley of Jehoshaphat, for there I will sit to judge all the nations on every side.
Joel3:13 Swing the sickle, for the harvest is ripe. Come, trample the grapes, for the winepress is full and the vats overflow--so great is their wickedness!'
Joel3:14 Multitudes, multitudes in the valley of decision! For the day of the LORD is near in the valley of decision.
Joel3:15 The sun and moon will be darkened, and the stars no longer shine.
Joel3:16 The LORD will roar from Zion and thunder from Jerusalem; the earth and the sky will tremble. But the LORD will be a refuge for His people, a stronghold for the people of Israel.
Mt24:29 "Immediately after the distress of those days "'the sun will be darkened, and the moon will not give its light; the stars will fall from the sky, and the heavenly bodies will be shaken.'
Mt24:30 "At that time the sign of the Son of Man will appear in the sky, and all the nations of the earth will mourn. They will see the Son of Man coming on the clouds of the sky, with power and great glory.
Mt24:31 And He will send His angels with a loud trumpet call, and they will gather His elect from the four winds, from one end of the heavens to the other.
Lk21:25 "There will be signs in the sun, moon and stars. On the earth, nations will be in anguish and perplexity at the roaring and tossing of the sea.

Lk21:26 Men will faint from terror, apprehensive of what is coming on the world, for the heavenly bodies will be shaken.
Lk21:27 At that time they will see the Son of Man coming in a cloud with power and great glory.
Lk21:28 When these things begin to take place, stand up and lift up

Chapter 7

1. **Chapter 7** is an insertion between the sixth seal and the seventh seal rather than a continuation. It shows how God will take care of His people when He is about to judge the earth.
2. Therefore, Chapter 8 is the continuation of chapter 6.
3. In the sixth seal, all the disasters will be changed from natural disasters to supernatural disasters. The sun, the moon, and the stars will be hurt, and these disasters will be the prelude to the seventh seal.
4. But God will preserve His many people (Israelites and the redeemed saints).
5. When the seventh seal is opened, the situation will be unbearable. The trumpet will sound shortly after the seventh seal is opened. The disaster of the trumpets will be far more severe than the disaster of the seals.
6. God created this land for people to live in, but because all the people are evil, He will not tolerate them and will judge the land, the sea, the river, all the water springs, and the celestial bodies.
7. In the Old Testament and the New Testament, we see something called 'the Day of the Lord.' This very day is the 'Great Tribulation'. The Day of the Lord is the day of God's wrath when He comes to intervene in the world with supernatural

---

your heads, because your redemption is drawing near."

Rev16:18 Then there came flashes of lightning, rumblings, peals of thunder and a severe earthquake. No earthquake like it has ever occurred since man has been on earth, so tremendous was the quake.

Rev16:19 The great city split into three parts, and the cities of the nations collapsed. God remembered Babylon the Great and gave her the cup filled with the wine of the fury of His wrath.

Rev16:20 Every island fled away and the mountains could not be found.

Rev16:21 From the sky huge hailstones of about a hundred pounds each fell upon men. And they cursed God on account of the plague of hail, because the plague was so terrible.

disaster. The Day of the Lord will be terrible and will be worse than has ever been or ever will be again.

8. The sixth seal will occur as a prelude to the Day of the Lord. This will be a sign shown in advance of the Great Tribulation (Joel 1:15, 2:1, 3:14, Mal 4:5)[255].

Verse 1 After this I saw four angels standing at the four corners of the earth, holding back the four winds of the earth to prevent any wind from blowing on the land or on the sea or on any tree.

1. The four angels of the earth refer to those who rule over all of the earth (Da 7:2)[256].
2. Holding back the wind means God is holding back His judgment (Jn 1:4, Isa 11:15)[257].
3. The wind was held back from blowing on the land (the first trumpet), or on the sea (the second trumpet), or on any tree (the first trumpet).
4. This is to protect the people of God as He works.

---

255)Joel1:15 Alas for that day! For the day of the LORD is near; it will come like destruction from the Almighty.
Joel2:1 Blow the trumpet in Zion; sound the alarm on My holy hill. Let all who live in the land tremble, for the day of the LORD is coming. It is close at hand--
Joel3:14 Multitudes, multitudes in the valley of decision! For the day of the LORD is near in the valley of decision.
Mal4:5 "See, I will send you the prophet Elijah before that great and dreadful day of the LORD comes.

256)Da7:2 Daniel said: "In my vision at night I looked, and there before me were the four winds of heaven churning up the great sea.

257)Jn1:4 Then the LORD sent a great wind on the sea, and such a violent storm arose that the ship threatened to break up.
Isa11:15 The LORD will dry up the gulf of the Egyptian sea; with a scorching wind He will sweep His hand over the Euphrates River. He will break it up into seven streams so that men can cross over in sandals.

Verse 2-3 Then I saw another angel coming up from the east, having the seal of the living God. He called out in a loud voice to the four angels who had been given power to harm the land and the sea: "Do not harm the land or the sea or the trees until we put a seal on the foreheads of the servants of our God."

1. 'another angel' means Christ (Rev 8:3, 10:1, 18:1)[258]. In the Old Testament Christ operated as the 'Angel of the Lord' (Ge 22:11 ~12, Ex 3:2~6, Jdg 6:11~14)[259].

---

258)Rev8:3 Another angel, who had a golden censer, came and stood at the altar. He was given much incense to offer, with the prayers of all the saints, on the golden altar before the throne.
Rev10:1 Then I saw another mighty angel coming down from heaven. He was robed in a cloud, with a rainbow above His head; His face was like the sun, and His legs were like fiery pillars.
Rev18:1 After this I saw another angel coming down from heaven. He had great authority, and the earth was illuminated by His splendor.

259)Ge22:11 But the angel of the LORD called out to him from heaven, "Abraham! Abraham!" "Here I am," he replied.
Ge22:12 "Do not lay a hand on the boy," He said. "Do not do anything to him. Now I know that you fear God, because you have not withheld from Me your son, your only son."
Ex3:2 There the angel of the LORD appeared to him in flames of fire from within a bush. Moses saw that though the bush was on fire it did not burn up.
Ex3:3 So Moses thought, "I will go over and see this strange sight--why the bush does not burn up."
Ex3:4 When the LORD saw that he had gone over to look, God called to him from within the bush, "Moses! Moses!" And Moses said, "Here I am."
Ex3:5 "Do not come any closer," God said. "Take off your sandals, for the place where you are standing is holy ground."
Ex3:6 Then He said, "I am the God of your father, the God of Abraham, the God of Isaac and the God of Jacob." At this, Moses hid his face, because he was afraid to look at God.
Jdg6:11 The angel of the LORD came and sat down under the oak in Ophrah that belonged to Joash the Abiezrite, where his son Gideon was threshing wheat in a winepress to keep it from the Midianites.
Jdg6:12 When the angel of the LORD appeared to Gideon, He said, "The LORD is with you, mighty warrior."

2. In order to put a seal of God on the foreheads of the servants of God, he commands not to harm the land or the sea or the trees.
3. <u>The work of the seal</u>
   a. The seal of the living God: (Rev 7:2)[260].
   b. The seal of the Spirit (2Co 1:22, Eph 1:13, Eph 4:30)[261].
   c. The seal of the Lamb and of God: (Rev 14:1)[262]
   d. The seal of God, the new Jerusalem and Christ: (Rev 3:12)[263]
4. They put a seal on God's chosen Israel in order to protect

---

Jdg6:13 "But sir," Gideon replied, "if the LORD is with us, why has all this happened to us? Where are all His wonders that our fathers told us about when they said, 'Did not the LORD bring us up out of Egypt?' But now the LORD has abandoned us and put us into the hand of Midian."

Jdg6:14 The LORD turned to him and said, "Go in the strength you have and save Israel out of Midian's hand. Am I not sending you?"

260)Rev7:2 Then I saw another angel coming up from the east, having the seal of the living God. He called out in a loud voice to the four angels who had been given power to harm the land and the sea:

261)2Co1:22 set His seal of ownership on us, and put His Spirit in our hearts as a deposit, guaranteeing what is to come.

Eph1:13 And you also were included in Christ when you heard the word of truth, the gospel of your salvation. Having believed, you were marked in Him with a seal, the promised Holy Spirit,

Eph4:30 And do not grieve the Holy Spirit of God, with whom you were sealed for the day of redemption.

262)Rev14:1 Then I looked, and there before me was the Lamb, standing on Mount Zion, and with Him 144,000 who had His name and His Father's name written on their foreheads.

263)Rev3:12 Him who overcomes I will make a pillar in the temple of My God. Never again will he leave it. I will write on him the name of My God and the name of the city of My God, the new Jerusalem, which is coming down out of heaven from My God; and I will also write on him My new name.

them from the supernatural disasters that are to be performed by the trumpets before the first to fourth trumpets sound.
5. The seal of the living God is sealed on the forehead of those in Israel who are worthy to be called servants of God.

Verse 4-6 Then I heard the number of those who were sealed: 144,000 from all the tribes of Israel. From the tribe of Judah 12,000 were sealed, from the tribe of Reuben 12,000, from the tribe of Gad 12,000, from the tribe of Asher 12,000, from the tribe of Naphtali 12,000, from the tribe of Manasseh 12,000,

1. Among the Jews, those 12,000 from each tribe who have received a seal during the time of the Great Tribulation will keep the word of God as they live, and receive special care from God (Rev 12:14~16)[264].

2. For those who receive the seal of the living God, the seal will be a distinguishing sign to the angels that are sent to judge the land. This is how God will protect the chosen Israelites while judging the land (Ex 12:13, Rev 12:14~16)[265].
3. The reason why the tribe of Judah is mentioned first is because,

---

264)Rev12:14 The woman was given the two wings of a great eagle, so that she might fly to the place prepared for her in the desert, where she would be taken care of for a time, times and half a time, out of the serpent's reach.
Rev12:15 Then from his mouth the serpent spewed water like a river, to overtake the woman and sweep her away with the torrent.
Rev12:16 But the earth helped the woman by opening its mouth and swallowing the river that the dragon had spewed out of his mouth.
265)Ex12:13 The blood will be a sign for you on the houses where you are; and when I see the blood, I will pass over you. No destructive plague will touch you when I strike Egypt.
Rev12:14~16 ☝See footnote 264).

although Reuben was the eldest son, because of his sin (committing adultery with Bilhah) he lost his birthright. So, Judah ended up rising above his brothers (Ge 49:3~4, 8~9, Mic 5:2, 1Co 5:1~2)[266].

4. The tribe of Dan has been excluded. This is because they were the very first tribe of the twelve tribes to fall into idolatry after Israel entered Canaan (Jdg 18:30~31, Ge 49:17)[267].
5. But during the Millennial Kingdom period, the tribe of Dan will be counted as well (Eze 48:1)[268]. This is because they

---

266)Ge49:3 "Reuben, you are my firstborn, my might, the first sign of my strength, excelling in honor, excelling in power.
Ge49:4 Turbulent as the waters, you will no longer excel, for you went up onto your father's bed, onto my couch and defiled it.
Ge49:8 "Judah, your brothers will praise you; your hand will be on the neck of your enemies; your father's sons will bow down to you.
Ge49:9 You are a lion's cub, O Judah; you return from the prey, my son. Like a lion he crouches and lies down, like a lioness--who dares to rouse him?
Mic5:2 "But you, Bethlehem Ephrathah, though you are small among the clans of Judah, out of you will come for Me One who will be ruler over Israel, whose origins are from of old, from ancient times."
1Ch5:1 The sons of Reuben the firstborn of Israel (he was the firstborn, but when he defiled his father's marriage bed, his rights as firstborn were given to the sons of Joseph son of Israel; so he could not be listed in the genealogical record in accordance with his birthright,
1Ch5:2 and though Judah was the strongest of his brothers and a ruler came from him, the rights of the firstborn belonged to Joseph)--

267)Jgd18:30 There the Danites set up for themselves the idols, and Jonathan son of Gershom, the son of Moses, and his sons were priests for the tribe of Dan until the time of the captivity of the land.
Jgd18:31 They continued to use the idols Micah had made, all the time the house of God was in Shiloh.
268)Eze48:1 "These are the tribes, listed by name: At the northern frontier, Dan will have one portion; it will follow the Hethlon road to Lebo Hamath; Hazar Enan and the northern border of

had Jacob's blessing (Ge 49:18)[269], through the Lord's salvation the tribe of Dan will be included in the tribes of Israel (Ge 49:16~17)[270].

6. Because Joseph (Rev 7:8)[271] and one of his sons Manasseh each represent one tribe, Joseph will still receive a double portion of his birthright (1Ch 5:1~2)[272] even in the Millennial Kingdom (Eze 48:4~5, Dt 21:17)[273].

Verse 7-8: From the tribe of Simeon 12,000, from the tribe of Levi 12,000, from the tribe of Issachar 12,000, from the tribe of Zebulun 12,000, from the tribe of Joseph 12,000, from the tribe of Benjamin 12,000.

Damascus next to Hamath will be part of its border from the east side to the west side.

269)Ge49:18 "I look for Your deliverance, O LORD.

270)Ge49:16 "Dan will provide justice for his people as one of the tribes of Israel.
Ge49:17 Dan will be a serpent by the roadside, a viper along the path, that bites the horse's heels so that its rider tumbles backward.

271)Rev7:8 from the tribe of Zebulun 12,000, from the tribe of Joseph 12,000, from the tribe of Benjamin 12,000.

272)1Ch5:1 The sons of Reuben the firstborn of Israel (he was the firstborn, but when he defiled his father's marriage bed, his rights as firstborn were given to the sons of Joseph son of Israel; so he could not be listed in the genealogical record in accordance with his birthright,
1Ch5:2 and though Judah was the strongest of his brothers and a ruler came from him, the rights of the firstborn belonged to Joseph)--

273)Eze48:4 "Manasseh will have one portion; it will border the territory of Naphtali from east to west.
Dt21:17 He must acknowledge the son of his unloved wife as the firstborn by giving him a double share of all he has. That son is the first sign of his father's strength. The right of the firstborn belongs to him.

■ <u>The people who have been sealed in Israel will be protected during the Great Tribulation and be admitted into the Millennial Kingdom. There, they will be priests, teaching the nations to know and serve God</u> (Isa 2:2~4, 61:4~9, Zec 8:20~23, Mic 4:1~4)[274].

---

274)Isa2:2 In the last days the mountain of the LORD'S temple will be established as chief among the mountains; it will be raised above the hills, and all nations will stream to it.

Isa2:3 Many peoples will come and say, "Come, let us go up to the mountain of the LORD, to the house of the God of Jacob. He will teach us His ways, so that we may walk in His paths." The law will go out from Zion, the word of the LORD from Jerusalem.

Isa2:4 He will judge between the nations and will settle disputes for many peoples. They will beat their swords into plowshares and their spears into pruning hooks. Nation will not take up sword against nation, nor will they train for war anymore.

Isa61:4 They will rebuild the ancient ruins and restore the places long devastated; they will renew the ruined cities that have been devastated for generations.

Isa61:5 Aliens will shepherd your flocks; foreigners will work your fields and vineyards.

Isa61:6 And you will be called priests of the LORD, you will be named ministers of our God. You will feed on the wealth of nations, and in their riches you will boast.

Isa61:7 Instead of their shame My people will receive a double portion, and instead of disgrace they will rejoice in their inheritance; and so they will inherit a double portion in their land, and everlasting joy will be theirs.

Isa61:8 "For I, the LORD, love justice; I hate robbery and iniquity. In My faithfulness I will reward them and make an everlasting covenant with them.

Isa61:9 Their descendants will be known among the nations and their offspring among the peoples. All who see them will acknowledge that they are a people the LORD has blessed."

Zec8:20 This is what the LORD Almighty says: "Many peoples and the inhabitants of many cities will yet come,

Zec8:21 and the inhabitants of one city will go to another and say, 'Let us go at once to entreat the LORD and seek the LORD Almighty. I myself am going.'

Zec8:22 And many peoples and powerful nations will come to Jerusalem to seek the LORD Almighty and to entreat him."

Zec8:23 This is what the LORD Almighty says: "In those days ten men from all languages and nations will take firm hold of one Jew by the hem of his robe and say, 'Let us go with you, because we have heard that God is with you.'" An Oracle

Verse 9-10 After this I looked, and there before me was a great multitude that no one could count, from every nation, tribe, people and language, standing before the throne and before the Lamb. They were wearing white robes and were holding palm branches in their hands. And they cried out in a loud voice: "Salvation belongs to our God, who sits on the throne, and to the Lamb."

[A great multitude wearing white robes]

1. After sealing the 144,000 among Israel
2. 'a great multitude that no one could count, from every nation, tribe, people and language' refers to those among all nations who have been raptured before the heavenly throne as redeemed saints (Lk 21:36)[275].
3. The fact that they were wearing white clothes means that their deeds were righteous and clean, that their clothes have been washed with the blood of Christ (Rev 7:14)[276] and are

---

Mic4:1 In the last days the mountain of the LORD'S temple will be established as chief among the mountains; it will be raised above the hills, and peoples will stream to it.
Mic4:2 Many nations will come and say, "Come, let us go up to the mountain of the LORD, to the house of the God of Jacob. He will teach us His ways, so that we may walk in His paths." The law will go out from Zion, the word of the LORD from Jerusalem.
Mic4:3 He will judge between many peoples and will settle disputes for strong nations far and wide. They will beat their swords into plowshares and their spears into pruning hooks. Nation will not take up sword against nation, nor will they train for war anymore.
Mic4:4 Every man will sit under his own vine and under his own fig tree, and no one will make them afraid, for the LORD Almighty has spoken.

275)Lk21:36 Be always on the watch, and pray that you may be able to escape all that is about to happen, and that you may be able to stand before the Son of Man."
276)Rev7:14 I answered, "Sir, you know." And he said, "These are they who have come out of the great tribulation; they have washed their robes and made them white in the blood of the Lamb.

wearing the white robes.

4. 'and were holding palm branches in their hands' means that the saints have overcome the tribulation and have triumphed (Jn 12:13, Lev 23:40, Ne 8:15)[277]. It shows that they have overcome great suffering for the Lord.
5. Standing before the throne and in front of the Lamb means that they have ascended into heaven (raptured) and they sing in a loud voice the joy of salvation, meaning that they give praise and glory before God and the Lamb.

Verse 11-12 All the angels were standing around the throne and around the elders and the four living creatures. They fell down on their faces before the throne and worshiped God, 12 saying: "Amen! Praise and glory and wisdom and thanks and honor and power and strength be to our God for ever and ever. Amen!"

1. When the redeemed saints sing and praise their salvation before God and before the throne, all the angels chime in together with them to give glory to God.
2. The particulars of praise to God in heaven.
   a. (Rev 4:9~11)[278] ⇒ The four living creatures and the twenty

277)Jn12:13 They took palm branches and went out to meet Him, shouting, "Hosanna!" "Blessed is He who comes in the name of the Lord!" "Blessed is the King of Israel!"
Lev23:40 On the first day you are to take choice fruit from the trees, and palm fronds, leafy branches and poplars, and rejoice before the LORD your God for seven days.
Ne8:15 and that they should proclaim this word and spread it throughout their towns and in Jerusalem: "Go out into the hill country and bring back branches from olive and wild olive trees, and from myrtles, palms and shade trees, to make booths"--as it is written.

278)Rev4:9 Whenever the living creatures give glory, honor and thanks to Him who sits on the throne and who lives for ever and ever,
Rev4:10 the twenty-four elders fall down before Him who sits on the throne, and worship Him who lives for ever and ever. They lay their crowns before the throne and say:
Rev4:11 "You are worthy, our Lord and God, to receive glory and

-four elders praise God.

b. (Rev 5:11~12)[279) ⇒ The twenty-four elders and the four living creatures give praise to the Lord, for it was through His death as the Lamb, that mankind received salvation, and He was the One worthy to take the sealed scroll.

c. (Rev 19:4~5)[280) ⇒ After the judgment of Babylon the Great, the four creatures and the twenty-four elders praise God.

Verse 13-14 Then one of the elders asked me, "These in white robes—who are they, and where did they come from?" I answered, "Sir, you know." And he said, "These are they who have come out of the great tribulation; they have washed their robes and made them white in the blood of the Lamb.

1. One of the elders asked John this question in order to tell him in more detail about those in white robes.
2. 'These are they who have come out the great tribulations' - the "great tribulations" is referring to the great hardships in their life that they have gone through from the time of the church to the first three and a half years of Antichrist (Ac 14:22, Heb 12:5~8, Mt 5:11~12)[281).

---

honor and power, for You created all things, and by Your will they were created and have their being."

279)Rev5:11 Then I looked and heard the voice of many angels, numbering thousands upon thousands, and ten thousand times ten thousand. They encircled the throne and the living creatures and the elders.

Rev5:12 In a loud voice they sang: "Worthy is the Lamb, who was slain, to receive power and wealth and wisdom and strength and honor and glory and praise!"

280)Rev19:4 The twenty-four elders and the four living creatures fell down and worshiped God, who was seated on the throne. And they cried: "Amen, Hallelujah!"

Rev19:5 Then a voice came from the throne, saying: "Praise our God, all you His servants, you who fear Him, both small and great!"

281)Ac14:22 strengthening the disciples and encouraging them to remain

3. 'they have washed their robes and made them white in the blood of the Lamb' means that the saints have washed their acts with the precious blood as if washing dirty clothes (Lev 8:30, 1Jn 1:7~9)[282].

Verse 15-17 Therefore, "they are before the throne of God and serve Him day and night in His temple; and He who sits on the throne will shelter them with His presence. 'Never again will they hunger; never again will they thirst. The sun will not beat down on them,' nor any scorching heat. For the Lamb at the center of the

---

true to the faith. "We must go through many hardships to enter the kingdom of God," they said.

Heb12:5 And you have forgotten that word of encouragement that addresses you as sons: "My son, do not make light of the Lord's discipline, and do not lose heart when He rebukes you,

Heb12:6 because the Lord disciplines those He loves, and He punishes everyone He accepts as a son."

Heb12:7 Endure hardship as discipline; God is treating you as sons. For what son is not disciplined by his father?

Heb12:8 If you are not disciplined (and everyone undergoes discipline), then you are illegitimate children and not true sons.

Mt5:11 "Blessed are you when people insult you, persecute you and falsely say all kinds of evil against you because of Me.

Mt5:12 Rejoice and be glad, because great is your reward in heaven, for in the same way they persecuted the prophets who were before you.

282)Lev8:30 Then Moses took some of the anointing oil and some of the blood from the altar and sprinkled them on Aaron and his garments and on his sons and their garments. So he consecrated Aaron and his garments and his sons and their garments.

1Jn1:7 But if we walk in the light, as He is in the light, we have fellowship with one another, and the blood of Jesus, His Son, purifies us from all sin.

1Jn1:8 If we claim to be without sin, we deceive ourselves and the truth is not in us.

1Jn1:9 If we confess our sins, He is faithful and just and will forgive us our sins and purify us from all unrighteousness.

throne will be their shepherd; 'he will lead them to springs of living water.' 'And God will wipe away every tear from their eyes.' "

1. This large crowd is those who have suffered the great tribulations and have washed their robes in the blood of the Lamb, so they are worthy to stand before the throne of God, and will become priests of the temple who serve God day and night (Heb 3:1, Heb 4:14, Heb 5:5~6)[283]. Christ works as the high priest in the temple.
2. The work of the priest who serves God day and night in the heavenly temple will be performed in the Millennial Kingdom. In the eternal state (New Heaven, New Earth, New Jerusalem) there is no night (Rev 21:23)[284].
3. 'He will spread His tent over them' just like when God made the tabernacle in the house of Israel when the Israelites were in the desert, He will make a tent over them and will take care of them (Rev 21:2~3)[285].

---

283)Heb3:1 Therefore, holy brothers, who share in the heavenly calling, fix your thoughts on Jesus, the apostle and high priest whom we confess.
Hev4:14 Therefore, since we have a great high priest who has gone through the heavens, Jesus the Son of God, let us hold firmly to the faith we profess.
Hev5:5 So Christ also did not take upon Himself the glory of becoming a high priest. But God said to Him, "You are My Son; today I have become Your Father."
Hev5:6 And He says in another place, "You are a priest forever, in the order of Melchizedek."

284)Rev21:23 The city does not need the sun or the moon to shine on it, for the glory of God gives it light, and the Lamb is its lamp.

285)Rev21:2 I saw the Holy City, the new Jerusalem, coming down out of heaven from God, prepared as a bride beautifully dressed for her husband.
Rev21:3 And I heard a loud voice from the throne saying, "Now the dwelling of God is with men, and He will live with them. They will be His people, and God Himself will be with them and be their God.

4. 'Never again will they hunger; never again will they thirst. The sun will not beat upon them nor any scorching heat' means that when they were in the world they had suffered all these pains, but since they have already received salvation they will enjoy peace and rest forever.
5. 'The Lamb at the center of the throne will be their shepherd' means that they will be taken care of even during the Millennial Kingdom; even though they are in the Millennial Kingdom, they still need to be led to reach the springs of living water. And they will be in the comfort and grace of God! Amen!

Chapter 8 (seventh seal ⇒ first trumpet~fourth trumpet)

Verse 1-2 When He opened the seventh seal, there was silence in heaven for about half an hour. And I saw the seven angels who stand before God, and seven trumpets were given to them.

1. Seals are opened in secret (it is hard to perceive the time and contents the seals are opened), but trumpets are opened in public.
2. When He opens the seventh seal, there is silence in heaven. This silence is the heavenly quiet before the storm indicating the tolerance of God is turning into His wrath.
3. When the seventh seal is opened, seven trumpets of God's wrath are given to be sounded by the seven angels.

Verse 3-4 Another angel, who had a golden censer, came and stood at the altar. He was given much incense to offer, with the prayers of all God's people, on the golden altar in front of the throne. The smoke of the incense, together with the prayers of God's people, went up before God from the angel's hand.

1. The altar in this scripture represents the altar of the burnt offering in the heavenly temple, and the golden altar before the throne means the altar of incense (Ex 27:1~2, 29:15~16, 30:7~10)[286].

---

286)Ex27:1 "Build an altar of acacia wood, three cubits high; it is to be square, five cubits long and five cubits wide.
Ex27:2 Make a horn at each of the four corners, so that the horns and the altar are of one piece, and overlay the altar with bronze.
Ex29:15 "Take one of the rams, and Aaron and his sons shall lay their hands on its head.
Ex29:16 Slaughter it and take the blood and sprinkle it against the altar on all sides.
Ex30:7 "Aaron must burn fragrant incense on the altar every morning when he tends the lamps.
Ex30:8 He must burn incense again when he lights the lamps at

2. After the seventh seal, the saints on the earth will continue to pray, and after all prayers, service, and works are offered to the temple of heaven, they are delivered to God by another angel.
3. In Revelation 5:8, the angelic elders served God with golden bowls full of incense, but in this scripture the incense of prayers are given to God through another angel. This other angel is Christ.
4. Every morning, only the high priest was able to burn fragrant incense on the altar (Ex 30:7~10)[287]. Therefore, only Christ, the heavenly high priest (Heb 5:5~6,10, 6:20,)[288] can accomplish that task, but as it is before the Lord's second coming, He works as an angel (Ex 3:2, 6, Jdg 6:11~12, 16, Zec 1:11~12, 2:8)[289].

---

twilight so incense will burn regularly before the LORD for the generations to come.

Ex30:9 Do not offer on this altar any other incense or any burnt offering or grain offering, and do not pour a drink offering on it.

Ex30:10 Once a year Aaron shall make atonement on its horns. This annual atonement must be made with the blood of the atoning sin offering for the generations to come. It is most holy to the LORD."

287)Ex30:7~10 ☝See footnote 286)

288)Heb5:5 So Christ also did not take upon Himself the glory of becoming a high priest. But God said to Him, "You are My Son; today I have become Your Father."

Heb5:6 And He says in another place, "You are a priest forever, in the order of Melchizedek."

Heb5:10 and was designated by God to be high priest in the order of Melchizedek.

Heb6:20 where Jesus, who went before us, has entered on our behalf. He has become a high priest forever, in the order of Melchizedek.

289)Ex3:2 There the angel of the LORD appeared to him in flames of fire from within a bush. Moses saw that though the bush was on fire it did not burn up.

Ex3:6 Then He said, "I am the God of your father, the God of Abraham, the God of Isaac and the God of Jacob." At this,

Verse 5-6 Then the angel took the censer, filled it with fire from the altar, and hurled it on the earth; and there came peals of thunder, rumblings, flashes of lightning and an earthquake. Then the seven angels who had the seven trumpets prepared to sound them.

1. As soon as the golden censer filled with the prayers of saints is offered on the golden altar before the throne, God responds by commencing the trumpet judgments.
2. As the angel took the censer, filled it with fire from the altar, and hurled it on the earth, then God's judgment began. Peals of thunder, rumbling and flashes of lightning, and an earthquake is the prelude that indicates the judgment of God.
3. The prayers in verses 3-4 are prayers by the saints who have come to understand, through supernatural disaster, that the kingdom of heaven is near for the fulfillment of God's kingdom and will.
4. In order for God's judgment to be executed, the prayer of saints is needed (Lk 18:7~8)[290]. Already in verse two, trumpets

---

Moses hid his face, because he was afraid to look at God.

Jdg6:11 The angel of the LORD came and sat down under the oak in Ophrah that belonged to Joash the Abiezrite, where his son Gideon was threshing wheat in a winepress to keep it from the Midianites.

Jdg6:12 When the angel of the LORD appeared to Gideon, He said, "The LORD is with you, mighty warrior."

Jdg6:16 The LORD answered, "I will be with you, and you will strike down all the Midianites together."

Zec1:11 And they reported to the angel of the LORD, who was standing among the myrtle trees, "We have gone throughout the earth and found the whole world at rest and in peace."

Zec1:12 Then the angel of the LORD said, "LORD Almighty, how long will You withhold mercy from Jerusalem and from the towns of Judah, which You have been angry with these seventy years?"

Zec2:8 For this is what the LORD Almighty says: "After he has honored Me and has sent Me against the nations that have plundered you--for whoever touches you touches the apple of His eye--

290)Lk18:7 And will not God bring about justice for His chosen ones, who cry out to Him day and night? Will He keep putting them off?

were given to the seven angels. But the preparing of the seven angels to sound the trumpets is done after the saints' prayers are offered.

Verse 7 The first angel sounded his trumpet, and there came hail and fire mixed with blood, and it was hurled down on the earth. A third of the earth was burned up, a third of the trees were burned up, and all the green grass was burned up.

[the first trumpet]

◈ In the time of **the first trumpet**, there will come hail and fire mixed with blood and the land and all things on the land, a third of the earth and trees and all the green grass will be burned up.

Verse 8-9 The second angel sounded his trumpet, and something like a huge mountain, all ablaze, was thrown into the sea. A third of the sea turned into blood, 9a third of the living creatures in the sea died, and a third of the ships were destroyed.

[the second trumpet]

◈ In the time of **the second trumpet**, something like a huge mountain all ablaze (unsure what this is) causes a third of the sea to be turned into blood, a third of all living creatures in the sea to die, and a third of the ships to be destroyed, resulting in a great disaster.

Verse 10-11 The third angel sounded his trumpet, and a great star, blazing like a torch, fell from the sky on a third of the rivers and on the springs of water — the name

---

Lk18:8 I tell you, He will see that they get justice, and quickly. However, when the Son of Man comes, will He find faith on the earth?"

of the star is Wormwood. A third of the waters turned bitter, and many people died from the waters that had become bitter.

[the third trumpet]

1. **The third trumpet** is the judgment of the rivers and the springs of water (Ex 7:17~21)[291].
2. The agony of the water being turned bitter and not being able to drink from it will be great suffering hard to imagine (Dt 29:19, Jer 9:15, 23:15)[292].

Verse 12 The fourth angel sounded his trumpet, and a third of the sun was struck, a third of the moon, and a third

---

291)Ex7:17 This is what the LORD says: By this you will know that I am the LORD: With the staff that is in My hand I will strike the water of the Nile, and it will be changed into blood.
Ex7:18 The fish in the Nile will die, and the river will stink; the Egyptians will not be able to drink its water.'"
Ex7:19 The LORD said to Moses, "Tell Aaron, 'Take your staff and stretch out your hand over the waters of Egypt--over the streams and canals, over the ponds and all the reservoirs'--and they will turn to blood. Blood will be everywhere in Egypt, even in the wooden buckets and stone jars."
Ex7:20 Moses and Aaron did just as the LORD had commanded. He raised his staff in the presence of Pharaoh and his officials and struck the water of the Nile, and all the water was changed into blood.
Ex7:21 The fish in the Nile died, and the river smelled so bad that the Egyptians could not drink its water. Blood was everywhere in Egypt.

292)Dt29:18 Make sure there is no man or woman, clan or tribe among you today whose heart turns away from the LORD our God to go and worship the gods of those nations; make sure there is no root among you that produces such bitter poison.
Jer9:15 Therefore, this is what the LORD Almighty, the God of Israel, says: "See, I will make this people eat bitter food and drink poisoned water.
Jer23:15 Therefore, this is what the LORD Almighty says concerning the prophets: "I will make them eat bitter food and drink poisoned water, because from the prophets of Jerusalem ungodliness has spread throughout the land."

of the stars, so that a third of them turned dark. A third of the day was without light, and also a third of the night.

1. In the time of the sixth seal, a supernatural disaster of the celestial bodies occurs as a warning of the natural great distress to come (Rev 6:12～13)[293].

[the fourth trumpet]

2. In the time of **the fourth trumpet**, a third of the sun, the moon, and the stars are struck as a warning of the man-made great distress to come (Rev 8:12)[294].
3. In the time of the seventh bowl judgment, by flashes of lightning, rumblings, peals of thunder, and a severe earthquake, the fall of Babylon the Great is forewarned (Rev 16:17)[295].

Verse 13 As I watched, I heard an eagle that was flying in midair call out in a loud voice: "Woe! Woe! Woe to the inhabitants of the earth, because of the trumpet blasts about to be sounded by the other three angels!"

1. The eagle that was flying in mid-air calling out "Woe! Woe! Woe" indicates that the disasters of the three trumpets that have not yet sounded, the fifth, sixth and seventh, will be progressively more serious than the first four trumpets.
2. The first to the seventh trumpet of disaster will occur during the last three and half years (Da 9:27)[296] that is the latter half

---

293)Rev6:12 I watched as He opened the sixth seal. There was a great earthquake. The sun turned black like sackcloth made of goat hair, the whole moon turned blood red,
Rev6:13 and the stars in the sky fell to earth, as late figs drop from a fig tree when shaken by a strong wind.

294)Rev8:12 The fourth angel sounded his trumpet, and a third of the sun was struck, a third of the moon, and a third of the stars, so that a third of them turned dark. A third of the day was without light, and also a third of the night.

295)Rev16:17 The seventh angel poured out his bowl into the air, and out of the temple came a loud voice from the throne, saying, "It is done!"

296)Da9:27 He will confirm a covenant with many for one 'seven.' In the

of one 'seven' (Da 7:25, 12:7, Rev 12:14)[297] or 42 months (Rev 11:2 13:5)[298], or 1,260 days (Rev 11:3, 12:6)[299].

3. In those days, as the Lord said, will be great distress, unequaled from the beginning of the world until now (Mt 24:15~22)[300].

---

middle of the 'seven' he will put an end to sacrifice and offering. And on a wing of the temple he will set up an abomination that causes desolation, until the end that is decreed is poured out on him."

297)Da7:25 He will speak against the Most High and oppress His saints and try to change the set times and the laws. The saints will be handed over to him for a time, times and half a time.

Da12:7 The man clothed in linen, who was above the waters of the river, lifted his right hand and his left hand toward heaven, and I heard him swear by Him who lives forever, saying, "It will be for a time, times and half a time. When the power of the holy people has been finally broken, all these things will be completed."

Rev12:14 The woman was given the two wings of a great eagle, so that she might fly to the place prepared for her in the desert, where she would be taken care of for a time, times and half a time, out of the serpent's reach.

298)Rev11:2 But exclude the outer court; do not measure it, because it has been given to the Gentiles. They will trample on the holy city for 42 months.

Rev13:5 The beast was given a mouth to utter proud words and blasphemies and to exercise his authority for forty-two months.

299)Rev11:3 And I will give power to My two witnesses, and they will prophesy for 1,260 days, clothed in sackcloth."

Rev12:6 The woman fled into the desert to a place prepared for her by God, where she might be taken care of for 1,260 days.

300)Mt24:15 "So when you see standing in the holy place 'the abomination that causes desolation,' spoken of through the prophet Daniel--let the reader understand--

Mt24:16 then let those who are in Judea flee to the mountains.

Mt24:17 Let no one on the roof of his house go down to take anything out of the house.

Mt24:18 Let no one in the field go back to get his cloak.

Mt24:19 How dreadful it will be in those days for pregnant women and nursing mothers!

Mt24:20 Pray that your flight will not take place in winter or on the

4. In this time, the elects will still remain on the earth. For their sake, those days will be shortened, the Lord said (Mt 24:22)[301].
5. During the Great Tribulation, a tremendous number of people will be killed. Until the power of the saints is broken, they will be in suffering (Da 7:21, 12:7, Rev 13:7, 10)[302].
6. As the scripture says, "Wherever there are many carcasses, there the vultures will gather". This saying symbolizes the tremendous number of dead (Mt 24:28, Rev 19:17~21)[303].

Sabbath.

Mt24:21 For then there will be great distress, unequaled from the beginning of the world until now--and never to be equaled again.

Mt24:22 If those days had not been cut short, no one would survive, but for the sake of the elect those days will be shortened.

301)Mt24:22 ☝ See footnote 300)

302)Da7:21 As I watched, this horn was waging war against the saints and defeating them,

Da12:7 The man clothed in linen, who was above the waters of the river, lifted his right hand and his left hand toward heaven, and I heard him swear by Him who lives forever, saying, "It will be for a time, times and half a time. When the power of the holy people has been finally broken, all these things will be completed."

Rev13:7 He was given power to make war against the saints and to conquer them. And he was given authority over every tribe, people, language and nation.

Rev13:10 If anyone is to go into captivity, into captivity he will go. If anyone is to be killed with the sword, with the sword he will be killed. This calls for patient endurance and faithfulness on the part of the saints.

303)Mt24:28 Wherever there is a carcass, there the vultures will gather.

Rev19:17 And I saw an angel standing in the sun, who cried in a loud voice to all the birds flying in midair, "Come, gather together for the great supper of God,

Rev19:18 so that you may eat the flesh of kings, generals, and mighty men, of horses and their riders, and the flesh of all people, free and slave, small and great."

Rev19:19 Then I saw the beast and the kings of the earth and their armies gathered together to make war against the rider on

Chapter 9

Verse 1 The fifth angel sounded his trumpet, and I saw a star that had fallen from the sky to the earth. The star was given the key to the shaft of the Abyss.

[star that had fallen from the sky to the earth]

1. A star that had fallen from the sky represents Satan. Until the first trumpet sounded, Satan held the power of the air, meaning he was able to accuse the saints even before the throne of God (Job 1:6~12, Rev 12:10)[304]. When the latter three and a half

---

the horse and his army.

Rev19:20 But the beast was captured, and with him the false prophet who had performed the miraculous signs on his behalf. With these signs he had deluded those who had received the mark of the beast and worshiped his image. The two of them were thrown alive into the fiery lake of burning sulfur.

Rev19:21 The rest of them were killed with the sword that came out of the mouth of the rider on the horse, and all the birds gorged themselves on their flesh.

304)Job1:6 One day the angels came to present themselves before the LORD, and Satan also came with them.

Job1:7 The LORD said to Satan, "Where have you come from?" Satan answered the LORD, "From roaming through the earth and going back and forth in it."

Job1:8 Then the LORD said to Satan, "Have you considered My servant Job? There is no one on earth like him; he is blameless and upright, a man who fears God and shuns evil."

Job1:9 "Does Job fear God for nothing?" Satan replied.

Job1:10 "Have You not put a hedge around him and his household and everything he has? You have blessed the work of his hands, so that his flocks and herds are spread throughout the land.

Job1:11 But stretch out Your hand and strike everything he has, and he will surely curse You to Your face."

Job1:12 The LORD said to Satan, "Very well, then, everything he has is in your hands, but on the man himself do not lay a finger." Then Satan went out from the presence of the LORD.

years begins, Satan falls to the earth. (Rev 12:7～10)[305].

[The key to the shaft of the Abyss]

2. After Satan has fallen from the sky, the latter three and a half years will begin because the Abyss is opened by the dragon with the key to the shaft of the Abyss, so that the spirit of Antichrist is released and begins to work. On the earth the Great Tribulation of the latter three and a half years will begin. This Great Tribulation will be unprecedented (Mt 24:21～22)[306].
3. The Abyss is the place of ghosts, endless, deep, and gloomy dungeons (Jude 1:6, 2Pe 2:4)[307].

Rev12:10 Then I heard a loud voice in heaven say: "Now have come the salvation and the power and the kingdom of our God, and the authority of His Christ. For the accuser of our brothers, who accuses them before our God day and night, has been hurled down.

305)Rev12:7 And there was war in heaven. Michael and his angels fought against the dragon, and the dragon and his angels fought back.

Rev12:8 But he was not strong enough, and they lost their place in heaven.

Rev12:9 The great dragon was hurled down--that ancient serpent called the devil, or Satan, who leads the whole world astray. He was hurled to the earth, and his angels with him.

Rev12:10 Then I heard a loud voice in heaven say: "Now have come the salvation and the power and the kingdom of our God, and the authority of His Christ. For the accuser of our brothers, who accuses them before our God day and night, has been hurled down.

306)Mt24:21 For then there will be great distress, unequaled from the beginning of the world until now--and never to be equaled again.

Mt24:22 If those days had not been cut short, no one would survive, but for the sake of the elect those days will be shortened.

307)Jude1:6 And the angels who did not keep their positions of authority but abandoned their own home--these He has kept in darkness, bound with everlasting chains for judgment on the great Day.

2Pe2:4 For if God did not spare angels when they sinned, but sent

Verse 2-3 When he opened the Abyss, smoke rose from it like the smoke from a gigantic furnace. The sun and sky were darkened by the smoke from the Abyss. And out of the smoke locusts came down on the earth and were given power like that of scorpions of the earth.

1. When the Abyss is opened, the sun and sky will be darkened by smoke like from a gigantic furnace, and then the army of locusts will come up out of the smoke.
2. The army of locusts will have power like that of scorpions.

Verse 4-6 They were told not to harm the grass of the earth or any plant or tree, but only those people who did not have the seal of God on their foreheads. They were not allowed to kill them but only to torture them for five months. And the agony they suffered was like that of the sting of a scorpion when it strikes. During those days people will seek death but will not find it; they will long to die, but death will elude them.

[The army of locusts]

1. The army of locusts has a king, but the One who controls them is God.
2. The work that the army of locusts has to do is not to harm the grass, or any plant or trees, but to harm the people who have not been sealed with the seal of God on their forehead. That is, the Jews, with the exception of the 144,000 Jews who have been sealed. The army of locusts will distinguish them by the seal of God (Rev 7:3～4)[308].

---

them to hell, putting them into gloomy dungeons to be held for judgment;

308)Rev7:3 "Do not harm the land or the sea or the trees until we put a seal on the foreheads of the servants of our God."

Rev7:4 Then I heard the number of those who were sealed: 144,000 from all the tribes of Israel.

3. They were not given power to kill them, but only to torture them for five months. And the agony they suffer will be like that of the sting of a scorpion when it strikes a man.
4. The agony they will suffer will be so bad that they will want to die. This inescapable agony will be given to them for five months.
5. It will be a punishment for those who are the people of God who have not lived a life of fearing Him and trusting in Him. It will also be a final opportunity to repent and return to God (Joel 2:1～14)[309].

---

309)Joel2:1 Blow the trumpet in Zion; sound the alarm on My holy hill. Let all who live in the land tremble, for the day of the LORD is coming. It is close at hand--

Joel2:2 a day of darkness and gloom, a day of clouds and blackness. Like dawn spreading across the mountains a large and mighty army comes, such as never was of old nor ever will be in ages to come.

Joel2:3 Before them fire devours, behind them a flame blazes. Before them the land is like the garden of Eden, behind them, a desert waste--nothing escapes them.

Joel2:4 They have the appearance of horses; they gallop along like cavalry.

Joel2:5 With a noise like that of chariots they leap over the mountaintops, like a crackling fire consuming stubble, like a mighty army drawn up for battle.

Joel2:6 At the sight of them, nations are in anguish; every face turns pale.

Joel2:7 They charge like warriors; they scale walls like soldiers. They all march in line, not swerving from their course.

Joel2:8 They do not jostle each other; each marches straight ahead. They plunge through defenses without breaking ranks.

Joel2:9 They rush upon the city; they run along the wall. They climb into the houses; like thieves they enter through the windows.

Joel2:10 Before them the earth shakes, the sky trembles, the sun and moon are darkened, and the stars no longer shine.

JoelJoel2:11 The LORD thunders at the head of His army; His forces are beyond number, and mighty are those who obey His command. The day of the LORD is great; it is dreadful. Who can endure it?

Joel2:12 'Even now,' declares the LORD, 'return to Me with all your heart, with fasting and weeping and mourning.'

Verse 7-10 The locusts looked like horses prepared for battle. On their heads they wore something like crowns of gold, and their faces resembled human faces. Their hair was like women's hair, and their teeth were like lions' teeth. They had breastplates like breastplates of iron, and the sound of their wings was like the thundering of many horses and chariots rushing into battle. They had tails with stingers, like scorpions, and in their tails they had power to torment people for five months.

◈ The shape and the characteristics of locusts coming up from the Abyss are seen (Joel 1:6, 2:4~11)[310].

Verse 11-12: They had as king over them the angel of the Abyss, whose name in Hebrew is Abaddon and in Greek is Apollyon (that is, Destroyer). The first woe is past; two other woes are yet to come.

1. The angel of the Abyss represents the Antichrist coming out of the Abyss and he becomes the king of the army of the locusts (Rev 11:7, 17:8)[311].

Joel2:13 Rend your heart and not your garments. Return to the LORD your God, for He is gracious and compassionate, slow to anger and abounding in love, and He relents from sending calamity.

Joel2:14 Who knows? He may turn and have pity and leave behind a blessing--grain offerings and drink offerings for the LORD your God.

310)Joel1:6 A nation has invaded My land, powerful and without number; it has the teeth of a lion, the fangs of a lioness.

Joe2:4~11 ☝ See footnote 309)

311)Rev11:7 Now when they have finished their testimony, the beast that comes up from the Abyss will attack them, and overpower and kill them.

Rev17:8 The beast, which you saw, once was, now is not, and will come up out of the Abyss and go to his destruction. The inhabitants of the earth whose names have not been written in the book of life from the creation of the world will be

2. Abaddon (In Hebrew) ⇒ Collapse
   Apollyon (In Greek) ⇒ Destroyer
3. After Satan is expelled from heaven, he will first open the Abyss and call out the spirit of Antichrist, making him king of the army of the locusts to attack Israel with the power of scorpions, and to torment those who have not been sealed with the seal of God for five months (Da 8:23～25)[312].
4. Then, the 144,000 people sealed with God's seal among the Jews, the servants of God, will be protected by God in a prepared place (Rev 12:13～16)[313].
5. The first woe, the fifth trumpet has passed, but the sixth and seventh trumpet - these two woes remain.

---

astonished when they see the beast, because he once was, now is not, and yet will come.

312)Da8:23 "In the latter part of their reign, when rebels have become completely wicked, a stern-faced king, a master of intrigue, will arise.
Da8:24 He will become very strong, but not by his own power. He will cause astounding devastation and will succeed in whatever he does. He will destroy the mighty men and the holy people.
Da8:25 He will cause deceit to prosper, and he will consider himself superior. When they feel secure, he will destroy many and take his stand against the Prince of princes. Yet he will be destroyed, but not by human power.

313)Rev12:13 When the dragon saw that he had been hurled to the earth, he pursued the woman who had given birth to the male child.
Rev12:14 The woman was given the two wings of a great eagle, so that she might fly to the place prepared for her in the desert, where she would be taken care of for a time, times and half a time, out of the serpent's reach.
Rev12:15 Then from his mouth the serpent spewed water like a river, to overtake the woman and sweep her away with the torrent.
Rev12:16 But the earth helped the woman by opening its mouth and swallowing the river that the dragon had spewed out of his mouth.

Verse 13-15 The sixth angel sounded his trumpet, and I heard a voice coming from the four horns of the golden altar that is before God. It said to the sixth angel who had the trumpet, "Release the four angels who are bound at the great river Euphrates." And the four angels who had been kept ready for this very hour and day and month and year were released to kill a third of mankind.

[The sixth trumpet]

1. The blood of atonement was put on the four horns of the golden altar (the bull for Aaron's own sin offering and thc goat for the sin offering of the people) and was sprinkled seven times with fingers. This is an atonement for the Most Holy Place because of the transgressions and iniquities of the children of Israel, and atonement for the tabernacle in their midst (Ex 30:10, Lev 16:16~19)[314].
2. The voice coming from the horns of the golden altar is the voice of the Lord of judgment that judges all the sins and

314)Ex30:10 Once a year Aaron shall make atonement on its horns. This annual atonement must be made with the blood of the atoning sin offering for the generations to come. It is most holy to the LORD."

Lev16:16 In this way he will make atonement for the Most Holy Place because of the uncleanness and rebellion of the Israelites, whatever their sins have been. He is to do the same for the Tent of Meeting, which is among them in the midst of their uncleanness.

Lev16:17 No one is to be in the Tent of Meeting from the time Aaron goes in to make atonement in the Most Holy Place until he comes out, having made atonement for himself, his household and the whole community of Israel.

Lev16:18 "Then he shall come out to the altar that is before the LORD and make atonement for it. He shall take some of the bull's blood and some of the goat's blood and put it on all the horns of the altar.

Lev16:19 He shall sprinkle some of the blood on it with his finger seven times to cleanse it and to consecrate it from the uncleanness of the Israelites.

the uncleanness of the world. Through this voice the sixth trumpet is sounded. All sins and injustices that have not been redeemed are punished for being unable to commune with God and enter the temple.
3. 'The four angels who are bound at the great river Euphrates' refers to the disobedient corrupt angels of evil who follow Satan.
4. The four angels are released at a specific hour and day and month and year, and there will be a great war on the earth and a third of mankind will be killed.
5. Through this we must see that every war of mankind occurs under the permission of God, and even the killing of men happens at a specific time.

Verse 16-18 The number of the mounted troops was twice ten thousand times ten thousand. I heard their number. The horses and riders I saw in my vision looked like this: Their breastplates were fiery red, dark blue, and yellow as sulfur. The heads of the horses resembled the heads of lions, and out of their mouths came fire, smoke and sulfur. A third of mankind was killed by the three plagues of fire, smoke and sulfur that came out of their mouths.

1. The number of horsemen coming over the great river Euphrates is 20,000 x 10,000 which is two hundred million, and the four angels will use this army to kill a third of mankind.
2. The two hundred million horsemen will come from the East (Rev 16:12). They will pass through the great river Euphrates to the Middle East, which is the richest place in the world.
3. In the end, they will be the army of Antichrist that gathers at Armageddon. They will carry out the war of Armageddon, the last war of mankind (Rev1 6:12~16, 19:17~18)[315].

315)Rev16:12 The sixth angel poured out his bowl on the great river Euphrates, and its water was dried up to prepare the way for the kings from the East.
Rev16:13 Then I saw three evil spirits that looked like frogs; they came out of the mouth of the dragon, out of the mouth of

4. Before the war of Armageddon takes place, the Middle Eastern war will take place and at this time a third of mankind will be killed (a third of the Middle Eastern people will be killed).
5. The weapon that they will be using is described in verse 17 and 18, which will be artillery.

※N.B. Schlesinger, a former Defense Secretary under President Nixon, told newspaper reporters that China had trained 200 million troops.

Verse 19-21 The power of the horses was in their mouths and in their tails; for their tails were like snakes, having heads with which they inflict injury. The rest of mankind who were not killed by these plagues still did not repent of the work of their hands; they did not stop worshiping demons, and idols of gold, silver, bronze, stone and wood—idols that cannot see or hear or walk. Nor did they repent of their murders, their magic arts, their sexual immorality or their thefts.

1. 'did not repent of the work of their hands' refers to the sins committed with their own hands, including the making of idols and worshipping them (Dt 31:29, Jer 1:16)[316].

---

the beast and out of the mouth of the false prophet.

Rev16:14 They are spirits of demons performing miraculous signs, and they go out to the kings of the whole world, to gather them for the battle on the great day of God Almighty.

Rev16:15 "Behold, I come like a thief! Blessed is he who stays awake and keeps his clothes with him, so that he may not go naked and be shamefully exposed."

Rev16:16 Then they gathered the kings together to the place that in Hebrew is called Armageddon.

316)Dt31:29 For I know that after my death you are sure to become utterly corrupt and to turn from the way I have commanded you. In days to come, disaster will fall upon you because you will do evil in the sight of the LORD and provoke Him to anger by what your hands have made."

Jer1:16 I will pronounce My judgments on My people because of their wickedness in forsaking Me, in burning incense to other

2. There will be an idol who cannot see, hear, or walk, but will be a talking idol (Rev 13:15)[317].
3. Through the disaster of His judgments, God has urged people to repent, but in the end they will not repent.
4. All of these disasters will occur in the Middle East over the great river Euphrates.

---

gods and in worshiping what their hands have made.

317)Rev13:15 He was given power to give breath to the image of the first beast, so that it could speak and cause all who refused to worship the image to be killed.

Chapter 10

※ In chapter 9:13 the sixth trumpet is sounded. In chapter 11:15 the seventh trumpet is sounded. So chapter 10:1 to chapter 11:14 is an insert.

※ Chapter 7 was inserted between the sixth seal and the seventh seal.

▣ The insertion has three parts.

a. The vision of Christ coming to own the earth (Rev 10:1~3)[318].

b. The vision of Jerusalem on the earth being trampled by Antichrist and his army (Rev 11:1~2)[319].

c. The vision of the two witnesses (Rev 11:3~5)[320].

---

318)Rev10:1 Then I saw another mighty angel coming down from heaven. He was robed in a cloud, with a rainbow above His head; His face was like the sun, and His legs were like fiery pillars.
Rev10:2 He was holding a little scroll, which lay open in His hand. He planted His right foot on the sea and His left foot on the land,
Rev10:3 and he gave a loud shout like the roar of a lion. When he shouted, the voices of the seven thunders spoke.

319)Rev11:1 I was given a reed like a measuring rod and was told, "Go and measure the temple of God and the altar, and count the worshipers there.
Rev11:2 But exclude the outer court; do not measure it, because it has been given to the Gentiles. They will trample on the holy city for 42 months.

320)Rev11:3 And I will give power to My two witnesses, and they will prophesy for 1,260 days, clothed in sackcloth."
Rev11:4 These are the two olive trees and the two lampstands that stand before the Lord of the earth.
Rev11:5 If anyone tries to harm them, fire comes from their mouths and devours their enemies. This is how anyone who wants to harm them must die.

Verse 1 Then I saw another mighty angel coming down from heaven. He was robed in a cloud, with a rainbow above His head; His face was like the sun, and His legs were like fiery pillars.

[Another mighty angel]

1. 'another mighty angel' describes Christ coming down to possess the earth.

※ In the Old Testament Christ was revealed as an angel (Ge 32:29~32, Ex 3:2~6, Jdg 6:11~14, 13:15~18)[321].

---

321)Ge32:29 Jacob said, "Please tell me Your name." But He replied, "Why do you ask My name?" Then He blessed him there.

Ge32:30 So Jacob called the place Peniel, saying, "It is because I saw God face to face, and yet my life was spared."

Ge32:31 The sun rose above him as he passed Peniel, and he was limping because of his hip.

Ge32:32 Therefore to this day the Israelites do not eat the tendon attached to the socket of the hip, because the socket of Jacob's hip was touched near the tendon.

Ex3:2 There the angel of the LORD appeared to him in flames of fire from within a bush. Moses saw that though the bush was on fire it did not burn up.

Ex3:3 So Moses thought, "I will go over and see this strange sight--why the bush does not burn up."

Ex3:4 When the LORD saw that he had gone over to look, God called to him from within the bush, "Moses! Moses!" And Moses said, "Here I am."

Ex3:5 "Do not come any closer," God said. "Take off your sandals, for the place where you are standing is holy ground."

Ex3:6 Then He said, "I am the God of Your father, the God of Abraham, the God of Isaac and the God of Jacob." At this, Moses hid his face, because he was afraid to look at God.

Jdg6:11 The angel of the LORD came and sat down under the oak in Ophrah that belonged to Joash the Abiezrite, where his son Gideon was threshing wheat in a winepress to keep it from the Midianites.

Jdg6:12 When the angel of the LORD appeared to Gideon, He said, "The LORD is with you, mighty warrior."

Jdg6:13 "But sir," Gideon replied, "if the LORD is with us, why has all this happened to us? Where are all His wonders that our fathers told us about when they said, 'Did not the LORD bring us up out of Egypt?' But now the LORD has abandoned us and

※Christ works as an angel until Revelation chapter 19, where the wedding supper of the Lamb has ended, and He defeats the army of Antichrist, and throws Satan into the Abyss and seals him, and becomes the king of kings and the Lord of lords, and reigns over the Millennial Kingdom (Rev 7:2, 8:3, 18:1)[322].

(For the redemption of mankind, He works as the Lamb, and for performing God's work, He works as another angel).

2. 'coming down from heaven. He was robed in a cloud'. At this time He comes down from heaven into the atmosphere before the seventh trumpet is sounded. He will secretly come down being robed in a cloud (Comparison = Mt 24:36, 42~44, 1Th 5:2)[323].

---

put us into the hand of Midian."

Jdg6:14 The LORD turned to him and said, "Go in the strength you have and save Israel out of Midian's hand. Am I not sending you?"

Jdg13:15 Manoah said to the angel of the LORD, "We would like You to stay until we prepare a young goat for you."

Jdg13:16 The angel of the LORD replied, "Even though you detain Me, I will not eat any of Your food. But if you prepare a burnt offering, offer it to the LORD." (Manoah did not realize that it was the angel of the LORD.)

Jdg13:17 Then Manoah inquired of the angel of the LORD, "What is Your name, so that we may honor You when Your word comes true?"

Jdg13:18 He replied, "Why do you ask My name? It is beyond understanding."

322)Rev7:2 Then I saw another angel coming up from the east, having the seal of the living God. He called out in a loud voice to the four angels who had been given power to harm the land and the sea:

Rev8:3 Another angel, who had a golden censer, came and stood at the altar. He was given much incense to offer, with the prayers of all the saints, on the golden altar before the throne.

Rev18:1 After this I saw another angel coming down from heaven. He had great authority, and the earth was illuminated by His splendor.

※ However, when the Lord comes down to the earth, He will come riding on the clouds visible to everyone (Mt 24:30, Mt 26:64, Ac 1:9~11)[324].

※ When we are raptured, we will be lifted up into the clouds, so we are to be ascended in secret. Therefore, non-believers and sleeping believers will not see the rapture of the true believers (1Th 4:17)[325].

3. 'with a rainbow above His head' refers to His promise never again to judge the earth with a flood (Ge 9:8~13)[326].

---

323)Mt24:36 "No one knows about that day or hour, not even the angels in heaven, nor the Son, but only the Father.
Mt24:42 "Therefore keep watch, because you do not know on what day Your Lord will come.
Mt24:43 But understand this: If the owner of the house had known at what time of night the thief was coming, he would have kept watch and would not have let his house be broken into.
Mt24:44 So you also must be ready, because the Son of Man will come at an hour when you do not expect Him.
1Th5:2 for you know very well that the day of the Lord will come like a thief in the night.

324)Mt24:30 "At that time the sign of the Son of Man will appear in the sky, and all the nations of the earth will mourn. They will see the Son of Man coming on the clouds of the sky, with power and great glory.
Mt26:64 "Yes, it is as you say," Jesus replied. "But I say to all of you: In the future you will see the Son of Man sitting at the right hand of the Mighty One and coming on the clouds of heaven."
Ac1:9 After He said this, He was taken up before their very eyes, and a cloud hid Him from their sight.
Ac1:10 They were looking intently up into the sky as He was going, when suddenly two men dressed in white stood beside them.
Ac1:11 "Men of Galilee," they said, "why do you stand here looking into the sky? This same Jesus, who has been taken from you into heaven, will come back in the same way you have seen Him go into heaven."

325)1Th4:17 After that, we who are still alive and are left will be caught up together with them in the clouds to meet the Lord in the air. And so we will be with the Lord forever.

4. 'His face was like the sun, and His legs were like fiery pillars' means that the Lord will come as the Lord of judgment (Rev 1:15~16)[327].

Verse 2-3 He was holding a little scroll, which lay open in His hand. He planted His right foot on the sea and His left foot on the land, and he gave a loud shout like the roar of a lion. When he shouted, the voices of the seven thunders spoke.

1. The little scroll is mentioned in Revelation 5:1. Christ has already received this scroll, that was sealed with seven seals. Now, all the seals up to the seventh seal have been opened; because little remains in the scroll, it has become a little scroll (the first six trumpets have been concluded).

※ And he had in His hand a little book open (KJV).

2. 'He planted His right foot on the sea and His left foot on the land' signifies that he owns these things (Dt 11:24, Jos 1:3)[328]. This shows that Christ comes down to reclaim what

---

326)Ge9:8 Then God said to Noah and to his sons with him:
Ge9:9 "I now establish My covenant with you and with Your descendants after you
Ge9:10 and with every living creature that was with you--the birds, the livestock and all the wild animals, all those that came out of the ark with you--every living creature on earth.
Ge9:11 I establish My covenant with you: Never again will all life be cut off by the waters of a flood; never again will there be a flood to destroy the earth."
Ge9:12 And God said, "This is the sign of the covenant I am making between Me and you and every living creature with you, a covenant for all generations to come:
Ge9:13 I have set My rainbow in the clouds, and it will be the sign of the covenant between Me and the earth.

327)Rev1:15 His feet were like bronze glowing in a furnace, and His voice was like the sound of rushing waters.
Rev1:16 In His right hand He held seven stars, and out of His mouth came a sharp double-edged sword. His face was like the sun shining in all its brilliance.

is rightfully His. Although the land and the sea have been trampled by the enemy, Christ will now come down to set His feet on the land and in the sea.

3. In the four gospels, the Lord spoke as the lamb, with patience and forbearance, and had been gracious, but when He comes to possess the Earth He will give a loud shout like the roar of a lion, tread the winepress and rule them with an iron scepter (Rev 19:12, 15, 20:2)[329].

Verse 4-6 And when the seven thunders spoke, I was about to write; but I heard a voice from heaven say, "Seal up what the seven thunders have said and do not write it down." Then the angel I had seen standing on the sea and on the land raised his right hand to heaven. And he swore by Him who lives for ever and ever, who created the heavens and all that is in them, the earth and all that is in it, and the sea and all that is in it, and said, "There will be no more delay!

[The seven thunders]

1. 'And **the seven thunders** spoke' means that the wrath of God has finally fully appeared. We cannot know the contents of

---

328)Dt11:24 Every place where you set Your foot will be yours: Your territory will extend from the desert to Lebanon, and from the Euphrates River to the western sea.

Jos1:3 I will give you every place where you set Your foot, as I promised Moses.

329)Rev19:12 His eyes are like blazing fire, and on His head are many crowns. He has a name written on Him that no one knows but He Himself.

Rev19:15 Out of His mouth comes a sharp sword with which to strike down the nations. "He will rule them with an iron scepter." He treads the winepress of the fury of the wrath of God Almighty.

Rev20:2 He seized the dragon, that ancient serpent, who is the devil, or Satan, and bound him for a thousand years.

the seven thunders right now, because they have been sealed up, but we will know when the time comes.

2. After the sixth trumpet, there will be no more patience in God's judgment of the Earth. All judgment will soon end with the seventh trumpet.
3. The main creature in the heavens are angels, and the main creature on the land are men, and the main creature in the sea are demons.

Verse 7 But in the days when the seventh angel is about to sound his trumpet, the mystery of God will be accomplished, just as He announced to His servants the prophets."

1. All the mysteries of God are fulfilled when the seventh trumpet is sounded. The seventh trumpet will sound for a long period of time (in the days of the voice).
2. In the days of Adam, Moses, and Christ, all is revealed and there is no secret. But from Christ to the Millennial Kingdom (the church age) everything is secret. Incarnation (1Ti 3:16)[330], Christ, Himself (Col 2:2)[331], the gospel (Eph 6:19)[332], the church (Eph 3:4~6)[333], the Kingdom of Heaven

---

330)1Ti3:16 Beyond all question, the mystery of godliness is great: He **appeared in a body**, was vindicated by the Spirit, was seen by angels, was preached among the nations, was believed on in the world, was taken up in glory.

331)Col2:2 My purpose is that they may be encouraged in heart and united in love, so that they may have the full riches of complete understanding, in order that they may **know the mystery of God, namely, Christ**,

332)Eph6:19 Pray also for me, that whenever I open my mouth, words may be given me so that I will fearlessly make known the **mystery of the gospel**,

333)Eph3:4 In reading this, then, you will be able to understand my insight into the **mystery of Christ**,
Eph3:5 which was not made known to men in other generations as it has now been revealed by the Spirit to God's holy apostles and

(Mt 13:11)[334], Christ's indwelling (Col 1:26~27)[335], the resurrection and transformation of the saints (1Co 15:51~52)[336], etc. are all mysteries of God. All the secrets are completed and finished at the sounding of these seventh trumpet. Furthermore, the judgment of the earth by God is concluded.

3. Also, the gospel which had been given to His servants, the prophets, is accomplished (Isa 2:4)[337]. That is, the Millennial Kingdom will appear (Rev 11:15)[338], and the New Heaven and the New Earth in which the New Jerusalem stands will follow. Amen!

---

prophets.

Eph3:6 This mystery is that through the gospel the Gentiles are heirs together with Israel, members together of one body, and sharers together in the promise in Christ Jesus.

334)Mt13:11 He replied, "The knowledge of the **secrets of the kingdom of heaven** has been given to you, but not to them.

335)Col 1:26 the mystery that has been kept hidden for ages and generations, but is now disclosed to the saints.

Col 1:27 To them God has chosen to make known among the Gentiles the glorious riches of **this mystery, which is Christ in you**, the hope of glory.

336)1Co 15:51 Listen, I tell you a mystery: We will not all sleep, but **we will all be changed--**

1Co 15:52 in a flash, in the twinkling of an eye, at the last trumpet. For the trumpet will sound, the dead **will be raised imperishable, and we will be changed.**

337)Isa2:4 He will judge between the nations and will settle disputes for many peoples. They will beat their swords into plowshares and their spears into pruning hooks. Nation will not take up sword against nation, nor will they train for war anymore.

338)Rev11:15 The seventh angel sounded his trumpet, and there were loud voices in heaven, which said: "The kingdom of the world has become the kingdom of our Lord and of His Christ, and He will reign for ever and ever."

Verse 8-9 Then the voice that I had heard from heaven spoke to me once more: "Go, take the scroll that lies open in the hand of the angel who is standing on the sea and on the land." So I went to the angel and asked him to give me the little scroll. He said to me, "Take it and eat it. It will turn Your stomach sour, but 'in Your mouth it will be as sweet as honey.' "

[The little scroll]

1. John asked the angel to give the little scroll to him, and the angel told him to take it and eat it. We know that in order to read a book we use our eyes, but the angel told John to eat the little scroll. Through eating this, one's whole personality can receive it. We must eat the divine revelation instead of trying to see and understand it with our eyes (Jer 15:16, Eze 2:8, Eze 3:1～3)[339].
2. After it has been eaten, if it is to be digested in me and completely owned by me, my stomach will turn sour. When we hear, it will be sweet, and when we understand it, we will be deeply moved, but if it is to be digested by obeying it, it will make our stomach sour, because we must pay the price.

Verse 10-11 I took the little scroll from the angel's hand and ate it. It tasted as sweet as honey in my mouth, but

339)Jer15:16 When Your words came, I ate them; they were my joy and my heart's delight, for I bear Your name, O LORD God Almighty.

Eze2:8 But you, son of man, listen to what I say to you. Do not rebel like that rebellious house; open Your mouth and eat what I give you."

Eze3:1 And He said to me, "Son of man, eat what is before you, eat this scroll; then go and speak to the house of Israel."

Eze3:2 So I opened my mouth, and He gave me the scroll to eat.

Eze3:3 Then He said to me, "Son of man, eat this scroll I am giving you and fill Your stomach with it." So I ate it, and it tasted as sweet as honey in my mouth.

when I had eaten it, my stomach turned sour. Then I was told, "You must prophesy again about many peoples, nations, languages and kings."

1. The prophecy of this book consists of two parts. The first part is from the first seal to the sixth trumpet (Rev 6:1～11:14), and the second part is the content in the little scroll that John has taken and eaten, from the seventh trumpet to the New Heaven and the New Earth (Rev 11:15～22:5).
   John has prophesied the first part, and now must prophesy the second part as well.
2. The content in the second part involves the judgment of the bowls, the rapture of saints, the judgment throne of Christ, the wedding supper of the Lamb, the Lord's second coming with His chosen army to defeat Antichrist and the false prophets, the imprisonment of Satan, the Millennial Kingdom, the last betrayal of mankind by the instigation of Satan, the judgment of the great white throne, the New Jerusalem, and the New Heavens and the New Earth.
3. This is the content of the seventh trumpet, and of the little scroll, and the second part of John's prophecy. In order to prophesy this, we must take the contents in this scroll and digest it.

Chapter 11

◈ Chapter 10~11:14 is an insertion between the sixth trumpet and the seventh trumpet

Verse 1-2 I was given a reed like a measuring rod and was told, "Go and measure the temple of God and the altar, with its worshipers. But exclude the outer court; do not measure it, because it has been given to the Gentiles. They will trample on the holy city for 42 months.

1. A reed is for measuring and a rod represents punishment. So, a reed like a rod means that God protects in holiness everyone that is measured and punishes everyone that is not measured.
2. The outer court of the temple refers to the outside of the temple, that is the castle of Jerusalem (not the courtyard of the temple).
3. Among the Jews, those who worship God in the temple are measured, but the people of God who do not worship Him wholeheartedly are God's people in name only and are not measured. They will be trampled for 42 months (Lk 21:24, Mt 24:15~24)[340].

---

340)Lk21:24 They will fall by the sword and will be taken as prisoners to all the nations. Jerusalem will be trampled on by the Gentiles until the times of the Gentiles are fulfilled.
Mt24:15 "So when you see standing in the holy place 'the abomination that causes desolation,' spoken of through the prophet Daniel--let the reader understand--
Mt24:16 then let those who are in Judea flee to the mountains.
Mt24:17 Let no one on the roof of his house go down to take anything out of the house.
Mt24:18 Let no one in the field go back to get his cloak.
Mt24:19 How dreadful it will be in those days for pregnant women and nursing mothers!
Mt24:20 Pray that Your flight will not take place in winter or on the Sabbath.
Mt24:21 For then there will be great distress, unequaled from the beginning of the world until now--and never to be equaled again.
Mt24:22 If those days had not been cut short, no one would survive, but for the sake of the elect those days will be shortened.

4. The holy city in the outer court means the castle of Jerusalem (Mt 27:53, Isa 52:1)[341)]

Verse 3 And I will appoint My two witnesses, and they will prophesy for 1,260 days, clothed in sackcloth."

[Moses and Elijah]

1. The **two witnesses** are **Moses and Elijah**.
   a. The Old Testament reveals Moses and Elijah as the witnesses.
      1) All the prophets of the Old Testament are witnesses, but the representative persons are these two men.
      2) Moses, who represents the Law, and Elijah, who represents the prophet, are the witnesses of God (Mt 11:13~14, Lk 16:16)[342)].
2. Everything that is done by the two witnesses (Rev 11:5~6)[343)] has been done by Moses and Elijah (Ex 7:17, 19, 2Ki

---

Mt24:23 At that time if anyone says to you, 'Look, here is the Christ!' or, 'There He is!' do not believe it.
Mt24:24 For false Christs and false prophets will appear and perform great signs and miracles to deceive even the elect--if that were possible.

341)Mt27:53 They came out of the tombs, and after Jesus' resurrection they went into the holy city and appeared to many people.
Isa52:1 Awake, awake, O Zion, clothe yourself with strength. Put on Your garments of splendor, O Jerusalem, the holy city. The uncircumcised and defiled will not enter you again.

342)Mt11:13 For all the Prophets and the Law prophesied until John.
Mt11:14 And if you are willing to accept it, he is the Elijah who was to come.
Lk16:16 "The Law and the Prophets were proclaimed until John. Since that time, the good news of the kingdom of God is being preached, and everyone is forcing his way into it.

343)Rev11:5 If anyone tries to harm them, fire comes from their mouths and devours their enemies. This is how anyone who wants to harm them must die.

1:10, 1Ki 17:1)[344].

3. The two witnesses appeared before the Lord in the mountain of transfiguration and talked about the death of the Lord on the cross (Mt 17:1~3, Lk 9:30)[345].
4. Concerning Elijah, it has been prophesied that he will come before the Messiah (Mal 4:5, Mt 17:10~11, Mk 9:11~13)[346].
5. The Jews have the utmost respect for Moses and Elijah and

Rev11:6 These men have power to shut up the sky so that it will not rain during the time they are prophesying; and they have power to turn the waters into blood and to strike the earth with every kind of plague as often as they want.

344)Ex7:17 This is what the LORD says: By this you will know that I am the LORD: With the staff that is in My hand I will strike the water of the Nile, and it will be changed into blood.

Ex7:19 The LORD said to Moses, "Tell Aaron, 'Take Your staff and stretch out Your hand over the waters of Egypt--over the streams and canals, over the ponds and all the reservoirs'--and they will turn to blood. Blood will be everywhere in Egypt, even in the wooden buckets and stone jars."

2Ki1:10 Elijah answered the captain, "If I am a man of God, may fire come down from heaven and consume you and Your fifty men!" Then fire fell from heaven and consumed the captain and his men.

1Ki17:1 Now Elijah the Tishbite, from Tishbe in Gilead, said to Ahab, "As the LORD, the God of Israel, lives, whom I serve, there will be neither dew nor rain in the next few years except at my word."

345)Mt17:1 After six days Jesus took with Him Peter, James and John the brother of James, and led them up a high mountain by themselves.

Mt17:2 There He was transfigured before them. His face shone like the sun, and His clothes became as white as the light.

Mt17:3 Just then there appeared before them Moses and Elijah, talking with Jesus.

Lk9:30 Two men, Moses and Elijah,

346)Mal4:5 "See, I will send you the prophet Elijah before that great and dreadful day of the LORD comes.

Mt17:10 The disciples asked Him, "Why then do the teachers of the law say that Elijah must come first?"

Mt17:11 Jesus replied, "To be sure, Elijah comes and will restore all things.

believe in them (Jn 1:21, 25, 5:45, 8:5, 9:28)[347].

6. During the Great Tribulation against Antichrist, the two witnesses will urge the Jews in the castle of Jerusalem to repent (clothed in sackcloth) (Rev 11:3)[348]. They will testify for 1,260 days and urge the people to repent.
7. As 1,260 days is the same as 42 months in verse 2, during that time Antichrist will utter blasphemies (Rev 13:5~6)[349] and persecute the people of God, but God will take care of them in the place prepared (Rev 12:6, 14)[350].

Verse 4 They are "the two olive trees" and the two lampstands, and "they stand before the Lord of the earth."

["the two olive trees" and the two lampstands]

---

347)Jn1:21 They asked Him, "Then who are you? Are you Elijah?" He said, "I am not." "Are you the Prophet?" He answered, "No."
Jn1:25 questioned Him, "Why then do you baptize if you are not the Christ, nor Elijah, nor the Prophet?"
Jn5:45 "But do not think I will accuse you before the Father. Your accuser is Moses, on whom Your hopes are set.
Jn8:5 In the Law Moses commanded us to stone such women. Now what do you say?"
Jn9:28 Then they hurled insults at him and said, "You are this fellow's disciple! We are disciples of Moses!

348)Rev11:3 And I will give power to My two witnesses, and they will prophesy for 1,260 days, clothed in sackcloth."

349)Rev13:5 The beast was given a mouth to utter proud words and blasphemies and to exercise his authority for forty-two months.
Rev13:6 He opened his mouth to blaspheme God, and to slander His name and His dwelling place and those who live in heaven.

350)Rev12:6 **The woman fled into the desert** to a **place prepared for her by God**, where she might be taken care of for 1,260 days.
Rev12:14 The woman was given the two wings of a great eagle, so that she might fly to the place prepared for her in the desert, where she would be taken care of for a time, times and half a time, out of the serpent's reach.

1. The two olive trees and the two lampstands means the two lampstands are lit with oil of olive trees. Because these two witnesses are full of this oil, they are full of the Spirit, and are the two witnesses that shine brightly before the Lord (Zec 4:8～14)[351].
2. During the Great Tribulation, because the affliction and persecution will be very severe, Moses and Elijah, being full of the Spirit, will oppose Antichrist, urge the people not to receive the '666' sign, and not to worship idols. This will be God's last consideration for the Jews.
3. In the church age, the churches were the lampstands for the witness of God (Rev 1:20)[352]. But in this last three and a half years period, the two witnesses in Israel will work as the two lampstands for the witness of God.

Verse 5-6 If anyone wants to harm them, fire proceeds from their mouths and devours their enemies. In this way,

---

351)Zec4:8 Then the word of the LORD came to me:
Zec4:9 "The hands of Zerubbabel have laid the foundation of this temple; his hands will also complete it. Then you will know that the LORD Almighty has sent me to you.
Zec4:10 "Who despises the day of small things? Men will rejoice when they see the plumb line in the hand of Zerubbabel. "(These seven are the eyes of the LORD, which range throughout the earth.)"
Zec4:11 Then I asked the angel, "What are these two olive trees on the right and the left of the lampstand?"
Zec4:12 Again I asked him, **"What are these two olive branches beside the two gold pipes that pour out golden oil?"**
Zec4:13 He replied, "Do you not know what these are?" "No, my lord," I said.
Zec4:14 So he said, "These are the two who are anointed to serve the Lord of all the earth."

352)Rev1:20 The mystery of the seven stars that you saw in My right hand and of the seven golden lampstands is this: The seven stars are the angels of the seven churches, and the seven lampstands are the seven churches.

anyone who wants to harm them must be killed. These witnesses have power to shut the sky so that no rain will fall during the days of their prophecy, and power to turn the waters into blood and to strike the earth with every kind of plague as often as they wish.

1. On the one hand, the two witnesses will make the Jews keep their faith in God until the end, and on the other, they will fight against Antichrist.
2. The two witnesses will fight the enemies as Moses and Elijah did in the past. They will fight their enemies by consuming them with fire (2Ki 1:10～12)[353], and they will shut up the sky so it will not rain (1Ki 17:1)[354], and they will turn the waters into blood (Ex 7:17～19)[355].

Verse 7-8 When the two witnesses have finished their testimony, the beast that comes up from the Abyss will

---

353)2Ki 1:10 Elijah answered the captain, "If I am a man of God, may fire come down from heaven and consume you and Your fifty men!" Then fire fell from heaven and consumed the captain and his men.

2Ki 1:11 At this the king sent to Elijah another captain with his fifty men. The captain said to him, "Man of God, this is what the king says, 'Come down at once!'"

2Ki 1:12 "If I am a man of God," Elijah replied, "may fire come down from heaven and consume you and Your fifty men!" Then the fire of God fell from heaven and consumed him and his fifty men.

354)1Ki17:1 In the twelfth year of Ahaz king of Judah, Hoshea son of Elah became king of Israel in Samaria, and he reigned nine years.

355)Ex7:17 This is what the LORD says: By this you will know that I am the LORD: With the staff that is in My hand I will strike the water of the Nile, and it will be changed into blood.

Ex7:18 The fish in the Nile will die, and the river will stink; the Egyptians will not be able to drink its water.'"

Ex7:19 The LORD said to Moses, "Tell Aaron, 'Take Your staff and stretch out Your hand over the waters of Egypt--over the streams and canals, over the ponds and all the reservoirs'--and they will turn to blood. Blood will be everywhere in Egypt, even in the wooden buckets and stone jars."

wage war with them, and will overpower and kill them. Their bodies will lie in the street of the great city—figuratively called Sodom and Egypt—where their Lord was also crucified.

1. Nothing will happen to the two witnesses until they finish their testimony. In the end, when their mission has been completed and their testimony is finished, they will be attacked by the beast, which is Antichrist coming up from the Abyss, and be killed.

[The beast that comes up from the Abyss]

2. The beast that comes up from the Abyss is Antichrist. He comes up from the Abyss in spirit (Rev 11:7, 17:8)[356] and comes up out of the sea in flesh (Rev 13:1)[357]. Antichrist will fight the two witnesses (Rev 11:7)[358] and make war against the saints (Rev 13:7)[359].
3. The great city (Rev 11:2, 16:19)[360] refers to Jerusalem where

---

356)Rev11:7 Now when they have finished their testimony, the beast that comes up from the Abyss will attack them, and overpower and kill them.
Rev17:8 The beast, which you saw, once was, now is not, and will come up out of the Abyss and go to his destruction. The inhabitants of the earth whose names have not been written in the book of life from the creation of the world will be astonished when they see the beast, because he once was, now is not, and yet will come.

357)Rev13:1 And the dragon stood on the shore of the sea. And I saw a beast coming out of the sea. He had ten horns and seven heads, with ten crowns on his horns, and on each head a blasphemous name.

358)Rev11:7 ☝ See footnote 356)

359)Rev13:7 He was given power to make war against the saints and to conquer them. And he was given authority over every tribe, people, language and nation.

360)Rev11:2 But exclude the outer court; do not measure it, because it has been given to the Gentiles. They will trample on the holy city for 42 months.
Rev16:19 The great city split into three parts, and the cities of the

Jesus was crucified. It is figuratively called Sodom (Rev 11:8, Isa 1:9~10)[361] and Egypt (Rev 11:8, Eze 23:3,27)[362] which signifies the corruption of Jerusalem.

※ Sodom symbolizes immorality and Egypt symbolizes materialism.

Verse 9-10 For three and a half days all peoples and tribes and tongues and nations will view their bodies and will not permit them to be laid in a tomb. And those who dwell on the earth will gloat over them, and will celebrate and send one another gifts, because these two prophets had tormented them.

1. Their dead bodies will not be buried; they will be rejected in the street of the great city where their Lord was also crucified.
2. These two prophets were refused burial because they had tormented Antichrist and all the rebels.
3. At this time, all the people of the world will gaze on their dead bodies for three and a half days. In today's world, all the people of the world will be able to see through

---

nations collapsed. God remembered Babylon the Great and gave her the cup filled with the wine of the fury of His wrath.

361)Rev11:8 Their bodies will lie in the street of the great city, which is figuratively called Sodom and Egypt, where also their Lord was crucified.

Isa1:9 Unless the LORD Almighty had left us some survivors, we would have become like Sodom, we would have been like Gomorrah.

Isa1:10 Hear the word of the LORD, you rulers of Sodom; listen to the law of our God, you people of Gomorrah!

362)Rev11:8 ☝See footnote 361)

Eze23:3 They became prostitutes in Egypt, engaging in prostitution from their youth. In that land their breasts were fondled and their virgin bosoms caressed.

Eze23:27 So I will put a stop to the lewdness and prostitution you began in Egypt. You will not look on these things with longing or remember Egypt anymore.

television and other mass media.
4. They will celebrate by sending each other gifts as they gloat over them.

Verse 11-12 But after the three and a half days, the breath of life from God entered the two witnesses, and they stood on their feet, and great fear fell upon those who saw them. And the witnesses heard a loud voice from heaven saying, "Come up here." And they went up to heaven in a cloud as their enemies watched them.

1. 'they stood on their feet' means they are resurrected, and terror will strike those who see it.

[They ascend into heaven in a cloud]

2. They will be raptured following a loud voice from heaven saying "Come up here" (Rev 4:1)[363]. The overcomers will hear this voice from heaven and be raptured.
3. Unbelievers and believers will see the bodies of the two witnesses and see both their resurrection and rapture. Believers will receive assurance and encouragement of faith, and unbelievers will fear.

※ Even the two witnesses' dead bodies being left in the streets of the great city is the great will of God. Through this, believers will, without a doubt, overcome the Great Tribulation of Antichrist.

Verse 13-14 And in that hour there was a great earthquake, and a tenth of the city collapsed. Seven thousand were killed in the quake, and the rest were terrified and gave glory to the God of heaven. The second woe has passed. Behold, the third woe is coming shortly.

1. The city in verse 8 refers to Jerusalem. A tenth of the city will collapse, and in Revelation 16:19, the rest will be split

363)Rev4:1 After this I looked, and there before me was a door standing open in heaven. And the voice I had first heard speaking to me like a trumpet said, "Come up here, and I will show you what must take place after this."

into three parts in the last earthquake.

2. The city's trampling by the Gentiles, the great earthquake, and the death of seven thousand people (in the earthquake) are because Jerusalem was already full of sin. If they still don't believe even after suffering all this, God will show them compelling evidence that they cannot ignore, that they must believe.
3. After this, the third woe comes; this will be the seventh trumpet, a loud trumpet (Mt 24:31)[364], and the last trumpet (1Co 15:51)[365].

Verse 15 Then the seventh angel sounded his trumpet, and loud voices called out in heaven: "The kingdom of the world has become the kingdom of our Lord and of His Christ, and He will reign for ever and ever."

1. When **the seventh trumpet** sounds, the Great Tribulation will be over, and it will be the end of the era. Through this, all the mystery of God will be accomplished (Rev 10:7)[366] and the kingdom of this world will become the kingdom of our Lord and of His Christ.
2. This will be the fulfilment of what was prophesied in the Old Testament and New Testament. The time of Satan will end (Satan will be imprisoned in the Abyss) (Rev 20:2)[367], and the kingdom of heaven, the Millennial Kingdom will

---

364)Mt24:31 And He will send His angels with a loud trumpet call, and they will gather His elect from the four winds, from one end of the heavens to the other.

365)1Co15:51 Listen, I tell you a mystery: We will not all sleep, but we will all be changed--

366)Rev10:7 But in the days when the seventh angel is about to sound his trumpet, the mystery of God will be accomplished, just as He announced to His servants the prophets."

367)Rev20:2 He seized the dragon, that ancient serpent, who is the devil, or Satan, and bound him for a thousand years.

begin, and Christ will reign for ever and ever.

※ After the two witnesses are resurrected and ascend, a tenth of Jerusalem will collapse and seven thousand people will be killed (which can be compared with the death of Korah's descendants and others by an earthquake). At this very hour, the seventh trumpet will sound.

Verse 16-17 And the twenty-four elders who sit on their thrones before God fell on their faces and worshiped God, saying: "We give thanks to You, O Lord God Almighty, the One who is and who was, because You have taken Your great power and have begun to reign.

◆ Chapter 1 verse 4 says "the One who is to come", but that phrase is left out in this verse because the One who is to come has now arrived in chapter 11.

Verse 18 The nations were enraged, and Your wrath has come. The time has come to judge the dead and to reward Your servants the prophets, as well as the saints and those who fear Your name, both small and great—and to destroy those who destroy the earth."

1. The seventh trumpet
   a. It brings the end of the Great Tribulation. Because the seven bowls are included in the seventh trumpet, this will be the third woe, and the last disaster (Rev 15:1)[368], and the end of all disasters.
   b. The end of an era
   This era will be finished with the ending of the Great Tribulation, and the mystery of God will be accomplished (Rev 10:7)[369]. The kingdom of the world will become

368)Rev15:1 I saw in heaven another great and marvelous sign: seven angels with the seven last plagues--last, because with them God's wrath is completed.

the kingdom of Christ.

c. The eternal kingdom will come.

The seventh trumpet will bring forth the eternal Kingdom of Christ. In verse 15, "He will reign for ever and ever" means He will reign not only in the Millennial Kingdom, but also in the New Heaven and New Earth for ever and ever.

[In addition to the seven bowls]

d. The seventh trumpet includes the following:

1) The judgment of the dead

a) He judges the angry Gentile nations, the Antichrist and his army.

b) He judges people already dead to distinguish those who will come before the white throne from those who will be resurrected and participate in the life of resurrection of the Millennial Kingdom.

2) He rewards (Rev 22:12, Mt 16:27)[370].

a) The prophets and the saints

This will take place before the judgment seat of Christ (2Co 5:10)[371]. Among the saints who have received salvation, it will be decided who is worthy of reward and who will be punished (Ro 14:10~12, Mt 25:30)[372].

---

369)Rev10:7 But in the days when the seventh angel is about to sound his trumpet, the mystery of God will be accomplished, just as He announced to His servants the prophets."

370)Rev22:12 "Behold, I am coming soon! My reward is with Me, and I will give to everyone according to what he has done.

Mt16:27 For the Son of Man is going to come in His Father's glory with His angels, and then He will reward each person according to what he has done.

371)2Co5:10 For we must all appear before the judgment seat of Christ, that each one may receive what is due him for the things done while in the body, whether good or bad.

372)Ro14:10 You, then, why do you judge Your brother? Or why do you

b) <u>Those who fear God</u>
They are those who have heard the everlasting gospel (Rev 14:6)[373], worshipped God, have not worshipped idols, and those among the unbelievers who have taken care of believers (Mt 25:33~40)[374]. This will be fulfilled when the Lord comes down onto the earth and judges the nations.

c) <u>He destroys those who destroy the earth</u>
Those who destroy the earth (verse 18) are Babylon The Great (Rev 17:2, 18:3)[375], Antichrist (Rev 13:

---

look down on Your brother? For we will all stand before God's judgment seat.
Ro14:11 It is written: "'As surely as I live,' says the Lord, 'every knee will bow before me; every tongue will confess to God.'"
Ro14:12 So then, each of us will give an account of himself to God.
Mt25:30 And throw that worthless servant outside, into the darkness, where there will be weeping and gnashing of teeth.'

373)Rev14:6 Then I saw another angel flying in midair, and he had the eternal gospel to proclaim to those who live on the earth--to every nation, tribe, language and people.

374)Mt25:33 He will put the sheep on His right and the goats on His left.
Mt25:34 "Then the King will say to those on His right, 'Come, you who are blessed by My Father; take Your inheritance, the kingdom prepared for you since the creation of the world.
Mt25:35 For I was hungry and you gave Me something to eat, I was thirsty and you gave Me something to drink, I was a stranger and you invited Me in,
Mt25:36 I needed clothes and you clothed Me, I was sick and you looked after Me, I was in prison and you came to visit me.'
Mt25:37 "Then the righteous will answer Him, 'Lord, when did we see You hungry and feed You, or thirsty and give You something to drink?
Mt25:38 When did we see You a stranger and invite You in, or needing clothes and clothe You?
Mt25:39 When did we see You sick or in prison and go to visit you?'
Mt25:40 "The King will reply, 'I tell you the truth, whatever you did for one of the least of these brothers of Mine, you did for me.'

3)[376], the false prophet (Rev 13:14)[377], Satan (Rev 20:7~9)[378], and his followers (Rev 17:12~14)[379]. They are all arranged for destruction while the seventh trumpet is ringing.

---

375)Rev17:2 With her the kings of the earth committed adultery and the inhabitants of the earth were intoxicated with the wine of her adulteries."
Rev18:3 For all the nations have drunk the maddening wine of her adulteries. The kings of the earth committed adultery with her, and the merchants of the earth grew rich from her excessive luxuries."

376)Rev13:3 One of the heads of the beast seemed to have had a fatal wound, but the fatal wound had been healed. The whole world was astonished and followed the beast.

377)Rev13:14 Because of the signs he was given power to do on behalf of the first beast, he deceived the inhabitants of the earth. He ordered them to set up an image in honor of the beast who was wounded by the sword and yet lived.

378)Rev20:7 When the thousand years are over, Satan will be released from his prison
Rev20:8 and will go out to deceive the nations in the four corners of the earth--Gog and Magog--to gather them for battle. In number they are like the sand on the seashore.
Rev20:9 They marched across the breadth of the earth and surrounded the camp of God's people, the city He loves. But fire came down from heaven and devoured them.

379)Rev17:12 "The ten horns you saw are ten kings who have not yet received a kingdom, but who for one hour will receive authority as kings along with the beast.
Rev17:13 They have one purpose and will give their power and authority to the beast.
Rev17:14 They will make war against the Lamb, but the Lamb will overcome them because He is Lord of lords and King of kings--and with Him will be His called, chosen and faithful followers."

Verse 19 Then the temple of God in heaven was opened, and the ark of His covenant appeared in His temple. And there were flashes of lightning, and rumblings, and peals of thunder, and an earthquake, and a great hailstorm.

1. In verse 19 the temple in heaven is opened
   By this event, God's throne encircled by a rainbow (Rev 4:2~3)[380] becomes the center of the judgments being executed on earth in chapters 6~11, and the opening of the temple with the ark of the covenant is the fulfillment of God's righteousness from chapters 12 to 22. You will see these two sections:

※ The first section : the throne with a rainbow (Rev 4:2~3)[381] ⇒ For the judgment of God.
The second section : the temple with the Ark of the Covenant (Rev 11:19)[382] ⇒ For the building of God.

2. When the temple of God was opened and the ark of the covenant was seen, there were lightning, voices, thunder, earthquakes, and hail. These are the severe proclamations of God's wrath.

※ **[The four earthquakes seen in Revelation]**
a. At the sixth seal (Rev 6:12)[383]: the seventh seal (the warning of God's wrath)

---

380)Rev4:2 At once I was in the Spirit, and there before me was a throne in heaven with someone sitting on it.
Rev4:3 And the One who sat there had the appearance of jasper and carnelian. A rainbow, resembling an emerald, encircled the throne.

381)Rev4:2~3 ☞See footnote 380)

382)Rev11:19 Then God's temple in heaven was opened, and within His temple was seen the ark of His covenant. And there came flashes of lightning, rumblings, peals of thunder, an earthquake and a great hailstorm.

383)Rev6:12 I watched as He opened the sixth seal. There was a great earthquake. The sun turned black like sackcloth made of goat hair, the whole moon turned blood red,

b. Before the first trumpet (Rev 8:5)[384]: the warning of the disaster of the trumpets.
c. Between the sixth and the seventh trumpet (Rev 11:13)[385] : the wrath of God against corrupt Jerusalem.
d. Between the seventh trumpet and the seven bowls (Rev 11:19)[386] : reveals the warning of God's wrath against those who destroy the earth.

※ Revelation is divided into two main sections:

The first part : Chapter 1～11

The second part : Chapter 12～22

The first section has a brief overview and general illumination of events

In the second section, the judgment proceeds, supplementing the detailed progress of the main items in the first section. (This is similar to how Genesis chapter 1 is a general record of God's creation, and Genesis chapter 2 emphasizes the special process of the creation of man).

---

384)Rev8:5 Then the angel took the censer, filled it with fire from the altar, and hurled it on the earth; and there came peals of thunder, rumblings, flashes of lightning and an earthquake.

385)Rev11:13 At that very hour there was a severe earthquake and a tenth of the city collapsed. Seven thousand people were killed in the earthquake, and the survivors were terrified and gave glory to the God of heaven.

386)Rev11:19 Then God's temple in heaven was opened, and within His temple was seen the ark of His covenant. And there came flashes of lightning, rumblings, peals of thunder, an earthquake and a great hailstorm.

Chapter 12

※A woman and a male child, a red dragon and his persecution, and the war in heaven and Satan being hurled down.

Verse 1 And a great sign appeared in heaven: a woman clothed in the sun, with the moon under her feet and a crown of twelve stars on her head.

1. In the Old Testament, to God, everyone who believes in God is a woman (Isa 54:5, Jer 3:14)[387].

   In the New Testament, a virgin (the wise virgin (Mt 25:1~13))

   ⇒ **a bride** (Jn 3:29)[388]

   ⇒ **a wife** (Rev 19:6~7)[389]

   ⇒ **the new Jerusalem** (Rev 21:2)[390]

---

387)Isa54:5 For Your Maker is Your husband--the LORD Almighty is His name--the Holy One of Israel is Your Redeemer; He is called the God of all the earth.

Jer3:14 "Return, faithless people," declares the LORD, "for I am Your husband. I will choose you--one from a town and two from a clan--and bring you to Zion.

388)Jn3:29 The bride belongs to the bridegroom. The friend who attends the bridegroom waits and listens for him, and is full of joy when he hears the bridegroom's voice. That joy is mine, and it is now complete.

389)Rev19:6 Then I heard what sounded like a great multitude, like the roar of rushing waters and like loud peals of thunder, shouting: "Hallelujah! For our Lord God Almighty reigns.

Rev19:7 Let us rejoice and be glad and give Him glory! For the wedding of the Lamb has come, and His bride has made herself ready.

390)Rev21:2 I saw the Holy City, the new Jerusalem, coming down out of heaven from God, prepared as a bride beautifully dressed for her husband.

[A woman]

2. The woman in chapter 12:1 represents the whole of God's people:
   a. A crown of twelve stars was on her head (Ge 37:9)[391)]
      The saints who believed in God, shining like stars in the age of the patriarchs.
   b. The body part clothed with the sun (Mal 4:2, Lk 1:78)[392)]
      New Testament believers who shine like the sun.
   c. The part of her feet standing on the moon (Mt 4:16)[393)]
      Represents the saints of the Old Testament depicted in the dark night before the coming of Christ, the sun.

The woman consists of these

Verse 2 She was pregnant and crying out in the pain and agony of giving birth.

1. This woman is the entirety of believers: the saints in the age of the patriarchs who shine like stars, the saints of the Old Testament, the age of the law, and the saints of the New Testament. The meaning of "she was pregnant" with a male child is that the churches were pregnant with the overcomers.
2. This child in verse 2 is a male child (Rev 12:5)[394)]. This

---

391)Ge37:9 Then he had another dream, and he told it to his brothers. "Listen," he said, "I had another dream, and this time the sun and moon and eleven stars were bowing down to me."

392)Mal4:2 But for you who revere My name, the sun of righteousness will rise with healing in its wings. And you will go out and leap like calves released from the stall.
Lk1:78 because of the tender mercy of our God, by which the rising sun will come to us from heaven

393)Mt4:16 the people living in darkness have seen a great light; on those living in the land of the shadow of death a light has dawned."

394)Rev12:5 She gave birth to a son, a male child, who will rule all the nations with an iron scepter. And her child was snatched up

represents the overcomer among the saints of the church, who is stronger (Rev 12:5, 1Pe 3:7)[395].

3. When the woman obeys Christ and wholeheartedly accepts Him, she will bear a male child.
4. The church's pregnancy and birth of the male child will be accompanied by great pain (Gal 4:19, Isa 26:17)[396].
5. "Cried out in pain" means to cry out to God in prayer due to great pain.

Verse 3-4 Then another sign appeared in heaven: a huge red dragon with seven heads, ten horns, and seven royal crowns on his heads. His tail swept a third of the stars from the sky, tossing them to the earth. And the dragon stood before the woman who was about to give birth, ready to devour her child as soon as she gave birth.

1. In Genesis chapter 3, Satan moved around as a serpent, but now he has become a red dragon. For 6,000 years the serpent has grown eating dust (Ge 3:14)[397]. Also, for a long time it has been killing many saints and drinking blood, through which it has become a red dragon (Mt 23:35, Jn 8:44)[398].

---

to God and to His throne.

395)Rev12:5 ☝See footnote 394)
1Pe3:7 Husbands, in the same way be considerate as you live with Your wives, and treat them with respect as the weaker partner and as heirs with you of the gracious gift of life, so that nothing will hinder Your prayers.

396)Gal4:19 My dear children, for whom I am again in the pains of childbirth until Christ is formed in you,
Isa26:17 As a woman with child and about to give birth writhes and cries out in her pain, so were we in Your presence, O LORD.

397)Ge3:14 So the LORD God said to the serpent, "Because you have done this, "Cursed are you above all the livestock and all the wild animals! You will crawl on Your belly and you will eat dust all the days of Your life.

398)Mt23:35 And so upon you will come all the righteous blood that has been shed on earth, from the blood of righteous Abel to the

[The persecution an enormous red dragon]

2. An enormous red dragon with seven heads and ten horns is the same as the beast in chapter 13:1. Therefore, the beast, the Antichrist, is the incarnation of the dragon and his ambassador plenipotentiary (Rev 13:2)[399].
3. Seven crowns on seven heads (diadema) means that, until now, it has ruled and reigned through the seven heads. (Egypt ⇒ Assyria ⇒ Babylon ⇒ Media / Persia ⇒ Greece ⇒ Rome ⇒ Late Rome)
4. The ten horns of the dragon represent the ten kings under Antichrist in chapter 17:3[400]. These ten kings are the ten toes in Daniel chapter 2. In the end time, the dragon will perform his work through the ten horns.
5. The dragon has always stood before the woman. The dragon is always standing outside the church, i.e. the believers, taking a special interest in the male child, looking to devour him when she finally gives birth.

Verse 5 And she gave birth to a son, a male child, who will rule all the nations with an iron scepter. And her child

---

blood of Zechariah son of Berekiah, whom you murdered between the temple and the altar.

Jn8:44 You belong to Your father, the devil, and you want to carry out Your father's desire. He was a murderer from the beginning, not holding to the truth, for there is no truth in him. When he lies, he speaks his native language, for he is a liar and the father of lies.

399)Rev13:2 The beast I saw resembled a leopard, but had feet like those of a bear and a mouth like that of a lion. The dragon gave the beast his power and his throne and great authority.

400)Rev17:3 Then the angel carried me away in the Spirit into a desert. There I saw a woman sitting on a scarlet beast that was covered with blasphemous names and had seven heads and ten horns.

was caught up to God and to His throne.

1. a son, a male child ⇒ (Greek) (υἱὸν ἄρσεν)

↙ ↘

son strong man

2. This son is the strongest part of God's people, the overcomer.
3. The Bible does not describe him as a baby, but as a man amongst boys.

※ The woman who is pregnant with **a male child** represents the whole of God's people. A male child represents the few strong ones among them.

4. We must not only be part of the woman, but also a part of the male child. In the Bible, a woman is a symbol of a weaker figure (1Pe 3:7)[401] and a man is a symbol of a stronger figure.

The weaker woman becomes pregnant with the stronger male child. Christians are not all strong.

※ The most noble duty of the woman is more than just the matter of what she does, what work she does, how much she does, but accepting a man and bearing a son.

※ The most noble duty of the church is more than just service, works, or other things, but accepting the life in Christ by obeying Him and giving birth to a male child. Satan hates and fears this more than anything. Therefore, Satan rather deceives us and tempts us to be occupied in many ways.

5. "Gave birth to a male child" means the male child has been resurrected. The male child represents the powerful saints who have already been raised from the dead, saints who are overcomers. The Lord Jesus has also died and received life again in resurrection (born) (Rev 1:5)[402], through which He

401)1Pe3:7 Husbands, in the same way be considerate as you live with Your wives, and treat them with respect as the weaker partner and as heirs with you of the gracious gift of life, so that nothing will hinder Your prayers.

402)Rev1:5 and from Jesus Christ, who is the faithful witness, the

became the firstborn son (Ac 13:33~34)[403]. Among the saints that have already died, martyrs and overcomers (Rev 12:11)[404] will be reborn through resurrection as a male child.

6. A male child who will rule all the nations with an iron scepter means that the male child (like in Revelation 2:26)[405] will consist of overcomers (like the overcomers in the church of Thyatira in Revelation 2:26). They will reign over the nations during the Millennial Kingdom with the power of the Lord and with an iron scepter (Rev 20:4~6)[406].
7. The male child will ascend directly into the third heaven

---

firstborn from the dead, and the ruler of the kings of the earth. To Him who loves us and has freed us from our sins by His blood,

403)Ac13:33 He has fulfilled for us, their children, by raising up Jesus. As it is written in the second Psalm: "'You are My Son; today I have become Your Father.'
Ac13:34 The fact that God raised Him from the dead, never to decay, is stated in these words: "'I will give you the holy and sure blessings promised to David.'

404)Rev12:11 They overcame him by the blood of the Lamb and by the word of their testimony; they did not love their lives so much as to shrink from death.

405)Rev2:26 To him who overcomes and does My will to the end, I will give authority over the nations--

406)Rev20:4 I saw thrones on which were seated those who had been given authority to judge. And I saw the souls of those who had been beheaded because of their testimony for Jesus and because of the word of God. They had not worshiped the beast or his image and had not received his mark on their foreheads or their hands. They came to life and reigned with Christ a thousand years.
Rev20:5 (The rest of the dead did not come to life until the thousand years were ended.) This is the first resurrection.
Rev20:6 Blessed and holy are those who have part in the first resurrection. The second death has no power over them, but they will be priests of God and of Christ and will reign with him for a thousand years.

before God and His throne (Rev 7:9～17)[407]. When the last trumpet sounds, the saints of wheat will ascend into the air (1Th 4:17)[408].

8. The time when the male child is to ascend into heaven will be right before Satan is driven out of heaven onto the earth. When Satan is exiled to the earth, the Great Tribulation will begin and will last for the latter three and a half years, 1,260 days.

---

407)Rev7:9 After this I looked and there before me was a great multitude that no one could count, from every nation, tribe, people and language, standing before the throne and in front of the Lamb. They were wearing white robes and were holding palm branches in their hands.

Rev7:10 And they cried out in a loud voice: "Salvation belongs to our God, who sits on the throne, and to the Lamb."

Rev7:11 All the angels were standing around the throne and around the elders and the four living creatures. They fell down on their faces before the throne and worshiped God,

Rev7:12 saying: "Amen! Praise and glory and wisdom and thanks and honor and power and strength be to our God for ever and ever. Amen!"

Rev7:13 Then one of the elders asked me, "These in white robes--who are they, and where did they come from?"

Rev7:14 I answered, "Sir, you know." And he said, "These are they who have come out of the great tribulation; they have washed their robes and made them white in the blood of the Lamb.

Rev7:15 Therefore, "they are before the throne of God and serve Him day and night in His temple; and He who sits on the throne will spread His tent over them.

Rev7:16 Never again will they hunger; never again will they thirst. The sun will not beat upon them, nor any scorching heat.

Rev7:17 For the Lamb at the center of the throne will be their shepherd; He will lead them to springs of living water. And God will wipe away every tear from their eyes."

408)1Th4:17 After that, we who are still alive and are left will be caught up together with them in the clouds to meet the Lord in the air. And so we will be with the Lord forever.

Verse 6 The woman fled into the wilderness to a place prepared for her by God, where she might be taken care of for 1,260 days.

[A place prepared for her by God]

1. The desert the woman fled to in verse 14 is **the place God has prepared** for His people (the Israelites, who represent the feet standing on the moon) to protect them during the Great Tribulation.
2. They will be protected and taken care of in the desert during the time of the Great Tribulation, which can be seen as the latter three and a half years or 1,260 days. These people will be the Israelites who have been sealed by God (Rev 7:3～4)[409].

Verse 7-9 Then war broke out in heaven. Michael and his angels fought against the dragon, and the dragon and his angels fought back. But he was not strong enough, and they lost their place in heaven. The great dragon was hurled down—that ancient serpent called the devil, or Satan, who leads the whole world astray. He was hurled to the earth, and his angels with him.

[The war in heaven]

1. The war in heaven will begin right after the male child has been raptured. This war will be between Michael the archangel and his angels against the dragon and his follower angels who have betrayed God.
2. Satan did not just possess the power of the air (Eph 6:12)[410],

---

409)Rev7:3 "Do not harm the land or the sea or the trees until we put a seal on the foreheads of the servants of our God."
Rev7:4 Then I heard the number of those who were sealed: 144,000 from all the tribes of Israel.

410)Eph6:12 For our struggle is not against flesh and blood, but against

but also came and went before the throne of God (Job 1) slandering the saints. But, very soon after the male child is raptured, they are expelled from heaven onto the earth by Michael and his angels.

3. Satan is expelled onto the earth outwardly by the archangel Michael and his angels, and inwardly by the male child.

※ Devil ⇒ (Greek) diabolos (slanderer, accuser, tempter)
Satan ⇒ (Hebrew) Satan (means rival)
Satan is the head of the fallen spirits who now work as a devil in men to deceive and cause all people to stumble. In the end, he will persecute, kill, and torment, desperatcly trying to crush the faith of the saints. As he is especially afraid of the overcomers, he will attack them severely (Zec 3:1～2, Rev 12:12～17)[411].

---

the rulers, against the authorities, against the powers of this dark world and against the spiritual forces of evil in the heavenly realms.

411)Zec3:1 Then he showed me Joshua the high priest standing before the angel of the LORD, and Satan standing at his right side to accuse him.

Zec3:2 The LORD said to Satan, "The LORD rebuke you, Satan! The LORD, who has chosen Jerusalem, rebuke you! Is not this man a burning stick snatched from the fire?"

Rev12:12 Therefore rejoice, you heavens and you who dwell in them! But woe to the earth and the sea, because the devil has gone down to you! He is filled with fury, because he knows that his time is short."

Rev12:13 When the dragon saw that he had been hurled to the earth, he pursued the woman who had given birth to the male child.

Rev12:14 The woman was given the two wings of a great eagle, so that she might fly to the place prepared for her in the desert, where she would be taken care of for a time, times and half a time, out of the serpent's reach.

Rev12:15 Then from his mouth the serpent spewed water like a river, to overtake the woman and sweep her away with the torrent.

Rev12:16 But the earth helped the woman by opening its mouth and swallowing the river that the dragon had spewed out of his mouth.

Verse 10-11 Then I heard a loud voice in heaven say: "Now have come the salvation and the power and the kingdom of our God, and the authority of His Messiah. For the accuser of our brothers and sisters, who accuses them before our God day and night, has been hurled down. They triumphed over him by the blood of the Lamb and by the word of their testimony; they did not love their lives so much as to shrink from death.

1. Because the one who accuses before God has been hurled down, first and foremost, heaven and the throne have been cleansed.
2. Because Satan has been hurled down from heaven, the salvation, the power, the kingdom of God, and the authority of His Christ will come. This will be achieved after all the overcomers have ascended.
3. The coming of the kingdom of God will take place by the prayers of the saints (Mt 6:10)[412] and after the ascension of the male child into heaven.
4. The brothers in verse 11 represent the male child described in verse 5. Therefore, the male child is not one figure, but it represents all overcomers as a whole.
5. The ways in which our brothers overcome:
   a. by the blood of the Lamb
   Everytime we hear the accusations of Satan, we must reject them by the forgiveness of our sins through the blood of the Lamb (1Jn 1:7~9, Mt 9:2)[413]. Even

---

Rev12:17 Then the dragon was enraged at the woman and went off to make war against the rest of her offspring--those who obey God's commandments and hold to the testimony of Jesus.

412)Mt6:10 Your kingdom come, Your will be done on earth as it is in heaven.

413)1Jn1:7 But if we walk in the light, as He is in the light, we have fellowship with one another, and the blood of Jesus, His Son, purifies us from all sin.
1Jn1:8 If we claim to be without sin, we deceive ourselves and the

when Satan deceives, condemns and accuses us, we must confess out loud the blood of Jesus Christ.

b. by the word of our testimony
   We must bear witness to the Lord out loud.
   We must confess the fact that the Lord has defeated the devil on the cross. We must proclaim that, in the end, the devil will be thrown into the lake of fire. We must proclaim the cross, and we must proclaim out loud before the devil that Christ is the King of kings and the Lord of lords. We must live as witnesses.
c. by not loving their lives so much as to shrink from death
   Eventually, we can overcome with determination even to the point of being martyred. In the life we live today, giving up the life of the soul (thoughts, emotions, will) and the self, can be considered the life of a martyr (dying on the cross daily).

6. Therefore, this male child represents the martyrs.
7. The martyrs in Revelation chapter 12 are the martyrs that were waiting in chapter 6. When their number is complete, they become the male child and ascend before the throne.

Verse 12-13 Therefore rejoice, you heavens and you who dwell in them! But woe to the earth and the sea, because the devil has gone down to you! He is filled with fury, because he knows that his time is short." When the dragon saw that he had been hurled to the earth, he pursued the woman who had given birth to the male child.

---

truth is not in us.

1Jn1:9 If we confess our sins, He is faithful and just and will forgive us our sins and purify us from all unrighteousness.

Mt9:2 Some men brought to Him a paralytic, lying on a mat. When Jesus saw their faith, He said to the paralytic, "Take heart, son; Your sins are forgiven."

1. "You heavens and you who dwell in them" is referring to the saints that have already ascended who will rejoice in heaven.
2. But the earth and the sea (the others who are still living on the earth) will go through great suffering. This is because the devil knows that his time is short. After the devil has been thrown to the earth, he will severely persecute the people left on earth because he knows that he only has three and a half years left.
3. After the male child ascends before the throne, the dragon is hurled to the earth. Following this event, the woman, who represents the whole of the church, will be persecuted, and the Great Tribulation will begin (the first trumpet ~ the sixth trumpet); Satan will focus his hatred on God's people (Mt 24:15~22)[414].

Verse 14-15 The woman was given the two wings of a great eagle, so that she might fly to the place prepared for her in the wilderness, where she would be taken care of for a time, times and half a time, out of the serpent's reach. Then from his mouth the serpent spewed water like a river, to overtake the woman and sweep her away

---

414)Mt4:15 "So when you see standing in the holy place 'the abomination that causes desolation,' spoken of through the prophet Daniel--let the reader understand--

Mt24:16 then let those who are in Judea flee to the mountains.

Mt24:17 Let no one on the roof of his house go down to take anything out of the house.

Mt24:18 Let no one in the field go back to get his cloak.

Mt24:19 How dreadful it will be in those days for pregnant women and nursing mothers!

Mt24:20 Pray that Your flight will not take place in winter or on the Sabbath.

Mt24:21 For then there will be great distress, unequaled from the beginning of the world until now--and never to be equaled again.

Mt24:22 If those days had not been cut short, no one would survive, but for the sake of the elect those days will be shortened.

with the torrent.

1. The woman in this scripture represents the woman in Israel of the Old Testament, the part of the moon under her feet.
2. The two wings of a great eagle represent the mighty hands of God's power and will deliver Israel from Satan's persecution just as He did when He delivered the Israelites from Egypt (Ex 19:4, Dt 32:11~12)[415].
3. 'the place prepared for her in the desert' is another way of saying the place prepared for the people of God (the Israelites). Just like the time in Exodus when the Israelites crossed over the Red sea and were taken care of for 40 years in the desert, God's people will be taken care of for three and a half years in this 'desert' (Dt 8:2)[416].
4. 'out of the serpent's reach' means that while the Israelites are being taken care of, they will not face Satan directly and will not be under the reign of Antichrist.
5. 'the serpent spewed water like a river' means Antichrist will attack with a great army. The earth 'opening its mouth and swallowing the river' means that the great army will be wiped out by a devastating earthquake (Isa 8:7~8, Jer 46:7~9, Nu 16:31~33)[417].

---

415)Ex9:4 'You yourselves have seen what I did to Egypt, and how I carried you on eagles' wings and brought you to Myself.
Dt2:11 like an eagle that stirs up its nest and hovers over its young, that spreads its wings to catch them and carries them on its pinions.
Dt32:12 The LORD alone led him; no foreign god was with him.

416)Dt8:2 Remember how the LORD Your God led you all the way in the desert these forty years, to humble you and to test you in order to know what was in Your heart, whether or not you would keep His commands.

417)Isa8:7 therefore the Lord is about to bring against them the mighty floodwaters of the River--the king of Assyria with all his pomp. It will overflow all its channels, run over all its banks
Isa8:8 and sweep on into Judah, swirling over it, passing through it and reaching up to the neck. Its outspread wings will cover

Verse 16-17 But the earth helped the woman by opening its mouth and swallowing the river that the dragon had spewed out of his mouth. Then the dragon was enraged at the woman and went off to wage war against the rest of her offspring—those who keep God's commands and hold fast their testimony about Jesus.

1. The woman in chapter 12 clothed with the sun, with the moon under her feet, and a crown of twelve stars on her head, is the saints. The martyrs that the woman gives birth to will conquer heaven by resurrection.
2. The woman that the dragon attacked first represents the 144,000 of Israel sealed with God's seal (Rev 7:1～4)[418].

---

the breadth of Your land, O Immanuel!"

Jer46:7 "Who is this that rises like the Nile, like rivers of surging waters?

Jer46:8 Egypt rises like the Nile, like rivers of surging waters. She says, 'I will rise and cover the earth; I will destroy cities and their people.'

Jer46:9 Charge, O horses! Drive furiously, O charioteers! March on, O warriors--men of Cush and Put who carry shields, men of Lydia who draw the bow.

Nu16:31 As soon as he finished saying all this, the ground under them split apart

Nu16:32 and the earth opened its mouth and swallowed them, with their households and all Korah's men and all their possessions.

Nu16:33 They went down alive into the grave, with everything they owned; the earth closed over them, and they perished and were gone from the community.

418)Rev7:1 After this I saw four angels standing at the four corners of the earth, holding back the four winds of the earth to prevent any wind from blowing on the land or on the sea or on any tree.

Rev7:2 Then I saw another angel coming up from the east, having the seal of the living God. He called out in a loud voice to the four angels who had been given power to harm the land and the sea:

Rev7:3 "Do not harm the land or the sea or the trees until we put a seal on the foreheads of the servants of our God."

Rev7:4 Then I heard the number of those who were sealed: 144,000 from all the tribes of Israel.

He will attack with many armies, but with the help of God the armies of Antichrist will be destroyed by an earthquake in the desert.

3. The rest of the woman's offspring refers to all the believers in the world outside of the sealed Israelites. The dragon now stands on the shore of the sea (the nations) to fight against the saints.

※ In this scripture, the earth represents Israel (or the place where the Israelites are) and the sea represents all the nations apart from Israel.

Chapter 13

Verse 1 The dragon stood on the shore of the sea. And I saw a beast coming out of the sea. It had ten horns and seven heads, with ten crowns on its horns, and on each head a blasphemous name.

[A beast coming out of the sea]

1. 'A beast coming out of the sea' means that the beast comes out of a gentile nation. In this verse, the sea is the Mediterranean (Dal 7:2~3)[419].
2. The beast with the ten horns and seven heads is similar to the dragon (Rev 12:3)[420]. We conclude that Satan and the Antichrist-like beast are portrayed as one. Antichrist is the incarnation of Satan.
3. Ten horns represent the ten kings (Rev 17:12)[421]. These ten kings are symbolized by the ten toes of the large statue in Daniel 2:42.
4. In Revelation chapter 12:3, there are crowns on 7 heads, but in chapter 13:1 there are crowns on ten horns. What that means is that Satan works with 7 heads and Antichrist works with ten horns.
5. On the seven heads are blasphemous names. They all claim that they are gods and pressure others to serve them.

※ Antichrist

---

419)Da7:2 Daniel said: "In my vision at night I looked, and there before me were the four winds of heaven churning up the great sea.
Da7:3 Four great beasts, each different from the others, came up out of the sea.

420)Rev12:3 Then another sign appeared in heaven: an enormous red dragon with seven heads and ten horns and seven crowns on his heads.

421)Rev17:12 "The ten horns you saw are ten kings who have not yet received a kingdom, but who for one hour will receive authority as kings along with the beast.

a. comes out of the sea (Rev 13:1, Da 7:3)[422].
b. comes up from the Abyss (Rev 9:11, 11:7, 17:8)[423].
His body will come out of the nations of the districts along the shore of the Mediterranean and his spirit will come up from the Abyss.

Verse 2-3 The beast I saw resembled a leopard, but had feet like those of a bear and a mouth like that of a lion. The dragon gave the beast his power and his throne and great authority. One of the heads of the beast seemed to have had a fatal wound, but the fatal wound had been healed. The whole world was filled with wonder and followed the beast.

1. The Antichrist-like beast is a combination of the three creatures described in Daniel chapter 7 - swift like a leopard, rough like a bear, and roars like a lion. It will be the totality of all the most evil and cruel authority ever in the history of mankind. He is not a human anymore, but more like a beast.
2. This is because Satan has given the beast his power, his

---

422)Rev13:1 And the dragon stood on the shore of the sea. And I saw a beast coming out of the sea. He had ten horns and seven heads, with ten crowns on his horns, and on each head a blasphemous name.
Da7:3 Four great beasts, each different from the others, came up out of the sea.

423)Rev9:11 They had as king over them the angel of the Abyss, whose name in Hebrew is Abaddon, and in Greek, Apollyon.
Rev11:7 Now when they have finished their testimony, the beast that comes up from the Abyss will attack them, and overpower and kill them.
Rev17:8 The beast, which you saw, once was, now is not, and will come up out of the Abyss and go to his destruction. The inhabitants of the earth whose names have not been written in the book of life from the creation of the world will be astonished when they see the beast, because he once was, now is not, and yet will come.

authority, his throne, and everything he possesses. He is the embodiment of Satan.

3. Antichrist will look like he was dead with a fatal wound, but after the fatal wound has been healed, the whole world will follow him. The head is the seventh head that is involved with the late Roman Empire.

※ Before His death and resurrection, Jesus was limited to His own body but after His death and resurrection, all authority and power was given to Him (Mt 28:18)[424].
Satan will also try to testify to the world that his Antichrist is like Jesus. The Antichrist is not a remarkable figure before his death, but after resurrection he will be a remarkable figure and deceive many.

Verse 4-5 People worshiped the dragon because he had given authority to the beast, and they also worshiped the beast and asked, "Who is like the beast? Who can wage war against it?" The beast was given a mouth to utter proud words and blasphemies and to exercise its authority for forty-two months.

[The dragon has given authority to the beast,]

1. The dragon has given authority to the beast, so men will worship the beast, and ask "Who can make war against the beast who was dead and risen?"
2. After having a fatal wound and being healed, the beast will be given a mouth to utter proud words and blasphemies, so that he will speak eloquently, better than the average man, in order to pressure the people to serve him as a god (Da 7:8, 11, 20, 2Th 2:4)[425].

---

424)Mt28:18 Then Jesus came to them and said, "All authority in heaven and on earth has been given to Me.

425)Da7:8 "While I was thinking about the horns, there before me was another horn, a little one, which came up among them; and three of the first horns were uprooted before it. This horn had eyes like the eyes of a man and a mouth that spoke boastfully.

3. After he is healed, he will work for 42 months. This will be the Great Tribulation (Rev 11:2～3, Mt 24:21)[426].
4. At the end of this age, Antichrist will conclude a 7 year treaty with Israel (Da 9:27)[427]. After the three and a half years have passed and his fatal wound has been healed, he will one day break the covenant with Israel and put an end to all worship and service to God (Da 9:27), persecute the saints (Rev 13:7)[428], trample the holy city (Rev 11:2)[429], and for the last three and a half years he will commit extreme brutality.

Da7:11 "Then I continued to watch because of the boastful words the horn was speaking. I kept looking until the beast was slain and its body destroyed and thrown into the blazing fire.
Da7:20 I also wanted to know about the ten horns on its head and about the other horn that came up, before which three of them fell--the horn that looked more imposing than the others and that had eyes and a mouth that spoke boastfully.
2Th2:4 He will oppose and will exalt himself over everything that is called God or is worshiped, so that he sets himself up in God's temple, proclaiming himself to be God.

426)Rev11:2 But exclude the outer court; do not measure it, because it has been given to the Gentiles. They will trample on the holy city for 42 months.
Rev11:3 And I will give power to My two witnesses, and they will prophesy for 1,260 days, clothed in sackcloth."
Mt24:21 For then there will be great distress, unequaled from the beginning of the world until now--and never to be equaled again.

427)Da9:27 He will confirm a covenant with many for one 'seven.' In the middle of the 'seven' he will put an end to sacrifice and offering. And on a wing of the temple he will set up an abomination that causes desolation, until the end that is decreed is poured out on him."

428)Rev13:7 He was given power to make war against the saints and to conquer them. And he was given authority over every tribe, people, language and nation.

429)Rev11:2 But exclude the outer court; do not measure it, because it has been given to the Gentiles. They will trample on the holy city for 42 months.

[the Lamb's book of life]

Verse 6-8 It opened its mouth to blaspheme God, and to slander His name and His dwelling place and those who live in heaven. It was given power to wage war against God's holy people and to conquer them. And it was given authority over every tribe, people, language and nation. All inhabitants of the earth will worship the beast—all whose names have not been written in the Lamb's book of life, the Lamb who was slain from the creation of the world.

1. Antichrist will blaspheme God and those who live in heaven (Da 7:25)[430].
2. Antichrist will be given power to make war against the saints and conquer them. The saints are the rest of the woman's offspring (Rev 12:17)[431]. They are the saints outside the ones in His 'dwelling place' in verse 6, that is, those who live in heaven (they are the ones who have already ascended into heaven), and the 144,000 Jews who have been sealed with God's seal (they are the ones who were taken care of in the desert prepared for her), that is, the rest of the saints that are alive on the earth.
3. They are the Jews that obey God's commandments and the saints in the New Testament that have the testimony of Jesus. Some of them will be the last of the martyrs to enter into the company of overcomers (Rev 13:15)[432].

---

430)Da7:25 He will speak against the Most High and oppress His saints and try to change the set times and the laws. The saints will be handed over to him for a time, times and half a time.

431)Rev12:17 Then the dragon was enraged at the woman and went off to make war against the rest of her offspring--those who obey God's commandments and hold to the testimony of Jesus.

432)Rev13:15 He was given power to give breath to the image of the first beast, so that it could speak and cause all who refused to

There will also be many people who receive the mark of 666 or worship the idol of Antichrist because of the persecution of Antichrist and the difficulties of living (Rev 13:7, 8, 16)[433].

4. At this time everyone in the world will worship the beast, and all believers, except those written in the Lamb's book of life, will fall (Rev 13:7～8)[434]. *(Rev 21:27)

Verse 9-10 Whoever has ears, let them hear. "If anyone is to go into captivity, into captivity they will go. If anyone is to be killed with the sword, with the sword they will be killed." This calls for patient endurance and faithfulness on the part of God's people.

1. 'He who has an ear' refers to people whose inner man's ears are open (spiritual ears).
2. Those who are to be taken will be taken, and those who are to be killed by the sword will be killed by the sword (becoming the last martyrs).
3. Here, the saints must maintain their endurance and faith right to the end.

[another beast coming out of the earth]

Verse 11 Then I saw another beast, coming out of the earth. He had two horns like a lamb, but he spoke like a dragon.

---

worship the image to be killed.

433)Rev13:7 He was given power to make war against the saints and to conquer them. And he was given authority over every tribe, people, language and nation.

Rev13:8 All inhabitants of the earth will worship the beast--all whose names have not been written in the book of life belonging to the Lamb that was slain from the creation of the world.

Rev13:16 He also forced everyone, small and great, rich and poor, free and slave, to receive a mark on his right hand or on his forehead,

434)Rev 13:7～8 ☞See footnote 433)

1. ‘another beast, coming out of the earth’ is a false prophet (Rev 16:13)[435] and 'out of the earth' means he will come from among the Jews.

※ Geographically, 'coming out of the earth' means he will come from underneath the ground. Symbolically, it means he will come from Israel.

2. Another beast, aka the false prophet, looks like a lamb but will speak like a dragon. This means he is untrue and in appearance pretends to be Christ, like a lamb, but his words will be like the dragon, Satan.

Verse 12-13 It exercised all the authority of the first beast on its behalf, and made the earth and its inhabitants worship the first beast, whose fatal wound had been healed. And it performed great signs, even causing fire to come down from heaven to the earth in full view of the people.

1. The false prophet will make men worship Antichrist, the first beast. In other words, he will make men worship the Antichrist whose fatal wound has been healed, and he will be active during the latter three and a half years.
2. He will perform great and miraculous signs, even causing fire to come down from heaven. He will fight against the two witnesses (chapter 11) and make the Jews worship Antichrist, therefore making it difficult for the Jews to distinguish between the false prophet and the true prophets (the two witnesses).

[To give breath to the image of the first beast]

Verse 14-15 Because of the signs it was given power to perform on behalf of the first beast, it deceived the inhabitants of the earth. It ordered them to set up an

---

435)Rev16:13 Then I saw three evil spirits that looked like frogs; they came out of the mouth of the dragon, out of the mouth of the beast and out of the mouth of the false prophet.

image in honor of the beast who was wounded by the sword and yet lived. The second beast was given power to give breath to the image of the first beast, so that the image could speak and cause all who refused to worship the image to be killed.

1. The false prophet will perform many signs to deceive the inhabitants of the earth. He will use the fact that the beast was wounded yet lived to order them to set up an idol.
2. No idol that men have ever made has been able to speak, but this last idol will be able to speak like a living being. This will be a definitive miracle in the eyes of the inhabitants of the earth, which will cause many people to worship the idol.
3. Both Elijah and the false prophet will perform signs with fire. By just these signs, we will not be able to tell who is in God, but the life of God does not work in the false prophet (Mt 24:24, 2Th 2:9~10)[436].
4. In this generation, we must not pay any attention to miracles, wonders, or signs because Jesus said that a wicked and adulterous generation asks for a miraculous sign (Mt 12:38~39)[437]. Rather, we must tune in our ears to detect life. We cannot distinguish between truth and falsehood

---

436)Mt24:24 For false Christs and false prophets will appear and perform great signs and miracles to deceive even the elect--if that were possible.
2Th2:9 The coming of the lawless one will be in accordance with the work of Satan displayed in all kinds of counterfeit miracles, signs and wonders,
2Th2:10 and in every sort of evil that deceives those who are perishing. They perish because they refused to love the truth and so be saved.

437)Mt12:38 Then some of the Pharisees and teachers of the law said to Him, "Teacher, we want to see a miraculous sign from you."
Mt12:39 He answered, "A wicked and adulterous generation asks for a miraculous sign! But none will be given it except the sign of the prophet Jonah.

through signs.

5. All who refuse to worship the image will be killed. They will be the last martyrs and ascend as overcomers (Rev 15:2)[438].

[The mark of the beast 666]

Verse 16-18 It also forced all people, great and small, rich and poor, free and slave, to receive a mark on their right hands or on their foreheads, so that they could not buy or sell unless they had the mark, which is the name of the beast or the number of its name. This calls for wisdom. Let the person who has insight calculate the number of the beast, for it is the number of a man. That number is 666.

1. 'He also forced everyone, small and great, rich and poor, free and slave' to receive the mark of Antichrist. It will probably be on a woman's right hand and on a man's forehead.
2. This mark will be used to buy and sell. Without this mark, there will be no way to live.
3. Once a person receives this mark he will come under the authority of Antichrist and be controlled by him.
4. This mark will be the name of the beast or the number of his name. His number will be 666. This is already being partially used in the world today, which shows that there isn't much time left until the emergence of Antichrist.

---

438)Rev15:2 And I saw what looked like a sea of glass mixed with fire and, standing beside the sea, those who had been victorious over the beast and his image and over the number of his name. They held harps given them by God

Chapter 14

[Summary]

14:1～5 ⇒ the first fruits
14:6～7 ⇒ the eternal gospel
14:8 ⇒ the fall of Babylon the Great
14:9～12 ⇒ the beast and his image, the mark of his name 666
14:13 ⇒ the martyrs
14:14～16 ⇒ the wheat harvest
14:17～20 ⇒ the great winepress

Verse 1 Then I looked, and there before me was the Lamb, standing on Mount Zion, and with Him 144,000 who had His name and His Father's name written on their foreheads.

1. The Mount Zion described here is the heavenly Mount Zion because the Lamb has not yet come down to the earth (Heb 12:22, Ro 11:26, Isa 59:20)[439].
2. In chapter 7:2~4, the 144,000 are the Jews who have been sealed with God's seal on their foreheads (they have not been sealed with the Lamb's seal because they don't yet believe in the Lamb, Jesus). In chapter 14:1, the 144,000 who have the name of the Lamb and the name of His Father on their foreheads means that these saints believe in both God and the Lamb, Jesus. (They have become the possession of God and of the Lamb).

※ Being sealed means becoming God's possession (a mark that says "You are mine").

※ 144,000 simplified is 12 × 12 × 1000. 12 is the number of

---

439)Heb12:12 Therefore, strengthen Your feeble arms and weak knees.
Ro11:26 And so all Israel will be saved, as it is written: "The deliverer will come from Zion; He will turn godlessness away from Jacob.
Isa59:20 "The Redeemer will come to Zion, to those in Jacob who repent of their sins," declares the LORD.

fulfillment of God's dispensation; 1000 is the number of complete hardship: simplified as 10 × 10 × 10, 10 being the number of hardship. Therefore, the 144,000 represents those who have gone through trials and completely fulfilled God's dispensation.

The overcomers	The place of rapture	The role	The process
(Rev 7:9) A great multitude who are wearing white robes	Before the throne and the Lamb	They worship God in the temple	Those who have come out of Great Tribulations and washed their robes in the blood of the Lamb
(Rev 12:5) A male child	Before God's throne	He drives out Satan from heaven onto the earth	By the blood of the Lamb and by the word of their testimony
(Rev 14:1) The 144,000	In heaven on Mount Zion	On Mount Zion, after they become one with the body of Christ, they become the army of heaven and defeat the army of Antichrist on the earth	A life led by the Lamb
(Rev 15:2) The last martyrs	In heaven beside the sea of glass mixed with fire	They become kings in the kingdom, together with the overcomers	The martyrs who did not receive the mark of the beast, 666

Verse 2-3 And I heard a sound from heaven like the roar of rushing waters and like a loud peal of thunder. The sound I heard was like that of harpists playing their harps. And they sang a new song before the throne and before the four living creatures and the elders. No one

could learn the song except the 144,000 who had been redeemed from the earth.

1. In chapter 5:9, the new song is sung to the Lord, who is worthy to open the seals, by the four living creatures and the 24 elders, and in chapter 14, it is sung by the overcomers who have been redeemed from the earth (Isa 42:10, Ps 33:3)[440].
2. Those who had been specially redeemed from the earth 'standing on Mount Zion' means they have been raptured to the heavenly Mount Zion.
3. New songs are sung according to life experiences. Those who overcome can sing new songs by virtue of their special experience of Christ.

[The firstfruits]

Verse 4-5 These are those who did not defile themselves with women, for they remained virgins. They follow the Lamb wherever He goes. They were purchased from among mankind and offered as firstfruits to God and the Lamb. No lie was found in their mouths; they are blameless.

1. The principle of virginity means that we should not defile ourselves with anything in the earth (Mt 19:12, 1Co 7:7, 34, Rev 2:22)[441].

---

440)Isa42:10 Sing to the LORD a new song, His praise from the ends of the earth, you who go down to the sea, and all that is in it, you islands, and all who live in them.
Ps33:3 Sing to Him a new song; play skillfully, and shout for joy.

441)Mt19:12 For some are eunuchs because they were born that way; others were made that way by men; and others have renounced marriage because of the kingdom of heaven. The one who can accept this should accept it."
1Co7:7 I wish that all men were as I am. But each man has his own gift from God; one has this gift, another has that.
1Co7:34 and his interests are divided. An unmarried woman or

※ To be overcomers, we must be kept from all defilement by the grace of the Lord and live like virgins on earth. We must be changed until we can live a life of virginity, or purity. We must also have a desire to preserve ourselves as virgins for the Lord.

※ We must not say not to do something because the Church or the Bible says not to do something. It is a matter of love and desire for the Lord. We are to live a life in which all these things are consumed by love for the Lord. This is the way to becoming the 'firstfruits'.

2. We must live in this world following the Lamb, wherever and whenever He goes. These people are the ones that become firstfruits and are redeemed among men; they will be raptured first (Lev 23:10, Jas 1:18, Ro 8:23)[442].
3. Lies come from Satan. He is a liar and the father of lies, and he has been so from the very beginning (Jn 8:44)[443].
4. Being blameless means being sanctified by God and living

---

virgin is concerned about the Lord's affairs: Her aim is to be devoted to the Lord in both body and spirit. But a married woman is concerned about the affairs of this world--how she can please her husband.

Rev2:22 So I will cast her on a bed of suffering, and I will make those who commit adultery with her suffer intensely, unless they repent of her ways.

442)Lev23:10 "Speak to the Israelites and say to them: 'When you enter the land I am going to give you and you reap its harvest, bring to the priest a sheaf of the first grain you harvest.

Jas1:18 He chose to give us birth through the word of truth, that we might be a kind of firstfruits of all He created.

Ro8:23 Not only so, but we ourselves, who have the firstfruits of the Spirit, groan inwardly as we wait eagerly for our adoption as sons, the redemption of our bodies.

443)Jn8:44 You belong to Your father, the devil, and you want to carry out Your father's desire. He was a murderer from the beginning, not holding to the truth, for there is no truth in him. When he lies, he speaks his native language, for he is a liar and the father of lies.

in grace completely (Jude 1:24, 1Th 5:23, Eph 5:27)[444].

Verse 6-7 Then I saw another angel flying in midair, and he had the eternal gospel to proclaim to those who live on the earth—to every nation, tribe, language and people. He said in a loud voice, "Fear God and give Him glory, because the hour of His judgment has come. Worship Him who made the heavens, the earth, the sea and the springs of water."

1. **[the eternal gospel]**
   a. Preached when: During the Great Tribulation, after the rapture of the firstfruits.
   b. To whom: Among the nations, to those who are left on the earth during the Great Tribulation, especially believers.
   c. By whom: the angels
   ※ During the Great Tribulation, people will no longer be able to preach the gospel.
   d. Content of the message:
      1) "Fear God and give Him glory": do not worship Antichrist.
      2) "Only worship God who made the heavens, the earth, the sea and the springs of water": do not worship the image of Antichrist.
      3) The hour of God's judgment has come.
2. The divisions of the gospel
   a. The gospel of God's grace (Ac 20:24)[445] : Repentance

---

444)Jude1:24 To Him who is able to keep you from falling and to present you before His glorious presence without fault and with great joy--
1Th5:23 May God Himself, the God of peace, sanctify you through and through. May Your whole spirit, soul and body be kept blameless at the coming of our Lord Jesus Christ.
Eph5:27 and to present her to Himself as a radiant church, without stain or wrinkle or any other blemish, but holy and blameless.

445)Ac20:24 However, I consider my life worth nothing to me, if only I may finish the race and complete the task the Lord Jesus has

and faith (Mk 1:15)[446].

b. The gospel of the kingdom (Mt 24:14)[447] : emphasizes the conditions to enter the kingdom of heaven.

c. The eternal gospel (Rev 14:6～7)[448] : do not worship idols, but only worship God and give Him glory. Emphasizes that the hour of His judgment has come. Those who obey these words can enter the kingdom of heaven.

Verse 8 A second angel followed and said "Fallen! Fallen is Babylon the Great, which made all the nations drink the maddening wine of the adulteries."

[The Fall of Babylon]

1. Babylon the Great here is not talking about the material Babylon (Rev 18:2)[449], but the religious Babylon (Rev 17:1)[450], which is Roman Catholicism. Because they fornicated with all the nations and made them drink the wine of wrath.

※ The religious Babylon the Great is destroyed in the first

given me--the task of testifying to the gospel of God's grace.

446)Mk1:15 "The time has come," he said. "The kingdom of God is near. Repent and believe the good news!"

447)Mt24:14 And this gospel of the kingdom will be preached in the whole world as a testimony to all nations, and then the end will come.

448)Rev14:6 Then I saw another angel flying in midair, and he had the eternal gospel to proclaim to those who live on the earth--to every nation, tribe, language and people.

Rev14:7 He said in a loud voice, "Fear God and give Him glory, because the hour of His judgment has come. Worship Him who made the heavens, the earth, the sea and the springs of water."

449)Rev18:2 With a mighty voice he shouted: "Fallen! Fallen is Babylon the Great! She has become a home for demons and a haunt for every evil spirit, a haunt for every unclean and detestable bird.

450) Rev17:1 One of the seven angels who had the seven bowls came and said to me, "Come, I will show you the punishment of the great prostitute, who sits on many waters.

three and a half years, and the material Babylon the Great is destroyed in the latter three and a half years (Rev 18:2)[451].

2. Antichrist will put himself above all other gods and make the people worship him as God (Da 8:9~11, 2Th 2:3~4, Rev 13:12, 14,15)[452].

※ The tower of Babel (Genesis 11:1-9) ⇒ Babylon the Great (Daniel 2) ⇒ a. Religious Babylon (chapter 17) / b. Material Babylon (chapter 18)

[The image and mark of 666]

Verse 9-10 A third angel followed them and said in a loud

---

451)Rev18:2 ☝See footnote 449)

452)Da8:9 Out of one of them came another horn, which started small but grew in power to the south and to the east and toward the Beautiful Land.

Da8:10 It grew until it reached the host of the heavens, and it threw some of the starry host down to the earth and trampled on them.

Da8:11 It set itself up to be as great as the Prince of the host; it took away the daily sacrifice from him, and the place of his sanctuary was brought low.

2Th2:3 Don't let anyone deceive you in any way, for that day will not come until the rebellion occurs and the man of lawlessness is revealed, the man doomed to destruction.

2Th2:4 He will oppose and will exalt himself over everything that is called God or is worshiped, so that he sets himself up in God's temple, proclaiming himself to be God.

Rev13:12 He exercised all the authority of the first beast on his behalf, and made the earth and its inhabitants worship the first beast, whose fatal wound had been healed.

REv13:14 Because of the signs he was given power to do on behalf of the first beast, he deceived the inhabitants of the earth. He ordered them to set up an image in honor of the beast who was wounded by the sword and yet lived.

Rev13:15 He was given power to give breath to the image of the first beast, so that it could speak and cause all who refused to worship the image to be killed.

voice: "If anyone worships the beast and its image and receives its mark on their forehead or on their hand, they, too, will drink the wine of God's fury, which has been poured full strength into the cup of His wrath. They will be tormented with burning sulfur in the presence of the holy angels and of the Lamb.

1. The warning of the third angel is for the saints who obey God's commandments and remain faithful to Jesus (Rev 14:12)[453].
   a. They must not worship the beast and his image and receive his mark on the forehead or on the hand.
   b. If they do not obey this, they too will drink of the wine of God's fury and be tormented with burning sulfur. This suffering has a different meaning from the lake of fire. The lake of fire is a place of eternal and severe suffering in a lake of fire and burning sulfur, but the burning sulfur mentioned here is like the suffering experienced by the second death (Rev 2:11)[454], the most severe pain of hell. Also, because they are in the presence of the holy angels and of the Lamb, after these believers are judged by Christ (2Co 5:10)[455] they will suffer in hell, and be the last ones to receive salvation (Rev 16:15)[456]. Because they are awake, and keep their clothes and are not naked, even if their souls are not born again, they have clothes

---

453)Rev14:12 This calls for patient endurance on the part of the saints who obey God's commandments and remain faithful to Jesus.

454)Rev2:11 He who has an ear, let him hear what the Spirit says to the churches. He who overcomes will not be hurt at all by the second death.

455)2Co5:10 For we must all appear before the judgment seat of Christ, that each one may receive what is due him for the things done while in the body, whether good or bad.

456)Rev16:15 "Behold, I come like a thief! Blessed is he who stays awake and keeps his clothes with him, so that he may not go naked and be shamefully exposed."

to cover their shamefulness (Greek: Himation) so their bodies can receive salvation. In Revelation19, after the wedding supper of Christ has ended, they are raptured and will be judged before Christ's throne of judgment.

c. After the judgment of Christ, they will have no rest day and night, and experience temporary suffering (1,000 years).

※ "They, too" (Rev 14:10)[457] ⇒ they (those who have faith in Jesus)

d. If anyone whose name has not been written in the book of life belonging to the Lamb (Rev 13:8) suffers during the severe Great Tribulation (latter three and a half years), one might think that it is better to receive the mark of 666, worship the beast and his image, and just suffer in the burning sulfur, but compared to the thousand years of the Millennial Kingdom, the three and a half years will be over in a flash.

Verse 11-12 And the smoke of their torment will rise for ever and ever. There will be no rest day or night for those who worship the beast and its image, or for anyone who receives the mark of its name." This calls for patient endurance on the part of the people of God who keep His commands and remain faithful to Jesus.

1. To be tormented with burning sulfur means to be punished in a hell resembling a lake of fire. 'for ever and ever' (Greek: αἰῶνας αἰώνωὶ, pronounced aio-n, meaning an extremely long time). This refers to a period of time, not eternity (hell).
2. Those who worship the beast and his image, and anyone who receives the mark of his name, will be punished with burning sulfur like that of the lake of fire, so those who die before the Great Tribulation are blessed (Rev 14:13)[458].

---

457)Rev14:10 he, too, will drink of the wine of God's fury, which has been poured full strength into the cup of His wrath. He will be tormented with burning sulfur in the presence of the holy angels and of the Lamb.

3. The people in the Great Tribulation will consist of non-believers, Jews who obey God's commandments, and the believers in Christ.

※ From verse 9~12, those addressed by the third angel are the saints who believe in Jesus and the Jews who obey God's commandments.

[Those who die in the Lord]

Verse 13 Then I heard a voice from heaven say, "Write this: Blessed are the dead who die in the Lord from now on." "Yes," says the Spirit, "they will rest from their labor, for their deeds will follow them."

1. Those who die in the Lord from now on (meaning those who die after hearing this gospel) are blessed. This is because they will not worship idols in the latter three and a half years or receive the mark of 666, therefore, they will not be punished with the lake of fire and be rewarded with the fruits of their labor.
2. This is because after death, they will rest from their labor in the world, and their souls will enter deep rest, and after resurrection, they will be rewarded for their deeds.

[The harvest of the wheat]

Verse 14-16 I looked, and there before me was a white cloud, and seated on the cloud was One like a son of man with a crown of gold on His head and a sharp sickle in His hand. Then another angel came out of the temple and called in a loud voice to Him who was sitting on the cloud, "Take Your sickle and reap, because the

---

458)Rev14:13 Then I heard a voice from heaven say, "Write: Blessed are the dead who die in the Lord from now on." "Yes," says the Spirit, "they will rest from their labor, for their deeds will follow them."

time to reap has come, for the harvest of the earth is ripe." So He who was seated on the cloud swung His sickle over the earth, and the earth was harvested.

1. The harvest of the earth will be reaped by Christ, the Son of man. He has come as the Son of man to sow His seed and He will come again to harvest (Mt 3:12, Mk 4:26~29)[459].
2. When He comes to harvest the grain, He will not be robed in a cloud, but seated on a cloud. He will sit on a judgment seat and judge. At this time, the Lord will reveal Himself and judge openly (Ro 14:10, 2Co 5:10)[460].
3. 'with a crown of gold on His head' means that He has the authority of a king who reigns. 'a sharp sickle' indicates that He is the One who reaps the field of God.

※ To the overcomers, He will come as their bridegroom, but to the harvested grain, because He will come with a crown on His head, He will come as the One who reigns.

4. 'the time to reap has come, for the harvest of earth is ripe' means that a few among those who remain on the earth have become ripe grain while passing through the Great Tribulation.

※ When the Lord first came down onto the earth, He sowed

---

459)Mt3:12 His winnowing fork is in His hand, and He will clear His threshing floor, gathering His wheat into the barn and burning up the chaff with unquenchable fire."
Mk4:26 He also said, "This is what the kingdom of God is like. A man scatters seed on the ground.
Mk4:27 Night and day, whether he sleeps or gets up, the seed sprouts and grows, though he does not know how.
Mk4:28 All by itself the soil produces grain--first the stalk, then the head, then the full kernel in the head.
Mk4:29 As soon as the grain is ripe, he puts the sickle to it, because the harvest has come."

460)Ro14:10 You, then, why do you judge Your brother? Or why do you look down on Your brother? For we will all stand before God's judgment seat.
2Co5:10 For we must all appear before the judgment seat of Christ, that each one may receive what is due him for the things done while in the body, whether good or bad.

Himself as a seed in the believers (Mt 13:3~8, 24)[461]. Every believer who received Him as the seed of life becomes a grain of God on the earth (1Co 3:9)[462].

※ In the parable of the sower in Matthew 13, the sun means tribulation, and by the last tribulation, which is the blazing sun, the grain is ripened (Mt 13:21)[463].

5. <u>The sickle represents the angels the Lord has sent to reap the grain.</u> When the Lord comes again, He will send angels and take the believers from the world, which is the field (Mt 13:39)[464].

※ The grain of the harvest will all be gathered, as if reaped with a sickle, into the clouds when the last trumpet sounds (1Th 4:15~17, 1Co 15:51~52)[465].

---

461)Mt13:3 Then He told them many things in parables, saying: "A farmer went out to sow his seed.
Mt13:4 As he was scattering the seed, some fell along the path, and the birds came and ate it up.
Mt13:5 Some fell on rocky places, where it did not have much soil. It sprang up quickly, because the soil was shallow.
Mt13:6 But when the sun came up, the plants were scorched, and they withered because they had no root.
Mt13:7 Other seed fell among thorns, which grew up and choked the plants.
Mt13:8 Still other seed fell on good soil, where it produced a crop--a hundred, sixty or thirty times what was sown.
Mt13:24 Jesus told them another parable: "The kingdom of heaven is like a man who sowed good seed in his field.

462)1Co3:9 For we are God's fellow workers; you are God's field, God's building.

463)Mt13:21 But since he has no root, he lasts only a short time. When trouble or persecution comes because of the word, he quickly falls away.

464)Mt13:39 and the enemy who sows them is the devil. The harvest is the end of the age, and the harvesters are angels.

465)1Th4:15 According to the Lord's own word, we tell you that we who are still alive, who are left till the coming of the Lord, will certainly not precede those who have fallen asleep.
1Th4:16 For the Lord Himself will come down from heaven, with a

※ The already ripe firstfruits are reaped before the Great Tribulation and gathered before the throne of heaven (on heavenly Mount Zion).

[the great winepress]

Verse 17-18 Another angel came out of the temple in heaven, and he too had a sharp sickle. Still another angel, who had charge of the fire, came from the altar and called in a loud voice to him who had the sharp sickle, "Take Your sharp sickle and gather the clusters of grapes from the earth's vine, because its grapes are ripe."

1. Judgment of evil among nonbelievers begins with the voice from the altar.

※ In the time of the flood of Noah, He judged with water, but now He judges with fire (the altar fire).

2. In the Bible, Jews are compared to a fig tree (Mt 24:32)[466], the believers are compared to wheat (Mt 13:25, 30)[467], and

---

loud command, with the voice of the archangel and with the trumpet call of God, and the dead in Christ will rise first.

1Th4:17 After that, we who are still alive and are left will be caught up together with them in the clouds to meet the Lord in the air. And so we will be with the Lord forever.

1Co15:51 Listen, I tell you a mystery: We will not all sleep, but we will all be changed--

1Co15:52 in a flash, in the twinkling of an eye, at the last trumpet. For the trumpet will sound, the dead will be raised imperishable, and we will be changed.

466)Mt24:32 "Now learn this lesson from the fig tree: As soon as its twigs get tender and its leaves come out, you know that summer is near.

467)Mt13:25 But while everyone was sleeping, his enemy came and sowed weeds among the wheat, and went away.

Mt13:30 Let both grow together until the harvest. At that time I will tell the harvesters: First collect the weeds and tie them in bundles to be burned; then gather the wheat and bring it into My barn.'"

the judgment of the wicked Gentiles is compared to a great winepress (Rev 14:19, Isa 63:1~3, 5:1~5)[468]. The wicked Gentiles are an imitation of the true vine which consists of the body of Christ (Jn 15:1~6)[469].

---

468)Rev14:19 The angel swung His sickle on the earth, gathered its grapes and threw them into the great winepress of God's wrath.
Isa63:1 Who is this coming from Edom, from Bozrah, with His garments stained crimson? Who is this, robed in splendor, striding forward in the greatness of His strength? "It is I, speaking in righteousness, mighty to save."
Isa63:2 Why are Your garments red, like those of one treading the winepress?
Isa63:3 "I have trodden the winepress alone; from the nations no one was with Me. I trampled them in My anger and trod them down in My wrath; their blood spattered My garments, and I stained all My clothing.
Isa5:1 I will sing for the one I love a song about his vineyard: My loved one had a vineyard on a fertile hillside.
Isa5:2 He dug it up and cleared it of stones and planted it with the choicest vines. He built a watchtower in it and cut out a winepress as well. Then he looked for a crop of good grapes, but it yielded only bad fruit.
Isa5:3 "Now you dwellers in Jerusalem and men of Judah, judge between Me and My vineyard.
Isa5:4 What more could have been done for My vineyard than I have done for it? When I looked for good grapes, why did it yield only bad?
Isa5:5 Now I will tell you what I am going to do to My vineyard: I will take away its hedge, and it will be destroyed; I will break down its wall, and it will be trampled.

469)Jn15:1 "I am the true vine, and My Father is the gardener.
Jn15:2 He cuts off every branch in Me that bears no fruit, while every branch that does bear fruit He prunes so that it will be even more fruitful.
Jn15:3 You are already clean because of the word I have spoken to you.
Jn15:4 Remain in Me, and I will remain in you. No branch can bear fruit by itself; it must remain in the vine. Neither can you bear fruit unless you remain in Me.
Jn15:5 "I am the vine; you are the branches. If a man remains in Me and I in Him, he will bear much fruit; apart from Me you can do nothing.

Verse 19-20 The angel swung His sickle on the earth, gathered its grapes and threw them into the great winepress of God's wrath. They were trampled in the winepress outside the city, and blood flowed out of the press, rising as high as the horses' bridles for a distance of 1,600 stadia.

1. The great winepress of God's wrath represents the war of Armageddon (Rev 16:12~16)[470]. There, all the evil armies of the world are gathered and fight against the army of Christ, consisting of the overcomers, and are ultimately defeated (Rev 19:11, 12, Joel 3:11~13, Isa 63:1~6)[471].

Jn15:6 If anyone does not remain in Me, he is like a branch that is thrown away and withers; such branches are picked up, thrown into the fire and burned.

470)Rev16:12 The sixth angel poured out his bowl on the great river Euphrates, and its water was dried up to prepare the way for the kings from the East.
Rev16:13 Then I saw three evil spirits that looked like frogs; they came out of the mouth of the dragon, out of the mouth of the beast and out of the mouth of the false prophet.
Rev16:14 They are spirits of demons performing miraculous signs, and they go out to the kings of the whole world, to gather them for the battle on the great day of God Almighty.
Rev16:15 "Behold, I come like a thief! Blessed is he who stays awake and keeps his clothes with him, so that he may not go naked and be shamefully exposed."
Rev16:16 Then they gathered the kings together to the place that in Hebrew is called Armageddon.

471)Rev19:11 I saw heaven standing open and there before me was a white horse, whose rider is called Faithful and True. With justice He judges and makes war.
Rev19:12 His eyes are like blazing fire, and on His head are many crowns. He has a name written on Him that no one knows but He Himself.
Jeol3:11 Come quickly, all you nations from every side, and assemble there. Bring down Your warriors, O LORD!
Jeol3:12 'Let the nations be roused; let them advance into the Valley of Jehoshaphat, for there I will sit to judge all the nations on

2. The great winepress will be trampled by Christ. Here, outside the city refers to outside of Jerusalem. The blood flowing out of the press is talking about the blood of the army of Antichrist defeated in the valley of Megiddo, which will be a river of blood (280 kilometers). This is the distance from Bozrah (Isa 63:1)[472] to Megiddo (Rev 16:16)[473]. This river will rise as high as a horse's bridle. This will be Christ's judgment of Antichrist.

※ With the trampling of the great winepress, the Great Tribulation will be over and this age will come to an end.

---

every side.

Jeol3:13 Swing the sickle, for the harvest is ripe. Come, trample the grapes, for the winepress is full and the vats overflow--so great is their wickedness!'

Isa63:1 Who is this coming from Edom, from Bozrah, with His garments stained crimson? Who is this, robed in splendor, striding forward in the greatness of His strength? "It is I, speaking in righteousness, mighty to save."

Isa63:2 Why are Your garments red, like those of one treading the winepress?

Isa63:3 "I have trodden the winepress alone; from the nations no one was with Me. I trampled them in My anger and trod them down in My wrath; their blood spattered My garments, and I stained all My clothing.

Isa63:4 For the day of vengeance was in My heart, and the year of My redemption has come.

Isa63:5 I looked, but there was no one to help, I was appalled that no one gave support; so My own arm worked salvation for Me, and My own wrath sustained Me.

Isa63:6 I trampled the nations in My anger; in My wrath I made them drunk and poured their blood on the ground."

472)Isa63:1 Who is this coming from Edom, from Bozrah, with His garments stained crimson? Who is this, robed in splendor, striding forward in the greatness of His strength? "It is I, speaking in righteousness, mighty to save."

473)RevIsa63:1 Who is this coming from Edom, from Bozrah, with His garments stained crimson? Who is this, robed in splendor, striding forward in the greatness of His strength? "It is I, speaking in righteousness, mighty to save."

Chapter 15 The latter overcomers and the seven bowls

Verse 1-2 I saw in heaven another great and marvelous sign: seven angels with the seven last plagues—last, because with them God's wrath is completed. And I saw what looked like a sea of glass glowing with fire and, standing beside the sea, those who had been victorious over the beast and its image and over the number of its name. They held harps given them by God

[The last martyr]

1. The seven last plagues of the seven angels represent the seven bowls (Rev 16:1)[474] of God's wrath. This will be a great disaster, the third woe (Rev 11:4)[475] and will be the last plague of God's wrath.
2. As the judgment of God's wrath proceeds, the sea of glass like a crystal before the throne of God seen in chapter 4:6 will become the sea of glass mixed with fire (1Co 3:14~15)[476].
3. Those who had been victorious over the beast and his image and over the number of his name (Rev 14:12)[477] means that they are the last martyrs. They will have become those who overcame and passed a trial like fire, symbolizing that they will have passed the sea of glass mixed with fire.

---

474)Rev16:1 Then I heard a loud voice from the temple saying to the seven angels, "Go, pour out the seven bowls of God's wrath on the earth."

475)Rev11:4 These are the two olive trees and the two lampstands that stand before the Lord of the earth.

476)1Co3:14 If what he has built survives, he will receive his reward.
1Co3:15 If it is burned up, he will suffer loss; he himself will be saved, but only as one escaping through the flames.

477)Rev14:12 This calls for patient endurance on the part of the saints who obey God's commandments and remain faithful to Jesus.

4. They will reign as kings with Christ during the Millennial Kingdom (Rev 20:4)[478].
5. Because the sea of glass is before the throne (Rev 4:6)[479], they were resurrected and passed through the sea of glass mixed with fire and ascended before the throne of God.

Verse 3-4 and sang the song of God's servant Moses and of the Lamb: "Great and marvelous are Your deeds, Lord God Almighty. Just and true are Your ways, King of the nations. Who will not fear You, Lord, and bring glory to Your name? For You alone are holy. All nations will come and worship before You, for Your righteous acts have been revealed."

1. They sang the song of Moses and the song of the Lamb means that they are composed of reverent Jews who obey God's commandments and the Law of Moses, and the saints who believe in Christ.
2. Among the Jews, those who do not worship the image of Antichrist or receive his mark under his reign will be martyred with the later believers in Christ (Ro 11:25)[480].
3. These martyrs will praise, even though they have been put

---

478)Rev20:4 I saw thrones on which were seated those who had been given authority to judge. And I saw the souls of those who had been beheaded because of their testimony for Jesus and because of the word of God. They had not worshiped the beast or his image and had not received his mark on their foreheads or their hands. They came to life and reigned with Christ a thousand years.

479)Rev4:6 Also before the throne there was what looked like a sea of glass, clear as crystal. In the center, around the throne, were four living creatures, and they were covered with eyes, in front and in back.

480)Ro11:25 I do not want you to be ignorant of this mystery, brothers, so that you may not be conceited: Israel has experienced a hardening in part until the full number of the Gentiles has come in.

through a fiery trial and have been persecuted, they will praise how great and marvellous the deeds of the Lord are and how just and true the ways of the Lord are!

4. They will be the ones who fear and bring glory to the name of the Lord.

Verse 5-6 After this I looked, and I saw in heaven the temple —that is, the tabernacle of the covenant law—and it was opened. Out of the temple came the seven angels with the seven plagues. They were dressed in clean, shining linen and wore golden sashes around their chests.

[The seven angels with the seven plagues]

1. "After this" means that the seven bowls of God's wrath will appear after the martyrs have sung the Song of Moses, the servant of God, and the Song of the Lamb, beside the sea of glass, and ascended before the throne.
2. The temple of the tabernacle of the Testimony (in Greek, naos = ναος) contains the Holy Place and the Most Holy Place where the ark is (Mt 23:16, 2Th 2:4, Rev 11:1)[481]. The meaning of the Tabernacle of the Testimony is the Most Holy Place where the ark of the covenant is (the ark of the Law). The bigger meaning indicates the Holy Place and the Most Holy Place.
3. The temple of God is opened by the praise of the last martyrs, the latter-day overcomers (Rev 15:2～3)[482].

---

481)Mt23:16 "Woe to you, blind guides! You say, 'If anyone swears by the temple, it means nothing; but if anyone swears by the gold of the temple, he is bound by his oath.'

2Th2:4 He will oppose and will exalt himself over everything that is called God or is worshiped, so that he sets himself up in God's temple, proclaiming himself to be God.

Rev11:1 I was given a reed like a measuring rod and was told, "Go and measure the temple of God and the altar, and count the worshipers there.

4. The seven angels with the seven plagues were dressed in the clothes of priests (Eze 44:17)[483]. As the angels have been carrying out the priest's duty, the last mission of the priests of the angels will be completed by pouring the last seven plagues of God's wrath over Antichrist and his followers.
5. These seven plagues come in response to the praise of the overcomers.

Verse 7-8 Then one of the four living creatures gave to the seven angels seven golden bowls filled with the wrath of God, who lives for ever and ever. And the temple was filled with smoke from the glory of God and from His power, and no one could enter the temple until the seven plagues of the seven angels were completed.

1. The fact that one of the four creatures, the representative of creation, gave the seven angels the golden bowls of the wrath of God, means that the representative of creation entrusted the angels with the plagues that the creature deserves (Antichrist and his followers).
2. The gold in 'golden bowls filled with the wrath of God' signifies that the wrath of God is holy and is to achieve

---

482)Rev15:2 And I saw what looked like a sea of glass mixed with fire and, standing beside the sea, those who had been victorious over the beast and his image and over the number of his name. They held harps given them by God

Rev15:3 and sang the song of Moses the servant of God and the song of the Lamb: "Great and marvelous are Your deeds, Lord God Almighty. Just and true are Your ways, King of the ages.

483)Eze15:2 And I saw what looked like a sea of glass mixed with fire and, standing beside the sea, those who had been victorious over the beast and his image and over the number of his name. They held harps given them by God

Eze15:3 and sang the song of Moses the servant of God and the song of the Lamb: "Great and marvelous are Your deeds, Lord God Almighty. Just and true are Your ways, King of the ages.

the kingdom of God and His righteousness.

3. The bowl means that the wrath of God is limited and is for the fulfillment of the kingdom of God.
4. The smoke in the temple is due to the glory and power of God, which means that it is the wrath of God will be satisfied (= poured out) through the seven plagues.
5. The seven plagues of the seven angels must be completed in order for the way to the temple to be opened. From then, the saints will be given the duty of priests of the temple.

Chapter 16

※ The first bowl ~ The seventh bowl and the destruction of Babylon the Great

[The first bowl]

Verse 1-2 Then I heard a loud voice from the temple saying to the seven angels, “Go, pour out the seven bowls of God’s wrath on the earth.” The first angel went and poured out his bowl on the land, and ugly, festering sores broke out on the people who had the mark of the beast and worshiped its image.

1. The events occurring through the temple
   a. Chapter 8:5[484] ⇒ The angel takes the censer, fills it with fire from the altar, and hurls it on the earth, and through the coming peals of thunder, rumblings, flashes of lightning, and an earthquake, the seven trumpet plagues begin:
   b. Chapter 9:13[485] ⇒ When the sixth angel sounds his trumpet, a voice comes from the horns of the golden altar, and by this, the angels who are bound at the great river Euphrates are released and a third of mankind are killed by the two hundred million mounted troops.
   c. Chapter 11:9[486] ⇒ When the seventh angel blows the trumpet, the heavenly temple is opened, the ark of the

---

484)Rev8:5 Then the angel took the censer, filled it with fire from the altar, and hurled it on the earth; and there came peals of thunder, rumblings, flashes of lightning and an earthquake

485)Rev9:13 The sixth angel sounded his trumpet, and I heard a voice coming from the horns of the golden altar that is before God.

486)Rev11:9 For three and a half days men from every people, tribe, language and nation will gaze on their bodies and refuse them burial.

covenant is visible, and there is lightning, a voice, thunder, earthquake, and a great hailstorm. He rewards those who fear the name of the Lord and destroys those who destroy the earth.

d. Chapter 14:15[487] ⇒ Another angel comes out of the temple and calls in a loud voice, "Take Your sickle and reap", and the earth is harvested.

e. Chapter 14:18[488] ⇒ Another angel, who had charge of the fire, comes from the altar and calls in a loud voice to him who had the sharp sickle, "Take Your sharp sickle and gather the clusters of grapes from the earth's vine". Then the angel swings His sickle on the earth, gathers its grapes and throws them into the great winepress of God's wrath, and so gathers the grapes of the earth.

f. Chapter 15:5, 16:1[489] ⇒ The temple in heaven, the tabernacle of the Testimony, is opened, and a loud voice from the temple commands the seven angels, "Go, pour out the seven bowls of God's wrath on the earth." And so, the seven bowls of God's wrath are poured on the earth.

g. Chapter 16:17[490] ⇒ The seventh angel pours out his bowl

---

487)Rev14:15 Then another angel came out of the temple and called in a loud voice to him who was sitting on the cloud, "Take Your sickle and reap, because the time to reap has come, for the harvest of the earth is ripe."

488)Rev14:18 Still another angel, who had charge of the fire, came from the altar and called in a loud voice to him who had the sharp sickle, "Take Your sharp sickle and gather the clusters of grapes from the earth's vine, because its grapes are ripe."

Rev14:19 The angel swung His sickle on the earth, gathered its grapes and threw them into the great winepress of God's wrath.

489)Rev15:5 After this I looked and in heaven the temple, that is, the tabernacle of the Testimony, was opened.

Rev16:1 Then I heard a loud voice from the temple saying to the seven angels, "Go, pour out the seven bowls of God's wrath on the earth."

into the air, and out of the temple comes a loud voice from the throne, saying, "It is done!" Then come flashes of lightning, a voice, peals of thunder and a severe earthquake. The great city, and the cities of nations, and Babylon the Great are destroyed.

2. Those who receive the mark of the beast and worship his image will get boils on their skin. This is because they have the mark of the beast.

[The second bowl]

Verse 3 The second angel poured out his bowl on the sea, and it turned into blood like that of a dead person, and every living thing in the sea died.

▣ In the second bowl, the sea will die and every living thing in it.

[The third bowl]

Verse 4-7 The third angel poured out his bowl on the rivers and springs of water, and they became blood. Then I heard the angel in charge of the waters say: "You are just in these judgments, O Holy One, You who are and who were; for they have shed the blood of Your holy people and Your prophets, and You have given them blood to drink as they deserve." And I heard the altar respond: "Yes, Lord God Almighty, true and just are Your judgments."

1. In the third bowl, all drinking water will become blood and they will end up drinking it. This is because they have shed the blood of God's saints and prophets.
2. An angel has been appointed in God's administration to

---

490)Rev16:17 The seventh angel poured out his bowl into the air, and out of the temple came a loud voice from the throne, saying,

watch over the waters.

3. 'you who are and who were' – 'who is to come' is omitted (cf Rev 1:8, 4:8)[491]. This is because Christ is coming in the clouds in chapter 10:1[492].
4. After the third bowl, there is no more drinking water left, only blood, so they are left with no other choice but to drink it. This is the price they must pay for having shed the blood of saints.

[The fourth bowl]

Verse 8-9 The fourth angel poured out his bowl on the sun, and the sun was allowed to scorch people with fire. They were seared by the intense heat and they cursed the name of God, who had control over these plagues, but they refused to repent and glorify Him.

1. In the fourth bowl, a sunspot explosion (coronal mass ejection – CME) or extreme destruction of the ozone layer will damage and burn people's skin.
2. Their wickedness has become so great that even in this unbearable situation, they refuse to repent, and curse the name of God.

[The fifth bowl]

---

491)Rev1:8 "I am the Alpha and the Omega," says the Lord God, "who is, and who was, and who is to come, the Almighty."
Rev4:8 Each of the four living creatures had six wings and was covered with eyes all around, even under his wings. Day and night they never stop saying: "Holy, holy, holy is the Lord God Almighty, who was, and is, and is to come."

492)Rev10:1 Then I saw another mighty angel coming down from heaven. He was robed in a cloud, with a rainbow above His head; His face was like the sun, and His legs were like fiery pillars.

Verse 10-11 The fifth angel poured out his bowl on the throne of the beast, and its kingdom was plunged into darkness. People gnawed their tongues in agony and cursed the God of heaven because of their pains and their sores, but they refused to repent of what they had done.

1. The fifth bowl being poured out on the throne of the beast can be compared to when Moses brought plagues on Pharaoh and on Egypt.

※ When darkness covered all the land of Egypt, still the whole land wasn't covered (Ex 10:21～23)[493].

2. The seven bowls are for judgment against the beast and his kingdom and land.
3. Even with intolerable pain, they will refuse to repent of what they have done and will gnaw their tongues in agony, cursing the God of heaven.

※ If we are not changed in our hearts during the church age, we will become more wicked and will lose the opportunity to repent forever.

[The sixth bowl]

Verse 12-14 The sixth angel poured out his bowl on the great river Euphrates, and its water was dried up to prepare the way for the kings from the East. Then I saw three impure spirits that looked like frogs; they came out of the mouth of the dragon, out of the mouth of the beast and out of the mouth of the false prophet. They are demonic spirits that perform signs, and they go out to

---

493)Ex10:21 Then the LORD said to Moses, "Stretch out Your hand toward the sky so that darkness will spread over Egypt--darkness that can be felt."

Ex10:22 So Moses stretched out his hand toward the sky, and total darkness covered all Egypt for three days.

Ex10:23 No one could see anyone else or leave his place for three days. Yet all the Israelites had light in the places where they lived.

the kings of the whole world, to gather them for the battle on the great day of God Almighty.

1. At the sixth trumpet (Rev 9:13~18)[494], an army of two hundred million and all the other armies gathered at the great river Euphrates, and in the sixth bowl, its water will dry up and they will cross the river and advance into Armageddon.
2. The three evil spirits perform miraculous signs, and through this, the hearts of the kings of the whole world are moved and they assemble for battle on the great day of God Almighty, the second coming of Christ.
3. On that day, the army in <u>the West (the Roman Empire), the north (Russia), and the East (the place where the sun rises, China, the other Arab states)</u> will gather in Armageddon (Eze 38:1~16, Eze Chapter 39)[495].

---

494)Rev9:13 The sixth angel sounded his trumpet, and I heard a voice coming from the horns of the golden altar that is before God.
Rev9:14 It said to the sixth angel who had the trumpet, "Release the four angels who are bound at the great river Euphrates."
Rev9:15 And the four angels who had been kept ready for this very hour and day and month and year were released to kill a third of mankind.
Rev9:16 The number of the mounted troops was two hundred million. I heard their number.
Rev9:17 The horses and riders I saw in my vision looked like this: Their breastplates were fiery red, dark blue, and yellow as sulfur. The heads of the horses resembled the heads of lions, and out of their mouths came fire, smoke and sulfur.
Rev9:18 A third of mankind was killed by the three plagues of fire, smoke and sulfur that came out of their mouths.

495)Eze38:1 The word of the LORD came to me:
Eze38:2 "Son of man, set Your face against Gog, of the land of Magog, the chief prince of Meshech and Tubal; prophesy against him.
Eze38:3 and say: 'This is what the Sovereign LORD says: I am against you, O Gog, chief prince of Meshech and Tubal.

Eze38:4 I will turn you around, put hooks in Your jaws and bring

※ In 1976, Syria built the Tabka dam (length is 3 miles, height is 60 meters) on the upstream of the great river Euphrates. By this one dam, the height of the river can be controlled. The great river Euphrates currently has six

---

you out with Your whole army--your horses, Your horsemen fully armed, and a great horde with large and small shields, all of them brandishing their swords.

Eze38:5 Persia, Cush and Put will be with them, all with shields and helmets,

Eze38:6 also Gomer with all its troops, and Beth Togarmah from the far north with all its troops--the many nations with you.

Eze38:7 "'Get ready; be prepared, you and all the hordes gathered about you, and take command of them.

Eze38:8 After many days you will be called to arms. In future years you will invade a land that has recovered from war, whose people were gathered from many nations to the mountains of Israel, which had long been desolate. They had been brought out from the nations, and now all of them live in safety.

Eze38:9 You and all Your troops and the many nations with you will go up, advancing like a storm; you will be like a cloud covering the land.

Eze38:10 "'This is what the Sovereign LORD says: On that day thoughts will come into Your mind and you will devise an evil scheme.

Eze38:11 You will say, "I will invade a land of unwalled villages; I will attack a peaceful and unsuspecting people--all of them living without walls and without gates and bars.

Eze38:12 I will plunder and loot and turn my hand against the resettled ruins and the people gathered from the nations, rich in livestock and goods, living at the center of the land."

Eze38:13 Sheba and Dedan and the merchants of Tarshish and all her villages will say to you, "Have you come to plunder? Have you gathered Your hordes to loot, to carry off silver and gold, to take away livestock and goods and to seize much plunder?"

Eze38:14 "Therefore, son of man, prophesy and say to Gog: 'This is what the Sovereign LORD says: In that day, when My people Israel are living in safety, will you not take notice of it?

Eze38:15 You will come from Your place in the far north, you and many nations with you, all of them riding on horses, a great horde, a mighty army.

Eze38:16 You will advance against My people Israel like a cloud that covers the land. In days to come, O Gog, I will bring you against My land, so that the nations may know Me. when I show Myself holy through you before their eyes.

dams completely up and running, and by these dams it is quite possible for the entire river to be dried up.

[The last to be saved]

Verse 15-16 "Look, I come like a thief! Blessed is the one who stays awake and remains clothed, so as not to go naked and be shamefully exposed." Then they gathered the kings together to the place that in Hebrew is called Armageddon.

1. "I come like a thief!", the Lord says, right before the battle of Armageddon, at the end of the Great Tribulation. This means that there are still many Christians in the land, and they will be the last ones to be saved.
2. The last remaining saints are ordered to keep their clothes with them so that they may at least not go naked and be shamefully exposed. This is in contrast to the saints in chapter 7 who had washed their robes and made them white in the blood of the Lamb and with the saints who wear bright and clean fine linen in chapter 19 (Rev 7:9, 14, 19:8, 3:3~5)[496]. These saints also will be the saints in

---

496)Rev7:9 After this I looked and there before me was a great multitude that no one could count, from every nation, tribe, people and language, standing before the throne and in front of the Lamb. They were wearing white robes and were holding palm branches in their hands.

Rev7:14 I answered, "Sir, you know." And he said, "These are they who have come out of the great tribulation; they have washed their robes and made them white in the blood of the Lamb.

Rev19:8 Fine linen, bright and clean, was given her to wear." (Fine linen stands for the righteous acts of the saints.)

Rev3:3 Remember, therefore, what you have received and heard; obey it, and repent. But if you do not wake up, I will come like a thief, and you will not know at what time I will come to you.

Rev3:4 Yet you have a few people in Sardis who have not soiled their clothes. They will walk with Me, dressed in white, for they are worthy.

Rev3:5 He who overcomes will, like them, be dressed in white. I will never blot out his name from the book of life, but will

Revelation 2:11[497] that receive suffering like the second death, and the saints in Revelation 14:9~11[498]. Most of the last remaining saints will have received the mark of 666 and worshipped the image. Eventually, they will be punished with burning sulfur, the punishment of hell during the Millennial Kingdom.

3. These people will be the last remaining saints apart from the few overcomers and the grain saints. Their numbers will be overwhelming (Mt 22:14)[499].
4. Three evil spirits will incite the kings of the whole world and rally armies of two hundred million riders on horses, and the other armies as well, to Armageddon. They will attack Israel and so the war of Armageddon will begin as it will be the last battle of mankind. In the end, the army of Antichrist will be defeated by Christ and His army (Rev 19:20~21, Mic 4:11~13, Zec 14:3)[500].

---

acknowledge his name before My Father and His angels.

497)Rev2:11 He who has an ear, let him hear what the Spirit says to the churches. He who overcomes will not be hurt at all by the second death.

498)Rev14:9 A third angel followed them and said in a loud voice: "If anyone worships the beast and his image and receives his mark on the forehead or on the hand,

Rev14:10 he, too, will drink of the wine of God's fury, which has been poured full strength into the cup of His wrath. He will be tormented with burning sulfur in the presence of the holy angels and of the Lamb.

Rev14:11 And the smoke of their torment rises for ever and ever. There is no rest day or night for those who worship the beast and his image, or for anyone who receives the mark of his name."

499)Mt22:14 "For many are invited, but few are chosen."

500)Rev19:20 But the beast was captured, and with him the false prophet who had performed the miraculous signs on his behalf. With these signs he had deluded those who had received the mark of the beast and worshiped his image. The two of them were

[The seventh bowl]

Verse 17-18 The seventh angel poured out his bowl into the air, and out of the temple came a loud voice from the throne, saying, "It is done!" Then there came flashes of lightning, rumblings, peals of thunder and a severe earthquake. No earthquake like it has ever occurred since mankind has been on earth, so tremendous was the quake.

1. God's throne is for His reign. Eventually, biblical revelation leads from God's throne to the temple, God's expression. Ultimately, the book of Revelation, the final completion of the Bible, unites the throne and the temple (verse 17). At the end of Revelation, we see God on the throne in the New Jerusalem (Rev 22:3～4)[501].

※ God is on the throne for His administration, but He is in

---

thrown alive into the fiery lake of burning sulfur.

Rev19:21 The rest of them were killed with the sword that came out of the mouth of the rider on the horse, and all the birds gorged themselves on their flesh.

Mic4:11 But now many nations are gathered against you. They say, "Let her be defiled, let our eyes gloat over Zion!"

Mic4:12 But they do not know the thoughts of the LORD; they do not understand His plan, He who gathers them like sheaves to the threshing floor.

Mic4:13 "Rise and thresh, O Daughter of Zion, for I will give you horns of iron; I will give you hoofs of bronze and you will break to pieces many nations." You will devote their ill-gotten gains to the LORD, their wealth to the Lord of all the earth.

Zec14:3 Then the LORD will go out and fight against those nations, as He fights in the day of battle.

501)Rev22:3 No longer will there be any curse. The throne of God and of the Lamb will be in the city, and His servants will serve Him.

Rev22:4 They will see His face, and His name will be on their foreheads.

the temple for His self-revelation.

2. The loud voice that said "It is done" forewarns of the last great earthquake (Rev 11:19)[502]. This means that all things have been accomplished for God's testimony.

Verse 19-21 The great city split into three parts, and the cities of the nations collapsed. God remembered Babylon the Great and gave her the cup filled with the wine of the fury of His wrath. Every island fled away and the mountains could not be found. From the sky huge hailstones, each weighing about a hundred pounds, fell on people. And they cursed God on account of the plague of hail, because the plague was so terrible.

1. The great city is Jerusalem (Rev 11:8)[503]. This city will be split into three parts. At the same time, the corrupt cities of the nations will also collapse.
2. The Babylon the Great in Revelation 16:9 is talking about material Babylon in chapter 18, whereas Babylon the Great in Revelation 14:8[504] refers to the religious Babylon of chapter 17.

※ The religious Babylon is ruined by Antichrist after the Great Tribulation begins (the latter three and a half years), whereas material Babylon is destroyed at the end of the Great Tribulation (the latter three and a half years), right before the war of Armageddon takes place.

---

502)Rev11:19 Then God's temple in heaven was opened, and within His temple was seen the ark of His covenant. And there came flashes of lightning, rumblings, peals of thunder, an earthquake and a great hailstorm.

503)Rev11:8 Their bodies will lie in the street of the great city, which is figuratively called Sodom and Egypt, where also their Lord was crucified.

504)Rev14:8 A second angel followed and said, "Fallen! Fallen is Babylon the Great, which made all the nations drink the maddening wine of her adulteries."

3. Every island and mountain will disappear (partially).
4. Men will experience a tremendous amount of suffering because of hailstones weighing up to a hundred pounds each, yet they will still curse God.

Chapter 17 : the punishment of the great prostitute

※ The great prostitute that sits on a scarlet beast

- The one who sits on many waters
- The woman who has committed adultery with the kings of the earth
- The inhabitants of the earth were intoxicated with the wine of her adulteries
- The woman that sits on a scarlet beast
- The woman dressed in purple and scarlet
- The woman glittering with gold, precious stones and pearls
- The woman holding a golden cup, filled with abominable things and the filth of her adulteries
- The title was written on her forehead: this is the mystery, Babylon the Great
- The mother of prostitutes and of the abominations of the earth
- The woman was drunk with the blood of the saints, the blood of those who bore testimony to Jesus

[the wine of her adulteries]

Verse 1-2 One of the seven angels who had the seven bowls came and said to me, "Come, I will show you the punishment of the great prostitute, who sits by many waters. With her the kings of the earth committed adultery, and the inhabitants of the earth were intoxicated with the wine of her adulteries."

1. 'The great prostitute who sits on many waters' means that the apostate Roman Catholic Church sits on top of many peoples and nations all around the world (Rev 17:15)[505]. The Roman Catholic Church actually numbers approximately

---

505)17:15 Then the angel said to me, "The waters you saw, where the prostitute sits, are peoples, multitudes, nations and languages.

a third of the world population.

2. 'With her the kings of the earth committed adultery' means that the Roman Catholic Church and the rulers of the earth have a religious relationship filled with sin. Just as a prostitute commits adultery for money, so also the apostate church commits adultery by making sin-filled relationships with the rulers of the earth for money. The act of committing adultery for an apostate church is spiritual. As the Roman Catholic Church is intimately involved with the politics of the world, the rulers of the earth commit adultery with "her" directly and indirectly.
3. The wine of verse 2 refers to heretical doctrines in the sinful religious relationships of the apostate church. These doctrines intoxicate those involved in her religion, as wine does. This is the wine of her adulteries.
4. The heretical doctrines of an apostate church are like a drug. This causes men to become blind, mute, given to spewing out sophistry, and numbs the senses.
5. Ultimately, in verse 16, this prostitute will be forsaken by the beast and will be ruined, naked, and left to burn in fire.

[Seven heads and ten horns]

Verse 3 Then the angel carried me away in the Spirit into a wilderness. There I saw a woman sitting on a scarlet beast that was covered with blasphemous names and had seven heads and ten horns.

1. The wilderness is a desert, a barren land. This is where the apostate church is barren, like the desert, where there are no springs of water prepared by God.
2. A woman riding a red beast implies that the Roman Catholic Church is riding (controlling) the Seventh Emperor, the Antichrist. The color of this beast is red. This is the same color as the dragon, symbolizing that the dragon and

the beast are one in appearance and shed much blood of the saints.

3. 'covered with blasphemous names' means that the kings who are symbolized by the seven heads of the beast call themselves gods, which is blasphemous to God.
4. The seven heads represent the rulers of Egypt, Assur, Babylon, Media Persia, Greece, Rome, and the latter Roman Empire. The ten horns represent the ten kings (rulers) who will rise in the latter Roman Empire.

[the prostitute]

Verse 4-5 The woman was dressed in purple and scarlet, and was glittering with gold, precious stones and pearls. She held a golden cup in her hand, filled with abominable things and the filth of her adulteries. The name written on her forehead was a mystery: BABYLON THE GREAT THE MOTHER OF PROSTITUTES AND OF THE ABOMINATIONS OF THE EARTH.

1. Purple symbolizes dignity that possesses authority. This woman was also dressed in scarlet which can be found everywhere in the Vatican. Cardinals of the Vatican can be found wearing scarlet headwear and robes as their formal attire.
2. Gold, precious stones, and pearls are all materials used in building the Holy City, the New Jerusalem (Rev 21:18~21)[506], but

---

506)Rev21:18 The wall was made of jasper, and the city of pure gold, as pure as glass.
Rev21:19 The foundations of the city walls were decorated with every kind of precious stone. The first foundation was jasper, the second sapphire, the third chalcedony, the fourth emerald,
Rev21:20 the fifth sardonyx, the sixth carnelian, the seventh chrysolite, the eighth beryl, the ninth topaz, the tenth chrysoprase, the eleventh jacinth, and the twelfth amethyst.
Rev21:21 The twelve gates were twelve pearls, each gate made of a single pearl. The great street of the city was of pure gold, like transparent glass.

the apostate church decorates itself with precious stones, mimicking the New Jerusalem in appearance. This is the fake appearance of a prostitute.

3. She held a golden cup in her hand filled with abominable things and the filth of her adulteries. Gold symbolizes the divine nature of God, meaning that the apostate church superficially resembles God in some way, but is filled with abomination and the filth of her adulteries.
4. The great prostitute has a title but it is a mystery. This means that because she is mysterious, it is hard to understand her. Since her teachings and everything she does is a mystery of her adulteries, it is not easily exposed.
5. Babylon the Great, the Roman Catholic Church, is the mother of prostitutes and of the abominations of the earth. The Roman Catholic Church teaches that every religion is one, and so, "marries" all the religions of the world (44th International Eucharistic Congress in 1989, etc.)

[The mystery of the beast with seven heads and ten horns]

Verse 6-7 I saw that the woman was drunk with the blood of the saints, the blood of those who bore testimony to Jesus. When I saw her, I was greatly astonished. Then the angel said to me: "Why are you astonished? I will explain to you the mystery of the woman and of the beast she rides, which has the seven heads and ten horns.

1. The Roman Catholic Church killed many more saints and witnesses of Jesus than the Roman empire ever did.
2. The reason why John was greatly astonished when he saw the woman (Roman Catholic Church) is because as a woman (to Christ), she has persecuted God's church and its saints.
3. It is hard to understand the woman by just seeing her, but if you solve the mystery of the woman and the beast she rides,

you will understand why this woman persecutes the saints.

4. The beast with the seven heads and ten horns is one with Satan and is his embodiment (Rev 12:3)[507].

Verse 8-9 The beast, which you saw, once was, now is not, and yet will come up out of the Abyss and go to its destruction. The inhabitants of the earth whose names have not been written in the book of life from the creation of the world will be astonished when they see the beast, because it once was, now is not, and yet will come. "This calls for a mind with wisdom. The seven heads are seven hills on which the woman sits.

1. The beast John saw which once was, but now is not, represents all the beasts in the past; Egypt, Assur, Babylon the Great (lion), Media Persia (bear), Greece (leopard), the Roman Empire (a terrifying and powerful beast), the Latter Roman Empire. These beasts are all nations or men that have operated as Antichrist (Da 7:4～8)[508].

---

507)Rev12:3 Then another sign appeared in heaven: an enormous red dragon with seven heads and ten horns and seven crowns on his heads.

508)Da7:4 "The first was like a lion, and it had the wings of an eagle. I watched until its wings were torn off and it was lifted from the ground so that it stood on two feet like a man, and the heart of a man was given to it.

Da7:5 "And there before me was a second beast, which looked like a bear. It was raised up on one of its sides, and it had three ribs in its mouth between its teeth. It was told, 'Get up and eat Your fill of flesh!'

Da7:6 "After that, I looked, and there before me was another beast, one that looked like a leopard. And on its back it had four wings like those of a bird. This beast had four heads, and it was given authority to rule.

Da7:7 "After that, in my vision at night I looked, and there before me was a fourth beast--terrifying and frightening and very powerful. It had large iron teeth; it crushed and devoured its victims and trampled underfoot whatever was left. It was

2. Therefore, those who had operated as Antichrist are all dead and 'now are not' (they are imprisoned in the Abyss), but in the end, the imprisoned spirit of Antichrist will enter into the beast which was dead and act as the last Antichrist (1Jn 2:18, Rev 13:3, 14)[509].

Antichrist
- comes out of the Abyss (Rev 9:11, 11:7, 17:8)[510]
- comes out of the sea (Rev 13:1, Da7:3)[511]

---

different from all the former beasts, and it had ten horns.

Da:8 "While I was thinking about the horns, there before me was another horn, a little one, which came up among them; and three of the first horns were uprooted before it. This horn had eyes like the eyes of a man and a mouth that spoke boastfully.

509)1Jn2:18 Dear children, this is the last hour; and as you have heard that the antichrist is coming, even now many antichrists have come. This is how we know it is the last hour.

Rev13:3 One of the heads of the beast seemed to have had a fatal wound, but the fatal wound had been healed. The whole world was astonished and followed the beast.

Rev13:14 Because of the signs he was given power to do on behalf of the first beast, he deceived the inhabitants of the earth. He ordered them to set up an image in honor of the beast who was wounded by the sword and yet lived.

510)Rev9:11 They had as king over them the angel of the Abyss, whose name in Hebrew is Abaddon, and in Greek, Apollyon.

Rev11:7 Now when they have finished their testimony, the beast that comes up from the Abyss will attack them, and overpower and kill them.

Rev17:8 The beast, which you saw, once was, now is not, and will come up out of the Abyss and go to his destruction. The inhabitants of the earth whose names have not been written in the book of life from the creation of the world will be astonished when they see the beast, because he once was, now is not, and yet will come.

511)Rev13:1 And the dragon stood on the shore of the sea. And I saw a beast coming out of the sea. He had ten horns and seven heads, with ten crowns on his horns, and on each head a blasphemous name.

Da7:3 Four great beasts, each different from the others, came up

[The seven kings]

Verse 10-11 They are also seven kings. Five have fallen, one is, the other has not yet come; but when he does come, he must remain for only a little while. The beast who once was, and now is not, is an eighth king. He belongs to the seven and is going to his destruction.

1. The seven kings represent the kings of Egypt, Assur, Babylon, Media Persia, Greece, Rome, and the latter Roman empire.
   a. 'Five have fallen' - Egypt, Assur, Babylon, Media Persia, and Greece
   ※ In the apostle John's time, from his point of view, these nations had come and gone.
   b. 'one is' – the Roman Empire
   ※ John was living in the Roman Empire.
   c. 'the other has not yet come' - the latter Roman Empire but when he does come, he must remain for a little while' means that the latter Roman Empire will continue to stand for a short time.
2. The beast who once was, and now is not, belongs to the seven and will be the eighth king. The king of the latter Roman Empire will be the seventh king, but after Antichrist revives from his fatal wound, he will be the eighth king (Da 7:8, Rev 13:3, 14)[512].

---

out of the sea.

512)Da7:8 "While I was thinking about the horns, there before me was another horn, a little one, which came up among them; and three of the first horns were uprooted before it. This horn had eyes like the eyes of a man and a mouth that spoke boastfully.
Rev13:3 One of the heads of the beast seemed to have had a fatal wound, but the fatal wound had been healed. The whole world was astonished and followed the beast.
Rev13:14 Because of the signs he was given power to do on behalf of the first beast, he deceived the inhabitants of the earth. He ordered them to set up an image in honor of the beast who was wounded by the sword and yet lived.

[The ten horns are ten kings]

Verse 12-13 "The ten horns you saw are ten kings who have not yet received a kingdom, but who for one hour will receive authority as kings along with the beast. They have one purpose and will give their power and authority to the beast.

1. The ten horns are ten kings but are probably not kings who have received kingdoms. But because it says they will receive authority as kings for one hour, they will receive authority as kings for a short time. Indeed, the European Union, which is formed out of the latter Roman Empire, consists of representatives from each nation who were elected on behalf of their nations while not possessing kingdoms.
2. The ten kings will stand against God and become one with Antichrist as they persecute God's people. They will offer themselves and their authorities up to Antichrist.

※ The ten kings will not have kingdoms but will only hold power for a little while. They will not be kings, but they will just receive king-like authority. Their power will not last long and all their power will be centered on Antichrist.

Verse 14-15 They will wage war against the Lamb, but the Lamb will triumph over them because He is Lord of lords and King of kings—and with Him will be His called, chosen and faithful followers." Then the angel said to me, "The waters you saw, where the prostitute sits, are peoples, multitudes, nations and languages.

1. They will eventually make war against Christ the Lamb. This war will be the Armageddon war (Rev 19:11~21)[513]. In

513)Rev19:11 I saw heaven standing open and there before me was a white horse, whose rider is called Faithful and True. With justice He judges and makes war.

Rev19:12 His eyes are like blazing fire, and on His head are many crowns. He has a name written on Him that no one knows but He Himself.

this war the Lamb and His army will defeat them.
2. If one is called, he is saved and if one is chosen it means he is an overcomer who has been chosen by the Lord.

[The great city that rules over the kings of the earth (Roman Catholic church)]

Verse 16-18 The beast and the ten horns you saw will hate the prostitute. They will bring her to ruin and leave her naked; they will eat her flesh and burn her with fire. For God has put it into their hearts to accomplish His purpose by agreeing to hand over to the beast their royal authority, until God's words are fulfilled. The woman

---

Rev19:13 He is dressed in a robe dipped in blood, and His name is the Word of God.

Rev19:14 The armies of heaven were following Him, riding on white horses and dressed in fine linen, white and clean.

Rev19:15 Out of His mouth comes a sharp sword with which to strike down the nations. "He will rule them with an iron scepter." He treads the winepress of the fury of the wrath of God Almighty.

Rev19:16 On His robe and on His thigh He has this name written: KING OF KINGS AND LORD OF LORDS.

Rev19:17 And I saw an angel standing in the sun, who cried in a loud voice to all the birds flying in midair, "Come, gather together for the great supper of God,

Rev19:18 so that you may eat the flesh of kings, generals, and mighty men, of horses and their riders, and the flesh of all people, free and slave, small and great."

Rev19:19 Then I saw the beast and the kings of the earth and their armies gathered together to make war against the rider on the horse and his army.

Rev19:20 But the beast was captured, and with him the false prophet who had performed the miraculous signs on his behalf. With these signs he had deluded those who had received the mark of the beast and worshiped his image. The two of them were thrown alive into the fiery lake of burning sulfur.

Rev19:21 The rest of them were killed with the sword that came out of the mouth of the rider on the horse, and all the birds gorged themselves on their flesh.

you saw is the great city that rules over the kings of the earth."

1. The ten horns and the beast will hate the prostitute (Roman Catholic Church) and bring her to ruin, strip her of her glory and riches, and in the end, burn her with fire.
2. God will allow them to do as they please, as through it, Gods purpose will be accomplished and everything that has to do with the Roman Catholic Church will be owned by the beast until the word of God is fulfilled.
3. Although this prostitute is a small country, she is here described as the great city (the Vatican) that rules over the kings of the earth. This means that the kings of the earth have been ruled by this prostitute behind the scenes.

Chapter 18 The Fall of Material Babylon

Verse 1 After this I saw another angel coming down from heaven. He had great authority, and the earth was illuminated by His splendor.

1. Another angel coming down from heaven is talking about Christ. As He gradually descends, the earth is illuminated by His splendor.

※ In the Old Testament, Christ often appeared as an angel who had been sent by God. In the New Testament also, Christ is revealed as an angel until the Ascended Christ formally returns to rule the earth.

2. In chapter 10:1[514] Christ came down robed in a cloud, and in chapter 14:14[515] He was seated on a cloud, but in chapter 18:1[516] He illuminates the earth by His splendor, meaning that the Lord's descent onto the earth is much closer here than in chapters 10 and 14.

※ The Lord is first described as 'robed in a cloud' and 'descended in a cloud', in midair. When it is time for the Lord to judge in the air, and at the time of the wedding supper, He is described as 'seated on a cloud'. In the end, with great authority, He will come illuminating the whole earth by His splendor to destroy Babylon the Great. After He destroys Babylon the Great, the earth will completely be owned by Him and will be His kingdom!

---

514)Rev10:1 Then I saw another mighty angel coming down from heaven. He was robed in a cloud, with a rainbow above His head; His face was like the sun, and His legs were like fiery pillars.

515)Rev14:14 I looked, and there before me was a white cloud, and seated on the cloud was one "like a son of man" with a crown of gold on His head and a sharp sickle in His hand.

516)Rev18:1 After this I saw another angel coming down from heaven. He had great authority, and the earth was illuminated by His splendor.

[The maddening wine of her adulteries]

Verse 2-3 With a mighty voice He shouted: " 'Fallen! Fallen is Babylon the Great!' She has become a dwelling for demons and a haunt for every impure spirit, a haunt for every unclean bird, a haunt for every unclean and detestable animal. For all the nations have drunk the maddening wine of her adulteries. The kings of the earth committed adultery with her, and the merchants of the earth grew rich from her excessive luxuries."

1. Religious Babylon collapses as soon as the Great Tribulation begins. As for material Babylon, it falls near the end of the Great Tribulation (this scripture refers to the collapse of material Babylon).
2. A home for demons (Jer 50:34~39, 51:37)[517].
   A haunt for every evil spirit (Rev 16:13)[518].

---

517)Jer50:34 Yet their Redeemer is strong; the LORD Almighty is His name. He will vigorously defend their cause so that He may bring rest to their land, but unrest to those who live in Babylon.
Jer50:35 "A sword against the Babylonians!" declares the LORD--"against those who live in Babylon and against her officials and wise men!
Jer50:36 A sword against her false prophets! They will become fools. A sword against her warriors! They will be filled with terror.
Jer50:37 A sword against her horses and chariots and all the foreigners in her ranks! They will become women. A sword against her treasures! They will be plundered.
Jer50:38 A drought on her waters! They will dry up. For it is a land of idols, idols that will go mad with terror.
Jer50:39 "So desert creatures and hyenas will live there, and there the owl will dwell. It will never again be inhabited or lived in from generation to generation.
Jer51:37 Babylon will be a heap of ruins, a haunt of jackals, an object of horror and scorn, a place where no one lives.

518)Rev16:13 Then I saw three evil spirits that looked like frogs; they came out of the mouth of the dragon, out of the mouth of the beast and out of the mouth of the false prophet.

A haunt for every unclean and detestable bird (Isa 34:11~15, Mt 13:4)[519].

3. All the nations of the world have committed adultery with material Babylon. Through this, all the nations will fall.
4. The kings of the earth committed adultery with religious Babylon as well as material Babylon.

※ The kings of the earth committed adultery with religious Babylon to keep their power, and with material Babylon for wealth and honor.

5. The merchants (conglomerates) of the earth prospered by committing adultery with material Babylon, the power of excessive luxury.
6. The collapse of all the nations means that the cities of the nations, intoxicated with the maddening wine of her adulteries, have fallen (Rev 18:3, 16:19)[520].

---

519)Isa34:11 The desert owl and screech owl will possess it; the great owl and the raven will nest there. God will stretch out over Edom the measuring line of chaos and the plumb line of desolation.

Isa34:12 Her nobles will have nothing there to be called a kingdom, all her princes will vanish away.

Isa34:13 Thorns will overrun her citadels, nettles and brambles her strongholds. She will become a haunt for jackals, a home for owls.

Isa34:14 Desert creatures will meet with hyenas, and wild goats will bleat to each other; there the night creatures will also repose and find for themselves places of rest.

Isa34:15 The owl will nest there and lay eggs, she will hatch them, and care for her young under the shadow of her wings; there also the falcons will gather, each with its mate.

Mt13:4 As he was scattering the seed, some fell along the path, and the birds came and ate it up.

520)Rev18:3 For all the nations have drunk the maddening wine of her adulteries. The kings of the earth committed adultery with her, and the merchants of the earth grew rich from her excessive luxuries."

Rev16:19 The great city split into three parts, and the cities of the nations collapsed. God remembered Babylon the Great and gave

Verse 4-5 Then I heard another voice from heaven say: " 'Come out of her, My people,' so that you will not share in her sins, so that you will not receive any of her plagues; for her sins are piled up to heaven, and God has remembered her crimes.

1. The people of God must avoid these disasters by leaving those cities drunk with the maddening wine of her adulteries and Babylon the Great. We can see that the people of God (the Israelites - those who believe in God) will still be in Babylon the Great just before it collapses (Jer 50:8~9, 51:6)[521].

※ Just as Abram came out of Ur of the Chaldeans and Lot came out of Sodom right before destruction, the people of God must also come out of Babylon the Great.

2. The sins of the cities drunk with the maddening wine of her adulteries, which are destined for ruin, have piled up and reached the sky, meaning that God has remembered all her crimes (Jer 51:9, Ge 18:20~21)[522].

---

her the cup filled with the wine of the fury of His wrath.

521)Jer50:8 "Flee out of Babylon; leave the land of the Babylonians, and be like the goats that lead the flock.

Jer50:9 For I will stir up and bring against Babylon an alliance of great nations from the land of the north. They will take up their positions against her, and from the north she will be captured. Their arrows will be like skilled warriors who do not return empty-handed.

Jer51:6 "Flee from Babylon! Run for Your lives! Do not be destroyed because of her sins. It is time for the LORD'S vengeance; He will pay her what she deserves.

522)Jer51:9 "'We would have healed Babylon, but she cannot be healed; let us leave her and each go to his own land, for her judgment reaches to the skies, it rises as high as the clouds.'

Ge8:20 Then Noah built an altar to the LORD and, taking some of all the clean animals and clean birds, he sacrificed burnt offerings on it.

Ge8:21 The LORD smelled the pleasing aroma and said in His heart: "Never again will I curse the ground because of man, even though every inclination of His heart is evil from childhood. And never again will I destroy all living creatures, as I have

Verse 6-7 Give back to her as she has given; pay her back double for what she has done. Pour her a double portion from her own cup. Give her as much torment and grief as the glory and luxury she gave herself. In her heart she boasts, 'I sit enthroned as queen. I am not a widow; I will never mourn.'

1. Material Babylon is a prostitute who has enticed the hearts of many nations, kings and people into worldly materialism, and made them commit adultery. It is the righteousness of God to repay her as much she has done and given (Ps 137:8, Jer 16:18, 50:15)[523].
2. The glory and luxury we give ourselves are to be repaid with much suffering and grief. This is God's righteous judgment. Babylon the Great is a fortress in which glory and luxury has reached its climax (Lk 16:25, Mt 19:23)[524].
3. She sits as the queen of the world and boasts in her heart that she is not a widow and will never mourn.

[The kings of the earth who committed adultery with her]

Verse 8-10 Therefore in one day her plagues will overtake her:

---

done.

523)Ps137:8 O Daughter of Babylon, doomed to destruction, happy is He who repays you for what you have done to us--

Jer16:18 I will repay them double for their wickedness and their sin, because they have defiled My land with the lifeless forms of their vile images and have filled My inheritance with their detestable idols."

Jer50:15 Shout against her on every side! She surrenders, her towers fall, her walls are torn down. Since this is the vengeance of the LORD, take vengeance on her; do to her as she has done to others.

524)Lk16:25 "But Abraham replied, 'Son, remember that in Your lifetime you received Your good things, while Lazarus received bad things, but now he is comforted here and you are in agony.

Mt19:23 Then Jesus said to His disciples, "I tell you the truth, it is hard for a rich man to enter the kingdom of heaven.

death, mourning and famine. She will be consumed by fire, for mighty is the Lord God who judges her. "When the kings of the earth who committed adultery with her and shared her luxury see the smoke of her burning, they will weep and mourn over her. Terrified at her torment, they will stand far off and cry: " 'Woe! Woe to you, great city, you mighty city of Babylon! In one hour Your doom has come!'

1. In the early part of the latter three and a half years, religious Babylon the Great will be completely destroyed and consumed by fire (Rev 14:8, 17:16)[525]. The destruction of material Babylon in this text will take place towards the end of the latter three and a half years – at the time of the seventh bowl judgment (Rev 16:19, 18:16~21)[526].

---

525)Rev14:8 A second angel followed and said, "Fallen! Fallen is Babylon the Great, which made all the nations drink the maddening wine of her adulteries."
Rev17:16 The beast and the ten horns you saw will hate the prostitute. They will bring her to ruin and leave her naked; they will eat her flesh and burn her with fire.

526)Rev16:19 The great city split into three parts, and the cities of the nations collapsed. God remembered Babylon the Great and gave her the cup filled with the wine of the fury of His wrath.
Rev18:16 and cry out: "'Woe! Woe, O great city, dressed in fine linen, purple and scarlet, and glittering with gold, precious stones and pearls!
Rev18:17 In one hour such great wealth has been brought to ruin!' "Every sea captain, and all who travel by ship, the sailors, and all who earn their living from the sea, will stand far off.
Rev18:18 When they see the smoke of her burning, they will exclaim, 'Was there ever a city like this great city?'
Rev18:19 They will throw dust on their heads, and with weeping and mourning cry out: "'Woe! Woe, O great city, where all who had ships on the sea became rich through her wealth! In one hour she has been brought to ruin!
Rev18:20 Rejoice over her, O heaven! Rejoice, saints and apostles and prophets! God has judged her for the way she treated you.'"
Rev18:21 Then a mighty angel picked up a boulder the size of a

2. Babylon the Great will be destroyed in one day. This will be a day of death, mourning, and famine. Ultimately, she will be consumed by fire.

※ This one day of destruction will not be because of war, but by an earthquake.

3. Ultimately, Babylon the Great will be judged as a prostitute because she has stolen the hearts of the kings and all the people of the earth and made them commit adultery and live in luxury.

[The merchants of the earth grew rich from her excessive luxuries]

Verse 11-13 "The merchants of the earth will weep and mourn over her because no one buys their cargoes anymore— cargoes of gold, silver, precious stones and pearls; fine linen, purple, silk and scarlet cloth; every sort of citron wood, and articles of every kind made of ivory, costly wood, bronze, iron and marble; cargoes of cinnamon and spice, of incense, myrrh and frankincense, of wine and olive oil, of fine flour and wheat; cattle and sheep; horses and carriages; and bodies and souls of men.

1. The commodities listed in verses 12-13 speak of various material things, proving that Babylon in chapter 18 is material Babylon.
2. 'The merchants (conglomerates) of the earth will weep and mourn over her' is because there is no one left to buy their goods.
3. Among the merchandise, slaves, human lives, and even souls are auctioned.

Verse 14-16 "They will say, 'The fruit you longed for is gone from you. All Your luxury and splendor have vanished,

---

large millstone and threw it into the sea, and said: "With such violence the great city of Babylon will be thrown down, never to be found again.

never to be recovered.' The merchants who sold these things and gained their wealth from her will stand far off, terrified at her torment. They will weep and mourn and cry out: " 'Woe! Woe to you, great city, dressed in fine linen, purple and scarlet, and glittering with gold, precious stones and pearls!

1. This means that due to the collapse of Babylon, the fruit her soul has longed for is gone from her. We must not live for the satisfaction of our souls.
2. The merchants and conglomerates that have made money by her will weep and mourn in terror at her torment.
3. Babylon the Great has lived enjoying the things of the world, dressed in the luxuries of the world, glittering with gold, precious stones, and pearls. She has been living in this world as an imitation of New Jerusalem and decorating herself with worldly things to resemble heaven.
4. In the end, Babylon the Great has deceived all the people to enjoy riches and glory, heaven on earth, and a happy life.

Verse 17-19 In one hour such great wealth has been brought to ruin!' "Every sea captain, and all who travel by ship, the sailors, and all who earn their living from the sea, will stand far off. When they see the smoke of her burning, they will exclaim, 'Was there ever a city like this great city?' They will throw dust on their heads, and with weeping and mourning cry out: " 'Woe! Woe to you, great city, where all who had ships on the sea became rich through her wealth! In one hour she has been brought to ruin!'

1. It does not take long for luxurious precious stones and all the wondrous things of the world to be ruined; it happens in a moment.
2. They will throw dust on their heads, and with weeping and mourning cry out: "Woe! Woe, O great city".
3. In one hour, Antichrist and his army will fall by Christ

(Rev 17:12～14, 19:19～21)[527]. Material Babylon will also fall to the Lord in one hour (Rev 18:8)[528].

※ Those who have lived putting all their hope in this land and this world cry out with tears and mourning when their houses are burned down and family fortunes ruined.

[God has judged her to avenge the grief of the martyrs]

Verse 20-22 "Rejoice over her, you heavens! Rejoice, you people of God! Rejoice, apostles and prophets! For God has judged her with the judgment she imposed on you." Then a mighty angel picked up a boulder the size of a large millstone and threw it into the sea, and said: "With such violence the great city of Babylon will be thrown down, never to be found again. The music of

---

527)Rev17:12 "The ten horns you saw are ten kings who have not yet received a kingdom, but who for one hour will receive authority as kings along with the beast.

Rev17:13 They have one purpose and will give their power and authority to the beast.

Rev17:14 They will make war against the Lamb, but the Lamb will overcome them because He is Lord of lords and King of kings--and with Him will be His called, chosen and faithful followers."

Rev19:19 Then I saw the beast and the kings of the earth and their armies gathered together to make war against the rider on the horse and his army.

Rev19:20 But the beast was captured, and with him the false prophet who had performed the miraculous signs on his behalf. With these signs he had deluded those who had received the mark of the beast and worshiped his image. The two of them were thrown alive into the fiery lake of burning sulfur.

Rev19:21 The rest of them were killed with the sword that came out of the mouth of the rider on the horse, and all the birds gorged themselves on their flesh.

528)Rev18:8 Therefore in one day her plagues will overtake her: death, mourning and famine. She will be consumed by fire, for mighty is the Lord God who judges her.

harpists and musicians, pipers and trumpeters, will never be heard in you again. No worker of any trade will ever be found in you again. The sound of a millstone will never be heard in you again.

1. The heavens, saints, apostles and prophets rejoice for God has judged her (Babylon) for the way she treated them. This is because before the Great Tribulation (the latter three and a half years), many saints have ascended into heaven as overcomers after going through much pain and extreme suffering – having nothing to eat or drink or wear, and so on.
2. Those who have sought after and loved the things of the world will weep and cry out because of her. The overcomers will greatly rejoice in heaven, for God has heard their cry to avenge their grief, and because the kingdom of Christ is near.
3. In the end, Babylon the Great will be thrown into the sea and sink like a millstone, never to emerge again. This will be caused by the earthquake of chapter 16:18～20[529]

Verse 23-24 The light of a lamp will never shine in you again. The voice of bridegroom and bride will never be heard in you again. Your merchants were the world's important people. By Your magic spell all the nations were led astray. In her was found the blood of prophets and of God's holy people, of all who have been slaughtered on the earth."

---

529)Rev16:18 Then there came flashes of lightning, rumblings, peals of thunder and a severe earthquake. No earthquake like it has ever occurred since man has been on earth, so tremendous was the quake.

Rev16:19 The great city split into three parts, and the cities of the nations collapsed. God remembered Babylon the Great and gave her the cup filled with the wine of the fury of His wrath.

Rev16:20 Every island fled away and the mountains could not be found.

1. Because Your (her) merchants (or conglomerates) were the world's great men, by Your magic spell all the nations were led astray."
2. The blood of prophets and of the saints, and of all who have been killed on the earth, was found in the city. This is because all the martyrs led their lives naked and hungry and were beaten, persecuted, and finally killed (Rev 17:6, Mt 23:35~36)[530].
3. Many people were led astray by her magic (money, honor, all the good things in the world) into loving those things. They were led to live by the world and decorate it just like New Jerusalem.

---

530)Rev17:6 I saw that the woman was drunk with the blood of the saints, the blood of those who bore testimony to Jesus. When I saw her, I was greatly astonished.

Mt23:35 And so upon you will come all the righteous blood that has been shed on earth, from the blood of righteous Abel to the blood of Zechariah son of Berekiah, whom you murdered between the temple and the altar.

Mt23:36 I tell you the truth, all this will come upon this generation.

Chapter 19 <u>The wedding supper of the Lamb, The war of Armageddon</u>

Verse 1-3 After this I heard what sounded like the roar of a great multitude in heaven shouting: "Hallelujah! Salvation and glory and power belong to our God, for true and just are His judgments. He has condemned the great prostitute who corrupted the earth by her adulteries. He has avenged on her the blood of His servants." And again they shouted: "Hallelujah! The smoke from her goes up for ever and ever."

1. <u>After the collapse of material Babylon,</u> with a sound like the roar of a great multitude in heaven they shouted "Hallelujah!"
2. The words of this expression of praise is to show that His judgments are true and just, and that He has condemned the great prostitute who corrupted the earth by her adulteries and has avenged on her the blood of His servants.

※ Hallelujah: means "Praise the Lord"

Verse 4-6 The twenty-four elders and the four living creatures fell down and worshiped God, who was seated on the throne. And they cried: "Amen, Hallelujah!" Then a voice came from the throne, saying: "Praise our God, all you His servants, you who fear Him, both great and small!" Then I heard what sounded like a great multitude, like the roar of rushing waters and like loud peals of thunder, shouting: "Hallelujah! For our Lord God Almighty reigns.

1. After the collapse of Babylon the Great, the twenty-four elders and the four living creatures and His servants (the saints) worship and praise God. This is universal praise including all of God's creation.
2. After the collapse of Babylon the Great, material Babylon, God's reign begins.

[the wedding supper of the Lamb]

Verse 7-8 Let us rejoice and be glad and give Him glory! For the wedding of the Lamb has come, and His bride has made herself ready. Fine linen, bright and clean, was given her to wear." (Fine linen stands for the righteous acts of God's holy people.)

1. After the rapture of the believers, the wedding supper of the Lamb takes place and then the judgment seat of Christ.
2. His bride is the Church (Eph 5:24~25, 31~32)[531], meaning the bride of Christ (Jn 3:29)[532], which consists of the saints that believe and are awake (Mt 25:1~13)[533].

---

531)Eph5:24 Now as the church submits to Christ, so also wives should submit to their husbands in everything.
Eph5:25 Husbands, love Your wives, just as Christ loved the church and gave Himself up for her
Eph5:31 "For this reason a man will leave his father and mother and be united to his wife, and the two will become one flesh."
Eph5:32 This is a profound mystery--but I am talking about Christ and the church.

532)Jn3:29 The bride belongs to the bridegroom. The friend who attends the bridegroom waits and listens for him, and is full of joy when he hears the bridegroom's voice. That joy is mine, and it is now complete.

533)Mt25:1 "At that time the kingdom of heaven will be like ten virgins who took their lamps and went out to meet the bridegroom.
Mt25:2 Five of them were foolish and five were wise.
Mt25:3 The foolish ones took their lamps but did not take any oil with them.
Mt25:4 The wise, however, took oil in jars along with their lamps.
Mt25:5 The bridegroom was a long time in coming, and they all became drowsy and fell asleep.
Mt25:6 "At midnight the cry rang out: 'Here's the bridegroom! Come out to meet him!'
Mt25:7 "Then all the virgins woke up and trimmed their lamps.
Mt25:8 The foolish ones said to the wise, 'Give us some of Your oil; our lamps are going out.'

3. The preparation of the bride depends on the maturity of the life of the overcomers. The bride is a corporate group, not individuals, so the overcomers need to be built together as one (Eph 2:20～21)[534].
4. This fine linen stands for the righteous acts of our life. It means we reveal Christ through our lives.
5. The wedding of the Lamb is the completion of the New Testament's dispensation. Christ gains the church as His bride by His redemption and divine life.

Verse 9-10 Then the angel said to me, "Write this: Blessed are those who are invited to the wedding supper of the Lamb!" And he added, "These are the true words of God." At this I fell at his feet to worship him. But he said to me, "Don't do that! I am a fellow servant with you and with Your brothers and sisters who hold to the testimony of Jesus. Worship God! For it is the Spirit of prophecy who bears testimony to Jesus."

1. <u>Those who are invited</u> to the wedding supper of the Lamb in Matthew 22:1～14[535] are invited as guests (Lk 14:15

Mt25:9 "'No,' they replied, 'there may not be enough for both us and you. Instead, go to those who sell oil and buy some for yourselves.'
Mt25:10 "But while they were on their way to buy the oil, the bridegroom arrived. The virgins who were ready went in with him to the wedding banquet. And the door was shut.
Mt25:11 "Later the others also came. 'Sir! Sir!' they said. 'Open the door for us!'
Mt25:12 "But he replied, 'I tell you the truth, I don't know you.'
Mt25:13 "Therefore keep watch, because you do not know the day or the hour.

534)Eph2:20 built on the foundation of the apostles and prophets, with Christ Jesus Himself as the chief cornerstone.
Eph2:21 In Him the whole building is joined together and rises to become a holy temple in the Lord.
535)Mt22:1 Jesus spoke to them again in parables, saying:
Mt22:2 "The kingdom of heaven is like a king who prepared a

)[536]. They have been invited not as the bride, but as friends to celebrate the wedding. Brides are not invited, they are the called, chosen and faithful ones (Rev 17:14)[537]. The overcomers will have ascended before the throne before the guests are invited.

---

wedding banquet for his son.
Mt22:3 He sent his servants to those who had been invited to the banquet to tell them to come, but they refused to come.
Mt22:4 "Then he sent some more servants and said, 'Tell those who have been invited that I have prepared my dinner: My oxen and fattened cattle have been butchered, and everything is ready. Come to the wedding banquet.'
Mt22:5 "But they paid no attention and went off--one to his field, another to his business.
Mt22:6 The rest seized his servants, mistreated them and killed them.
Mt22:7 The king was enraged. He sent his army and destroyed those murderers and burned their city.
Mt22:8 "Then he said to his servants, 'The wedding banquet is ready, but those I invited did not deserve to come.
Mt22:9 Go to the street corners and invite to the banquet anyone you find.'
Mt22:10 So the servants went out into the streets and gathered all the people they could find, both good and bad, and the wedding hall was filled with guests.
Mt22:11 "But when the king came in to see the guests, he noticed a man there who was not wearing wedding clothes.
Mt22:12 'Friend,' he asked, 'how did you get in here without wedding clothes?' The man was speechless.
Mt22:13 "Then the king told the attendants, 'Tie him hand and foot, and throw him outside, into the darkness, where there will be weeping and gnashing of teeth.'
Mt22:14 "For many are invited, but few are chosen."

536)Lk14:15 When one of those at the table with him heard this, he said to Jesus, "Blessed is the man who will eat at the feast in the kingdom of God."

537)Rev17:14 They will make war against the Lamb, but the Lamb will overcome them because He is Lord of lords and King of kings--and with Him will be His called, chosen and faithful followers."

2. Blessed are those who are invited to the wedding supper of the Lamb because not all believers are invited as they cannot go there (Mt 22:1～14)[538]. Some of them will be placed in darkness outside while others will be the last to receive salvation (Rev 16:15)[539]. That is why it says those who eat bread in the wedding supper are blessed (Lk 14:15)[540].
3. The testimony of Jesus is the spirit of prophecy, so we must not worship angels but only God.

[The War of Armageddon]

Verse 11-13 I saw heaven standing open and there before me was a white horse, whose rider is called Faithful and True. With justice He judges and wages war. His eyes are like blazing fire, and on His head are many crowns. He has a name written on Him that no one knows but He Himself. He is dressed in a robe dipped in blood, and His name is the Word of God.

1. The wedding supper of the Lamb and the war of Armageddon are both seen in chapter 19. After the wedding supper of the Lamb there is the war of Armageddon. The war of Armageddon will get rid of all the obstacles preventing the coming Millennial Kingdom.
2. Even when Christ makes war, He does so with sincerity and truth. With justice He judges and makes war. Fighting is necessary to halt rebellion.
3. His eyes like blazing fire is the eyes of judgment. He judges

---

538) Mt22:1~14 ☞See footnote 535) on the previous page

539)Rev16:15 "Behold, I come like a thief! Blessed is he who stays awake and keeps his clothes with him, so that he may not go naked and be shamefully exposed."

540) Lk14:15 ☞See footnote 536) on the previous page

based on how He sees, with eyes of blazing fire, making war, and judging.

4. Christ has been crowned and glorified (Heb 2:9)[541]. The crown in this scripture symbolizes the crown of the king, the One who reigns.
5. He is dressed in a robe dipped in blood means that He trod the winepress of the fury of His wrath in the war of Armageddon (Verse 15, Isa 63:1~3)[542].
6. Christ makes war with the word of God. His fighting will be a powerful word. The word of God in John 1:1[543] is seen as light, life, and construction, but in Revelation 19, He uses the mighty word as a weapon and triumphs in the war. And He will judge the rebellion with the word of God.

---

541)Heb2:9 But we see Jesus, who was made a little lower than the angels, now crowned with glory and honor because He suffered death, so that by the grace of God He might taste death for everyone.

542)Rev19:15 Out of His mouth comes a sharp sword with which to strike down the nations. "He will rule them with an iron scepter." He treads the winepress of the fury of the wrath of God Almighty.
Isa63:1 Who is this coming from Edom, from Bozrah, with His garments stained crimson? Who is this, robed in splendor, striding forward in the greatness of His strength? "It is I, speaking in righteousness, mighty to save."
Isa63:2 Why are Your garments red, like those of one treading the winepress?
Isa63:3 "I have trodden the winepress alone; from the nations no one was with Me. I trampled them in My anger and trod them down in My wrath; their blood spattered My garments, and I stained all My clothing.

543)Jn1:1 In the beginning was the Word, and the Word was with God, and the Word was God.

[The armies of heaven]

Verse14-16 The armies of heaven were following Him, riding on white horses and dressed in fine linen, white and clean. Coming out of His mouth is a sharp sword with which to strike down the nations. "He will rule them with an iron scepter." He treads the winepress of the fury of the wrath of God Almighty. On His robe and on His thigh He has this name written: KING OF KINGS AND LORD OF LORDS.

1. The Lord does not make war alone, but with His army, His bride, which is His body (Rev 14:1, 17:14)[544].
2. The fine linen, white and clean, will not only be the formal attire for the wedding, but also a mighty battle uniform in the fight against Antichrist.
3. The word that comes out of His mouth will be a sharp sword. He will cast the Antichrist army into a winepress (the Megiddo plain) and trample them. Christ and His army will rule the nations with an iron scepter.
4. Today, in the church age, He watches over the saints with grace and love, but He rules over the disobedient with discipline and punishment (Heb 12:5~11)[545].

---

544)Rev14:1 "Do not let Your hearts be troubled. Trust in God; trust also in Me.
Rev17:14 I have given them Your word and the world has hated them, for they are not of the world any more than I am of the world.

545)Heb12:5 And you have forgotten that word of encouragement that addresses you as sons: "My son, do not make light of the Lord's discipline, and do not lose heart when He rebukes you,
Heb12:6 because the Lord disciplines those He loves, and He punishes everyone He accepts as a son."
Heb12:7 Endure hardship as discipline; God is treating you as sons. For what son is not disciplined by his father?
Heb12:8 If you are not disciplined (and everyone undergoes discipline), then you are illegitimate children and not true sons.

5. Christ's position as King of Kings and Lord of Lords was kept a secret during His earthly life, but now it is no longer a secret and is revealed for everyone to see (written on His robe and on His thigh) (Mt 16:20)[546].
6. Christ's robe represents His righteousness and His thigh represents His deeds and His life.

Verse 17-18 And I saw an angel standing in the sun, who cried in a loud voice to all the birds flying in midair, "Come, gather together for the great supper of God, so that you may eat the flesh of kings, generals, and the mighty, of horses and their riders, and the flesh of all people, free and slave, great and small."

▣ The great supper of God will be the destruction of Antichrist and his army, when Antichrist and the false prophet are thrown into the lake of burning sulfur, and when Satan is bound and cast into the Abyss (Eze 39:17~20, Jer 46:10, Mt 24:28)[547]. At this time, all the birds flying in the air will

---

Heb12:9 Moreover, we have all had human fathers who disciplined us and we respected them for it. How much more should we submit to the Father of our spirits and live!

Heb12:10 Our fathers disciplined us for a little while as they thought best; but God disciplines us for our good, that we may share in His holiness.

Heb12:11 No discipline seems pleasant at the time, but painful. Later on, however, it produces a harvest of righteousness and peace for those who have been trained by it.

546)Mt16:20 Then He warned His disciples not to tell anyone that He was the Christ.

547)Eze39:17 "Son of man, this is what the Sovereign LORD says: Call out to every kind of bird and all the wild animals: 'Assemble and come together from all around to the sacrifice I am preparing for you, the great sacrifice on the mountains of Israel. There you will eat flesh and drink blood.

Eze39:18 You will eat the flesh of mighty men and drink the blood of the princes of the earth as if they were rams and lambs, goats and bulls--all of them fattened animals from Bashan.

swoop down and eat their flesh (Mt 24:28, Isa 13:6~12)548).

[The Antichrist Army]

Verse 19-21 Then I saw the beast and the kings of the earth and their armies gathered together to wage war against the rider on the horse and his army. But the beast was captured, and with it the false prophet who had performed the signs on its behalf. With these signs he had deluded those who had received the mark of the

---

Eze39:19 At the sacrifice I am preparing for you, you will eat fat till you are glutted and drink blood till you are drunk.
Eze39:20 At My table you will eat Your fill of horses and riders, mighty men and soldiers of every kind,' declares the Sovereign LORD.
Jer46:10 But that day belongs to the Lord, the LORD Almighty--a day of vengeance, for vengeance on His foes. The sword will devour till it is satisfied, till it has quenched its thirst with blood. For the Lord, the LORD Almighty, will offer sacrifice in the land of the north by the River Euphrates.
Mt24:28 Wherever there is a carcass, there the vultures will gather.

548)Mt24:28 Wherever there is a carcass, there the vultures will gather.
Isa13:6 Wail, for the day of the LORD is near; it will come like destruction from the Almighty.
Isa13:7 Because of this, all hands will go limp, every man's heart will melt.
Isa13:8 Terror will seize them, pain and anguish will grip them; they will writhe like a woman in labor. They will look aghast at each other, their faces aflame.
Isa13:9 See, the day of the LORD is coming--a cruel day, with wrath and fierce anger--to make the land desolate and destroy the sinners within it.
Isa13:10 The stars of heaven and their constellations will not show their light. The rising sun will be darkened and the moon will not give its light.
Isa13:11 I will punish the world for its evil, the wicked for their sins. I will put an end to the arrogance of the haughty and will humble the pride of the ruthless.
Isa13:12 I will make man scarcer than pure gold, more rare than the gold of Ophir.

beast and worshiped its image. The two of them were thrown alive into the fiery lake of burning sulfur. The rest were killed with the sword coming out of the mouth of the rider on the horse, and all the birds gorged themselves on their flesh.

1. The enemies of Christ include the beast, the kings of the earth (Rev 17:12~14)[549], and their armies (the two hundred million mounted troops) (Rev 9:16, 16:12, 17:12~14)[550].

[Antichrist and the false prophet will enter the lake of fire]

2. Antichrist and the false prophet will enter the lake of fire first. The others will be killed by the sword of His mouth and their carcasses will be cleaned up by the birds in the air.

---

549)Rev17:12 "The ten horns you saw are ten kings who have not yet received a kingdom, but who for one hour will receive authority as kings along with the beast.
Rev17:13 They have one purpose and will give their power and authority to the beast.
Rev17:14 They will make war against the Lamb, but the Lamb will overcome them because He is Lord of lords and King of kings--and with Him will be His called, chosen and faithful followers."

550)Rev9:16 The number of the mounted troops was two hundred million. I heard their number.
Rev16:12 The sixth angel poured out his bowl on the great river Euphrates, and its water was dried up to prepare the way for the kings from the East.
Rev17:12~14 ☝See footnote 549

Chapter 20 Satan's Imprisonment, the Millennial Kingdom, and the White Throne Judgment

※ **The Millennial Kingdom** (the saints of the New Testament) : (Ps 2:6~9, 72:1~19, Isa 2:2~4, 11:1~10, 19:19~25, 35:1~10, 43:18~21, 61:11, 65:19~25, Zec 8:20~23, 14:16~21)

※ **The Kingdom of the Messiah** (the saints of the Old Testament) : (Isa 2:2~4, 61:4~11, Zec 8:20~23, 14:16-21)

Verse 1 And I saw an angel coming down out of heaven, having the key to the Abyss and holding in his hand a great chain.

▣ An angel comes down from heaven with a great chain and key to imprison Satan in the Abyss (the star seen in chapter 9 that had fallen from the sky to the earth was given the key to the shaft of the Abyss). This will happen after Antichrist and the false prophet (who are the embodiments of Satan) are thrown into the lake of fire and the army of Antichrist have all been killed.

※ The star that had fallen from the sky to the earth in chapter 9 (which is Satan) (Rev 12:9)[551] was given the key to the shaft of the Abyss to draw out the army of locusts.

※ After that, in the Millennial Kingdom, the Abyss is watched over by Christ. Later, Satan is unable to use his power if those who obey him (Antichrist and his army) are destroyed (Isa 14:10~17)[552].

---

551)Rev12:9 The great dragon was hurled down--that ancient serpent called the devil, or Satan, who leads the whole world astray. He was hurled to the earth, and his angels with him.

552)Isa14:10 They will all respond, they will say to you, "You also have become weak, as we are; you have become like us."
Isa14:11 All Your pomp has been brought down to the grave, along with the noise of Your harps; maggots are spread out beneath you and worms cover you.

[The imprisonment of Satan]

Verse 2-3 He seized the dragon, that ancient serpent, who is the devil, or Satan, and bound him for a thousand years. He threw him into the Abyss, and locked and sealed it over him, to keep him from deceiving the nations anymore until the thousand years were ended. After that, he must be set free for a short time.

▣ After Antichrist is defeated, in order to cleanse the earth, Satan is bound and imprisoned in the Abyss during the thousand years. Then, when the thousand years are over, he is set free again for a short time and deceives the nations.

※ Because the Antichrist and the false prophet are not needed anymore, they will be thrown into the lake of fire, but Satan will still be used as a tool by God to test the people of the nations.

[The martyr's first resurrection]

Verse 4-5 I saw thrones on which were seated those who had been given authority to judge. And I saw the souls of

---

Isa4:12 How you have fallen from heaven, O morning star, son of the dawn! You have been cast down to the earth, you who once laid low the nations!

Isa14:13 You said in Your heart, "I will ascend to heaven; I will raise my throne above the stars of God; I will sit enthroned on the mount of assembly, on the utmost heights of the sacred mountain.

Isa14:14 I will ascend above the tops of the clouds; I will make myself like the Most High."

Isa14:15 But you are brought down to the grave, to the depths of the pit.

Isa14:16 Those who see you stare at you, they ponder Your fate: "Is this the man who shook the earth and made kingdoms tremble,

Isa14:17 the man who made the world a desert, who overthrew its cities and would not let his captives go home?"

those who had been beheaded because of their testimony about Jesus and because of the word of God. They ahad not worshiped the beast or its image and had not received its mark on their foreheads or their hands. They came to life and reigned with Christ a thousand years. (The rest of the dead did not come to life until the thousand years were ended.) This is the first resurrection.

1. After the war of Armageddon, the Lord will hold court on His throne of glory in the valley of Jehoshaphat and gather before Him the people of the nations living on the earth (Joel 3:11～13)[553]. Then He will separate the people from one another just as a shepherd separates the sheep from the goats. The sheep will enter the Millennial Kingdom and the goats will go to the lake of fire (Mt 25:31～46)[554]. The

---

553)Joel3:11 Come quickly, all you nations from every side, and assemble there. Bring down Your warriors, O LORD!

Joel3:12 'Let the nations be roused; let them advance into the Valley of Jehoshaphat, for there I will sit to judge all the nations on every side.

Joel3:13 Swing the sickle, for the harvest is ripe. Come, trample the grapes, for the winepress is full and the vats overflow--so great is their wickedness!'

554)Mt25:31 "When the Son of Man comes in His glory, and all the angels with Him, He will sit on His throne in heavenly glory.

Mt25:32 All the nations will be gathered before Him, and He will separate the people one from another as a shepherd separates the sheep from the goats.

Mt25:33 He will put the sheep on His right and the goats on His left.

Mt25:34 "Then the King will say to those on His right, 'Come, you who are blessed by My Father; take Your inheritance, the kingdom prepared for you since the creation of the world.

Mt25:35 For I was hungry and you gave Me something to eat, I was thirsty and you gave Me something to drink, I was a stranger and you invited Me in,

Mt25:36 I needed clothes and you clothed Me, I was sick and you looked after Me, I was in prison and you came to visit me.'

Mt25:37 "Then the righteous will answer Him, 'Lord, when did we see You hungry and feed You, or thirsty and give You something to drink?

sheep will be ruled and taken care of during the Millennial Kingdom by Christ and the kings of Christ (Rev 20:4)[555]. But many who have not dealt with their rebellious nature will fall into temptation by Satan when he is freed from the Abyss again after the thousand years are ended (Rev 20:7 ~8)[556]. Ultimately, they will be thrown into the eternal lake of fire (Rev 20:15)[557].

Mt25:38 When did we see You a stranger and invite You in, or needing clothes and clothe You?
Mt25:39 When did we see You sick or in prison and go to visit you?'
Mt25:40 "The King will reply, 'I tell you the truth, whatever you did for one of the least of these brothers of Mine, you did for me.'
Mt25:41 "Then He will say to those on His left, 'Depart from Me, you who are cursed, into the eternal fire prepared for the devil and his angels.
Mt25:42 For I was hungry and you gave Me nothing to eat, I was thirsty and you gave Me nothing to drink,
Mt25:43 I was a stranger and you did not invite Me in, I needed clothes and you did not clothe Me, I was sick and in prison and you did not look after me.'
Mt25:44 "They also will answer, 'Lord, when did we see You hungry or thirsty or a stranger or needing clothes or sick or in prison, and did not help you?'
Mt25:45 "He will reply, 'I tell you the truth, whatever you did not do for one of the least of these, you did not do for me.'
Mt25:46 "Then they will go away to eternal punishment, but the righteous to eternal life."

555)Rev20:4 I saw thrones on which were seated those who had been given authority to judge. And I saw the souls of those who had been beheaded because of their testimony for Jesus and because of the word of God. They had not worshiped the beast or his image and had not received his mark on their foreheads or their hands. They came to life and reigned with Christ a thousand years.

556)Rev20:7 When the thousand years are over, Satan will be released from his prison
Rev20:8 and will go out to deceive the nations in the four corners of the earth--Gog and Magog--to gather them for battle. In number they are like the sand on the seashore.

[The Millennial Kingdom]

2. The saints who will reign as kings during the Millennial Kingdom.
   a. The overcomers in the last age of the church (Rev 3:21, Mt 19:28)[558].
   b. The martyrs who had been martyred for their testimony of Jesus and the Word of God (Rev 6:9, 20:4)[559].
   c. Those who were martyred during the last Great Tribulation (the latter three and a half years), who did not worship the image of the beast, and did not receive the mark of 666 (Rev 13:10, 15:2~3, 20:4)[560].

---

557)Rev20:15 If anyone's name was not found written in the book of life, he was thrown into the lake of fire.

558)Rev3:21 To him who overcomes, I will give the right to sit with Me on My throne, just as I overcame and sat down with My Father on His throne.
Mt19:28 Jesus said to them, "I tell you the truth, at the renewal of all things, when the Son of Man sits on His glorious throne, you who have followed Me will also sit on twelve thrones, judging the twelve tribes of Israel.

559)Rev6:9 When He opened the fifth seal, I saw under the altar the souls of those who had been slain because of the word of God and the testimony they had maintained.
Rev20:4 ☞See footnote 555) on the previous page

560)Rev13:10 If anyone is to go into captivity, into captivity he will go. If anyone is to be killed with the sword, with the sword he will be killed. This calls for patient endurance and faithfulness on the part of the saints.
Rev15:2 And I saw what looked like a sea of glass mixed with fire and, standing beside the sea, those who had been victorious over the beast and his image and over the number of his name. They held harps given them by God
Rev15:3 and sang the song of Moses the servant of God and the song of the Lamb: "Great and marvelous are Your deeds, Lord God Almighty. Just and true are Your ways, King of the ages.
Rev20:4 I saw thrones on which were seated those who had been given authority to judge. And I saw the souls of those who had been beheaded because of their testimony for Jesus and

3. The rest of the dead (the non-believers) will stay in Hades until the end of the Millennial Kingdom. When the Millennial Kingdom ends, they will be judged before the white throne. Those among the nations whose names have not been written in the book of life will also - by the white throne judgment - be thrown into the lake of fire.
4. Those among the nations whose names have been written in the book of life will live forever as the people of the nations of the New Earth (Rev 20:12~15, 21:3~4, 24~26, 22:2)[561].

---

because of the word of God. They had not worshiped the beast or his image and had not received his mark on their foreheads or their hands. They came to life and reigned with Christ a thousand years.

561)Rev20:12 And I saw the dead, great and small, standing before the throne, and books were opened. Another book was opened, which is the book of life. The dead were judged according to what they had done as recorded in the books.
Rev20:13 The sea gave up the dead that were in it, and death and Hades gave up the dead that were in them, and each person was judged according to what he had done.
Rev20:14 Then death and Hades were thrown into the lake of fire. The lake of fire is the second death.
Rev20:15 If anyone's name was not found written in the book of life, he was thrown into the lake of fire.
Rev21:3 And I heard a loud voice from the throne saying, "Now the dwelling of God is with men, and He will live with them. They will be His people, and God Himself will be with them and be their God.
Rev21:4 He will wipe every tear from their eyes. There will be no more death or mourning or crying or pain, for the old order of things has passed away."
Rev21:24 The nations will walk by its light, and the kings of the earth will bring their splendor into it.
Rev21:25 On no day will its gates ever be shut, for there will be no night there.
Rev21:26 The glory and honor of the nations will be brought into it.

Verse 6 Blessed and holy are those who share in the first resurrection. The second death has no power over them, but they will be priests of God and of Christ and will reign with Him for a thousand years.

1. The first resurrection ⇒ Greek: πρῶτοςς (protos), meaning 'the first' or 'the best' (Heb 11:35)[562].
2. The second death is the lake of fire (Rev 20:14)[563]. Those who have part in the first resurrection will not be thrown into the lake of fire but will be priests of Christ and will reign with Him as kings for the thousand years.
3. Those who take part in the first resurrection:
   a. Those who wear white robes in chapter 7:14[564]
   b. The male child in chapter 12:5[565]
   c. The last martyrs in chapter 15:2[566]
   d. The firstfruit saints in chapter 14:1～5[567]

---

562)Heb11:35 Women received back their dead, raised to life again. Others were tortured and refused to be released, so that they might gain a better resurrection.

563)Rev20:14 Then death and Hades were thrown into the lake of fire. The lake of fire is the second death.

564)Rev7:14 I answered, "Sir, you know." And he said, "These are they who have come out of the great tribulation; they have washed their robes and made them white in the blood of the Lamb.

565)Rev12:5 She gave birth to a son, a male child, who will rule all the nations with an iron scepter. And her child was snatched up to God and to His throne.

566)Rev15:2 And I saw what looked like a sea of glass mixed with fire and, standing beside the sea, those who had been victorious over the beast and his image and over the number of his name. They held harps given them by God

567)Rev14:1 Then I looked, and there before me was the Lamb, standing on Mount Zion, and with Him 144,000 who had His name and His Father's name written on their foreheads.

Rev14:2 And I heard a sound from heaven like the roar of rushing waters and like a loud peal of thunder. The sound I heard was like that of harpists playing their harps.

4. They will be priests of God and of Christ and will reign with Him for a thousand years.
5. Those who do not take part in the first resurrection will be hurt by the second death. (Mt 5:22, 25, 26, 29, 30, Lk 12:47～48)[568].

[The battle of Gog and Magog (Satan's deceit)]

Rev14:3 And they sang a new song before the throne and before the four living creatures and the elders. No one could learn the song except the 144,000 who had been redeemed from the earth.
Rev14:4 These are those who did not defile themselves with women, for they kept themselves pure. They follow the Lamb wherever He goes. They were purchased from among men and offered as firstfruits to God and the Lamb.
Rev14:5 No lie was found in their mouths; they are blameless.

568)Mt5:22 But I tell you that anyone who is angry with his brother will be subject to judgment. Again, anyone who says to his brother, 'Raca,' is answerable to the Sanhedrin. But anyone who says, 'You fool!' will be in danger of the fire of hell.
Mt5:25 "Settle matters quickly with Your adversary who is taking you to court. Do it while you are still with him on the way, or he may hand you over to the judge, and the judge may hand you over to the officer, and you may be thrown into prison.
Mt5:26 I tell you the truth, you will not get out until you have paid the last penny.
Mt5:29 If Your right eye causes you to sin, gouge it out and throw it away. It is better for you to lose one part of Your body than for Your whole body to be thrown into hell.
Mt5:30 And if Your right hand causes you to sin, cut it off and throw it away. It is better for you to lose one part of Your body than for Your whole body to go into hell.
Lk12:47 "That servant who knows his master's will and does not get ready or does not do what his master wants will be beaten with many blows.
Lk12:48 But the one who does not know and does things deserving punishment will be beaten with few blows. From everyone who has been given much, much will be demanded; and from the one who has been entrusted with much, much more will be asked.

Verse 7-8 When the thousand years are over, Satan will be released from his prison and will go out to deceive the nations in the four corners of the earth—Gog and Magog—and to gather them for battle. In number they are like the sand on the seashore.

1. The Abyss of Revelation 20:3[569] will be a prison where Satan is temporarily imprisoned, and at the end of the Millennial Kingdom, Satan will be released.
2. God will reign over the nations during the Millennial Kingdom and soon after, He will test their rebellious nature. When He does, He will use Satan (who has been imprisoned in the Abyss) to separate them once more, for the last time. At this time, just like Adam was deceived in the garden of Eden, a tremendous number of people - like the sand on the seashore - will be deceived. They will all be thrown into the eternal lake of fire.
3. In Ezekiel 38:1~3, 39:1~2[570], Gog and Magog are the princes of Meshech and Tubal, which indicate Moscow and Tobolsk in Russia. In Ezekiel, these two places are said to be in the far north (Ex-Soviet Union region).

---

569)Rev20:3 He threw him into the Abyss, and locked and sealed it over him, to keep him from deceiving the nations anymore until the thousand years were ended. After that, he must be set free for a short time.

570)Eze38:1 The word of the LORD came to me:
Eze38:2 "Son of man, set Your face against Gog, of the land of Magog, the chief prince of Meshech and Tubal; prophesy against him
Eze38:3 and say: 'This is what the Sovereign LORD says: I am against you, O Gog, chief prince of Meshech and Tubal.
Eze39:1 "Son of man, prophesy against Gog and say: 'This is what the Sovereign LORD says: I am against you, O Gog, chief prince of Meshech and Tubal.
Eze39:2 I will turn you around and drag you along. I will bring you from the far north and send you against the mountains of Israel.

[The devil who has deceived the nations is thrown into the lake of burning sulfur]

Verse 9-10 They marched across the breadth of the earth and surrounded the camp of God's people, the city He loves. But fire came down from heaven and devoured them. And the devil, who deceived them, was thrown into the lake of burning sulfur, where the beast and the false prophet had been thrown. They will be tormented day and night for ever and ever.

1. A rebellious crowd (those who have been deceived) will attack the camp of God's people and the city that God loves, Jerusalem.

※ Jerusalem is the place where the king dwells and the camp of the saints is where the saints dwell outside of the city, and this will be the camp of the saints (In the Old Testament, the tribes of Israel surrounded the Tabernacle as the center and camped around it on all four sides).

2. In the end, after the thousand years is over, the devil will be thrown into the eternal lake of burning sulfur after deceiving the nations once more.
3. If one wants to enter the eternal Kingdom which consisted of the New Heaven and the New Earth, as the people of the nations, he must overcome the devil's temptations. In order to set foot in the New Jerusalem, we must be able to withstand the devil's temptation and be victorious over him.

[The judgment of the white throne]

Verse 11-12 Then I saw a great white throne and Him who was seated on it. The earth and the heavens fled from His presence, and there was no place for them. And I saw the dead, great and small, standing before the throne, and books were opened. Another book was opened, which is the book of life. The dead were judged according to

what they had done as recorded in the books.

1. The One who is seated on the great white throne is Christ (Jn 5:22, Ac 10:42, 2Ti 4:1)[571].
2. The color white symbolizes righteousness, meaning that the Lord's throne for judgment is righteous, pure, and faithful.
3. After the thousand years has ended and the judgment of the great white throne is finished, the earth and sky will flee and the sky will be rolled up like a scroll (Heb 1:10~12, 2Pe 3:12, Ps 102:26)[572].
4. The dead refers to those who have died and not been born again in spirit. The believing saints have been raptured already, but the non-believers will not wake up until the thousand years are over (Rev 20:5)[573] and will be judged

---

571)Jn5:22 Moreover, the Father judges no one, but has entrusted all judgment to the Son,
Ac10:42 He commanded us to preach to the people and to testify that He is the One whom God appointed as judge of the living and the dead.
2Ti4:1 In the presence of God and of Christ Jesus, who will judge the living and the dead, and in view of His appearing and His kingdom, I give you this charge:

572)Isa34:4 All the stars of the heavens will be dissolved and the sky rolled up like a scroll; all the starry host will fall like withered leaves from the vine, like shriveled figs from the fig tree.
Heb1:10 He also says, "In the beginning, O Lord, You laid the foundations of the earth, and the heavens are the work of Your hands.
Heb1:11 They will perish, but You remain; they will all wear out like a garment.
Heb1:12 You will roll them up like a robe; like a garment they will be changed. But You remain the same, and Your years will never end."
2Pe3:12 as you look forward to the day of God and speed its coming. That day will bring about the destruction of the heavens by fire, and the elements will melt in the heat.
Ps102:26 They will perish, but You remain; they will all wear out like a garment. Like clothing You will change them and they will be discarded.

573)Rev20:5 (The rest of the dead did not come to life until the

before the great white throne according to what they had done and their souls will be thrown into the lake of fire (Da 7:9～11)[574].

[Then death and Hades were thrown into the lake of fire]

Verse 13-15 The sea gave up the dead that were in it, and death and Hades gave up the dead that were in them, and each person was judged according to what they had done. Then death and Hades were thrown into the lake of fire. The lake of fire is the second death. Anyone whose name was not found written in the book of life was thrown into the lake of fire.

1. Hades ⇒ Hell, Hades
   Hades: The dwelling place of dead spirits, the place of punishment, the underworld.
2. Death and Hades have held the souls of the dead but give them up in the time of the great white throne, for judgment, and Death, Hades (Hell) are thrown into the lake of fire. In other words, death is gone, and Hades, the abode of the dead, enters the lake of fire and is destroyed forever.
3. Because the judgment of the great white throne is a righteous judgment, the dead are judged according to what they have done.

---

thousand years were ended.) This is the first resurrection.

574)Da7:9 "As I looked, "thrones were set in place, and the Ancient of Days took His seat. His clothing was as white as snow; the hair of His head was white like wool. His throne was flaming with fire, and its wheels were all ablaze.
Da7:10 A river of fire was flowing, coming out from before Him. Thousands upon thousands attended Him; ten thousand times ten thousand stood before Him. The court was seated, and the books were opened.
Da7:11 "Then I continued to watch because of the boastful words the horn was speaking. I kept looking until the beast was slain and its body destroyed and thrown into the blazing fire.

4. The factor that decides whether one is thrown into the lake of fire is the book of life. That is, those who have faith in God and are born again in spirit will avoid the lake of fire after the great white throne judgment, as their spirits will be saved (angel-like salvation).
5. Ultimately, the great white throne judgment comes down to whether one's name is written in the book of life.

Chapter 21 A New Heaven and a New Earth, the New Jerusalem

Verse 1-2 Then I saw "a new heaven and a new earth," afor the first heaven and the first earth had passed away, and there was no longer any sea. I saw the Holy City, the new Jerusalem, coming down out of heaven from God, prepared as a bride beautifully dressed for her husband.

1. In chapter 21:1～2 the Holy city, the New Jerusalem comes down to the New Earth, completing God's eternal economy.

[four eras]

2. For this to be accomplished, God has gone through four eras to achieve His work.
   a. The Patriarch era (from the time of Adam to the time of Moses) (Ro 5:14)[575] : The time of the 12 stars.
   ※ God acquires chiefs of faith
   b. The Law of Moses era (from the time of Moses to the time of Christ) (Jn 1:17)[576] : The moon under the woman's feet.
   ※ God acquires the saints of the Old Testament
   c. The Grace era (from the time of Christ's first coming to His second coming) (Ac 3:20～21)[577] : The woman clothed with the sun.
   ※ God acquires the saints of the New Testament
   d. The Kingdom era (from the time of Christ's second

---

575)Ro5:14 Nevertheless, death reigned from the time of Adam to the time of Moses, even over those who did not sin by breaking a command, as did Adam, who was a pattern of the one to come.

576)Jn1:17 For the law was given through Moses; grace and truth came through Jesus Christ.

577)Ac3:20 and that He may send the Christ, who has been appointed for you--even Jesus.
Ac3:21 He must remain in heaven until the time comes for God to restore everything, as He promised long ago through His holy prophets.

coming to the judgment of the great white throne (Rev 11:15, 20:4~6)[578].

※ This is the period when God perfects the saints of the Old Testament (the Israelites) and immature Christians.

※ Among the non-believers, the chosen sheep are the people of the Millennial Kingdom. They will become the people of the nations to serve God (Mt 25:31~46, Rev 21:3)[579].

3. After the people of God have become complete through the four steps written above, God will no longer need the first heaven and earth (the old creation ends).
4. After the fourth stage, the completeness of God's people is fulfilled, and God possesses the city of New Jerusalem, a perfect, holy and universal woman (Rev 21:2)[580].

---

578)Rev11:15 The seventh angel sounded his trumpet, and there were loud voices in heaven, which said: "The kingdom of the world has become the kingdom of our Lord and of His Christ, and He will reign for ever and ever."

Rev20:4 I saw thrones on which were seated those who had been given authority to judge. And I saw the souls of those who had been beheaded because of their testimony for Jesus and because of the word of God. They had not worshiped the beast or his image and had not received his mark on their foreheads or their hands. They came to life and reigned with Christ a thousand years.

Rev20:5 (The rest of the dead did not come to life until the thousand years were ended.) This is the first resurrection.

Rev20:6 Blessed and holy are those who have part in the first resurrection. The second death has no power over them, but they will be priests of God and of Christ and will reign with Him for a thousand years.

579)Mt25:31~46 Bible text reference

Rev21:3 And I heard a loud voice from the throne saying, "Now the dwelling of God is with men, and He will live with them. They will be His people, and God Himself will be with them and be their God.

580)Rev21:2 I saw the Holy City, the new Jerusalem, coming down out of heaven from God, prepared as a bride beautifully dressed for her husband.

5. God has disciplined, refined, and transformed His people using many things to perfect them (Satan, Antichrist, false prophets, weakness, suffering, all filthiness, and the joy of the world).
6. After this, **[everything pertaining to the old creation]** (the first heaven, the first earth, Satan, Antichrist, false prophets, material things, death, hell, etc.) will be thrown into the lake of fire, the eternal trash can.
7. After the sea releases the dead that were in it (Rev 20:13)[581], it will no longer exist in the New Earth, the eternal earth.
8. In the end, the New Jerusalem will come down to the New Earth, meaning that we will live eternally NOT in heaven, but in the New Jerusalem on the New Earth (Rev 21:2)[582].

※ The New Jerusalem is, by turns, a living person composed of believers redeemed by God generation after generation (Rev 21:2, Gal 4:26)[583], His partner, His bride (Jn 3:2 9)[584], and the holy city of God, His dwelling place (Ex 29:45~46, 1Co 3:16~17, 1Ti 3:15, Heb 11:10, 12:22)[585].

---

581)Rev20:13 The sea gave up the dead that were in it, and death and Hades gave up the dead that were in them, and each person was judged according to what he had done.

582)Rev21:2 I saw the Holy City, the new Jerusalem, coming down out of heaven from God, prepared as a bride beautifully dressed for her husband.

583)Rev21:2 ☞See footnote 582
Gal4:26 But the Jerusalem that is above is free, and she is our mother.

584)Jn3:29 The bride belongs to the bridegroom. The friend who attends the bridegroom waits and listens for him, and is full of joy when he hears the bridegroom's voice. That joy is mine, and it is now complete.

585)Ex29:45 Then I will dwell among the Israelites and be their God.
Ex29:46 They will know that I am the LORD their God, who brought them out of Egypt so that I might dwell among them. I am the LORD their God.
1Co3:16 Don't you know that you yourselves are God's temple and that God's Spirit lives in you?

※ The New Jerusalem is for the satisfaction of God as a partner in love, but at the same time stands for God's rest as a dwelling place.

Verse 3-4 And I heard a loud voice from the throne saying, "Look! God's dwelling place is now among the people, and He will dwell with them. They will be His people, and God Himself will be with them and be their God. 'He will wipe every tear from their eyes. There will be no more death' or mourning or crying or pain, for the old order of things has passed away."

1. The tabernacle of God ⇒ tabernacle (tent, temporary building, barracks).
2. God dwells with the people by dwelling in the tabernacle. It will be like dwelling in the tabernacle of the Old Testament and living with the people of Israel, and they will be God's people, and they will be the peoples of the New Earth (Rev 21:24, 26)[586].
3. During the Millennial Kingdom, the people of the nations will believe in Christ and be born again. Their rebellious nature will be swept away (the rebels will be deceived by the devil and thrown into the lake of fire at the end of the Millennial Kingdom).

1Co3:17 If anyone destroys God's temple, God will destroy him; for God's temple is sacred, and you are that temple.

1Di3:15 if I am delayed, you will know how people ought to conduct themselves in God's household, which is the church of the living God, the pillar and foundation of the truth.

Heb11:10 For he was looking forward to the city with foundations, whose architect and builder is God.

Heb12:22 But you have come to Mount Zion, to the heavenly Jerusalem, the city of the living God. You have come to thousands upon thousands of angels in joyful assembly,

586)Rev21:24 The nations will walk by its light, and the kings of the earth will bring their splendor into it.

Rev21:26 The glory and honor of the nations will be brought into it.

4. In the New Heaven and the New Earth, the people of the nations will still have their bodies but there will be no more tears, suffering, pain, or death, only full satisfaction, joy, and rest.

※ The conditions will be prelapsarian - the state before Adam and Eve ate the fruit of the knowledge of good and evil; there will be no death and they will be fruitful and increase in number forever (Ge 1:28)[587].
(Death came after the fruit of the knowledge of good and evil was eaten.)

Verse 5-6 He who was seated on the throne said, "I am making everything new!" Then He said, "Write this down, for these words are trustworthy and true." He said to me: "It is done. I am the Alpha and the Omega, the Beginning and the End. To the thirsty I will give water without cost from the spring of the water of life.

1. God's eternal economy is to obtain sons and to give an inheritance to the overcomers, and to have an eternal resting place in the New Jerusalem.
2. The living water - our eternal drink - is the spirit that gives us life (Jn 4:10, 14, 7:37～39)[588]. We all need something

---

587)Ge1:28 God blessed them and said to them, "Be fruitful and increase in number; fill the earth and subdue it. Rule over the fish of the sea and the birds of the air and over every living creature that moves on the ground."

588)Jn4:10 Jesus answered her, "If you knew the gift of God and who it is that asks you for a drink, you would have asked Him and He would have given you living water."
Jn4:14 but whoever drinks the water I give him will never thirst. Indeed, the water I give him will become in him a spring of water welling up to eternal life."
Jn7:37 On the last and greatest day of the Feast, Jesus stood and said in a loud voice, "If anyone is thirsty, let him come to Me and drink.
Jn7:38 Whoever believes in Me, as the Scripture has said, streams of living water will flow from within him."

to eat and drink. In eternity, we will have the fruit of the tree of life as our food and the life-giving spirit as our drink. The life-giving spirit is actually God Himself; He flows to us and becomes our drink.

[The inheritance of the overcomers]

Verse 7-8 Those who are victorious will inherit all this, and I will be their God and they will be My children. But the cowardly, the unbelieving, the vile, the murderers, the sexually immoral, those who practice magic arts, the idolaters and all liars—they will be consigned to the fiery lake of burning sulfur. This is the second death."

1. During the Millennial Kingdom, those who become overcomers among the nations will receive God's inheritance that provides the water of life, and they will be the sons of God.
2. During the Millennial Kingdom, the cowards and the liars among the nations will be thrown into the lake of fire.

※ The message in chapter 21:3～8[589] is for the people of the

---

Jn7:39 By this He meant the Spirit, whom those who believed in Him were later to receive. Up to that time the Spirit had not been given, since Jesus had not yet been glorified.

589)Rev21:3 And I heard a loud voice from the throne saying, "Now the dwelling of God is with men, and He will live with them. They will be His people, and God Himself will be with them and be their God.

Rev21:4 He will wipe every tear from their eyes. There will be no more death or mourning or crying or pain, for the old order of things has passed away."

Rev21:5 He who was seated on the throne said, "I am making everything new!" Then He said, "Write this down, for these words are trustworthy and true."

Rev21:6 He said to me: "It is done. I am the Alpha and the Omega, the Beginning and the End. To him who is thirsty I will give to drink without cost from the spring of the water of life.

Rev21:7 He who overcomes will inherit all this, and I will be his God and He will be My son.

Rev21:8 But the cowardly, the unbelieving, the vile, the murderers,

nations of the Millennial Kingdom (The faithful saints have already finished these things before the beginning of the Millennial Kingdom).

Verse 9-10 One of the seven angels who had the seven bowls full of the seven last plagues came and said to me, "Come, I will show you the bride, the wife of the Lamb." And he carried me away in the Spirit to a mountain great and high, and showed me the Holy City, Jerusalem, coming down out of heaven from God.

1. One of the seven angels who had carried out the last seven bowls judgment showed John the New Jerusalem, the bride of the Lamb, meaning that the last seven bowls judgment is dedicated to the New Jerusalem.
2. The bride = the wife of the Lamb = the Holy City = the New Jerusalem
3. As John was carried away in the Spirit to a mountain great and high and was shown the New Jerusalem, this means that in order to see the New Jerusalem, we too must be on the great and high mountain in the Spirit.

※ In order to see the vision of the seven churches, John had to be on the Island of Patmos, and to see the great prostitute Babylon (Rev 17:3)[590], he had to go to the desert, and to see the New Jerusalem, he had to go to a great and high mountain.

4. The New Jerusalem is the Holy City. This city is the bride of the Lamb, His wife. Because Jerusalem City, the Holy City is God's dwelling place separated by holiness, the saints who are part of Jerusalem must be drenched in the holy nature of God (Eze 16:8, 2Co 11:2)[591].

---

the sexually immoral, those who practice magic arts, the idolaters and all liars--their place will be in the fiery lake of burning sulfur. This is the second death."

590)Rev17:3 Then the angel carried me away in the Spirit into a desert. There I saw a woman sitting on a scarlet beast that was covered with blasphemous names and had seven heads and ten horns.

※ The church comes out of Christ and becomes His bride. The church will become the New Jerusalem. This is analogous to Eve coming out of Adam and becoming his wife.

Verse 11-12 It shone with the glory of God, and its brilliance was like that of a very precious jewel, like a jasper, clear as crystal. It had a great, high wall with twelve gates, and with twelve angels at the gates. On the gates were written the names of the twelve tribes of Israel.

1. Gemstones symbolize people who have changed after being redeemed by God and born again. When we, who are born of dust, confess "You are the Christ, the Son of the living God", we become rocks (Mt 16:16~18)[592]. These rocks are refined and melted by the Spirit and eventually become gemstones.

※ We are in the process of transformation and are being built (Eph 2:20~21, 1Pe 2:4~5)[593]. The New Jerusalem is a

---

591)Eze16:8 "'Later I passed by, and when I looked at you and saw that you were old enough for love, I spread the corner of My garment over you and covered Your nakedness. I gave you My solemn oath and entered into a covenant with you, declares the Sovereign LORD, and you became Mine.

2Co11:2 I am jealous for you with a godly jealousy. I promised you to one husband, to Christ, so that I might present you as a pure virgin to Him.

592)Mt16:16 Simon Peter answered, "You are the Christ, the Son of the living God."

Mt16:17 Jesus replied, "Blessed are you, Simon son of Jonah, for this was not revealed to you by man, but by My Father in heaven.

Mt16:18 And I tell you that you are Peter, and on this rock I will build My church, and the gates of Hades will not overcome it.

593)Eph2:20 built on the foundation of the apostles and prophets, with Christ Jesus Himself as the chief cornerstone.

Eph2:21 In Him the whole building is joined together and rises to become a holy temple in the Lord.

1Pe2:4 As you come to Him, the living Stone--rejected by men but chosen by God and precious to him--

living construct made up of all the saints who have been transformed after being redeemed and born again by God.

2. The saints of the Old Testament are represented by the twelve names of the twelve tribes on the twelve gates. The names of the twelve tribes of Israel are written on the gates, and the gates of the temple symbolize living people.

※ The temple gates are for entering and leaving the New Jerusalem. Entering and leaving the New Jerusalem can only be achieved through the twelve tribes of Israel, which means that only those who have fulfilled the Law can enter and leave through these gates. Past these gates, the riches of the New Jerusalem are supplied to the people of the nations.

[The twelve pearl gates and twelve foundations of the New Jerusalem]

Verse 13-14 There were three gates on the east, three on the north, three on the south and three on the west. The wall of the city had twelve foundations, and on them were the names of the twelve apostles of the Lamb.

1. The believers of the New Testament are represented by the names of the twelve apostles of the Lamb on the twelve foundations. This means that the New Jerusalem is made up of the saints of the Old Testament (represented by the Israelites) and the saints of the New Testament (represented by the apostles).

※ The New Testament believers are not for the doors, but for the walls. The doors are for entering and exiting, but the walls are for separation and protection. In other words, entry into the holy city requires the fulfillment of God's law, and the condition required for dwelling in the city is that one be transformed and clothed in the holiness of God's grace.

2. The foundation of the New Jerusalem is the twelve apostles. Churches today are built on the foundation of the apostles

---

1Pe2:5 you also, like living stones, are being built into a spiritual house to be a holy priesthood, offering spiritual sacrifices acceptable to God through Jesus Christ.

and prophets (Eph 2:20)[594]. The wall of the city built on the twelve apostles - the foundations of the New Jerusalem - will be a shining wall made of jasper, which is made up of saints.

※ Churches today are composed of born-again living stones (1Pe 2:4~5)[595].

Verse 15-17 The angel who talked with me had a measuring rod of gold to measure the city, its gates and its walls. The city was laid out like a square, as long as it was wide. He measured the city with the rod and found it to be 12,000 stadia in length, and as wide and high as it is long. The angel measured the wall using human measurement, and it was 144 cubits thick.

1. The reed is for measuring. The reed like that of a rod in Revelation 11:1[596] is for the measurement of punishment (Pr 10:13, Isa 10:5, 11:4)[597], but a rod of gold stands for the divine nature of God. This means that anything that goes against the divine nature of God does not belong in the New

---

594)Eph2:20 built on the foundation of the apostles and prophets, with Christ Jesus Himself as the chief cornerstone.

595)1Pe2:4 As you come to Him, the living Stone--rejected by men but chosen by God and precious to him--
1Pe2:5 you also, like living stones, are being built into a spiritual house to be a holy priesthood, offering spiritual sacrifices acceptable to God through Jesus Christ.

596)Rev11:1 I was given a reed like a measuring rod and was told, "Go and measure the temple of God and the altar, and count the worshipers there.

597)Pr10:13 Wisdom is found on the lips of the discerning, but a rod is for the back of him who lacks judgment.
Isa10:5 "Woe to the Assyrian, the rod of My anger, in whose hand is the club of My wrath!
Isa11:4 but with righteousness He will judge the needy, with justice He will give decisions for the poor of the earth. He will strike the earth with the rod of His mouth; with the breath of His lips He will slay the wicked.

Jerusalem. The city, its gates and its wall, and all the things of the city conform to the divine nature of God. In other words, everything that is worthy to be possessed by God is within that city.

2. The New Jerusalem is 12,000 stadia (2,220 km) in length, width, and height, a cube-shaped city. This means that the New Jerusalem is the Most Holy Place massively enlarged.

※ The Most Holy Place of the tabernacle (in the desert): a cube of 10 cubits.

※ The Most Holy Place of Solomon's temple: a cube of 20 cubits (1Ki 6:20)[598].

※ The New Jerusalem: a cube of 12,000 stadia (1 stadia =185m).

3. The principle of the Most Holy Place is that man must live and act in the presence of God.

※ In the Old Testament, the high priest could enter only once a year, on the Day of Atonement. However, in the New Testament, through the blood of Christ, the way has been opened for all faithful saints to enter the Most Holy Place (Heb 10:19~22)[599]. Those who are redeemed believers who are attached to Christ, who have made up the body of Christ, can enter, live and enjoy life there in fellowship and grace in the presence of God.

※ In church life today, we must rise up to enjoy the life of the Most Holy Place.

---

598)1Ki6:20 The inner sanctuary was twenty cubits long, twenty wide and twenty high. He overlaid the inside with pure gold, and he also overlaid the altar of cedar.

599)Heb10:19 Therefore, brothers, since we have confidence to enter the Most Holy Place by the blood of Jesus,
Heb10:20 by a new and living way opened for us through the curtain, that is, His body,
Heb10:21 and since we have a great priest over the house of God,
Heb10:22 let us draw near to God with a sincere heart in full assurance of faith, having our hearts sprinkled to cleanse us from a guilty conscience and having our bodies washed with pure water.

4. 'By man's measurement, which the angel was using' means that angels went by man's unit of measurement. The wall of the city is 144 cubits thick (around 72 meters) and the actual size of the New Jerusalem is a cube, 2,220 km in length, width, and height.

Verse 18 The wall was made of jasper, and the city of pure gold, as pure as glass.

1. The wall is made of jasper, which is a jewel that has the appearance of God (Rev 4:3)[600]. This gem is crystal clear green. Green means abundance of life. In other words, jasper means being in the abundance of the life of God.
2. The New Jerusalem is made up of precious stones. The whole city and its roads are pure gold. Gold symbolizes God's divine nature and the twelve pearl gates symbolizes death, overcoming, and the resurrection which gives life. In other words, these twelve pearl gates stand for the sons of God that have completed the commandments through the life of resurrection. The twelve pearl gates are the entrances to the city. The wall and its foundations are made of precious stones. This symbolizes the work of the Spirit that transforms redeemed and born-again saints into precious stones used to make God's eternal dwelling place. This wall, as a whole, expresses the glory of God.

※ We were born of dust, but by believing in God, we have been born again and become rocks, and by the work, refinement, and discipline of the Spirit, these rocks are transformed into precious stones and come to reveal the image of God (Rev 4:3)[601].

Verse 19-20 The foundations of the city walls were decorated with

600)Rev4:3 And the One who sat there had the appearance of jasper and carnelian. A rainbow, resembling an emerald, encircled the throne.

601)Rev4:3 ☝See footnote 600)

every kind of precious stone. The first foundation was jasper, the second sapphire, the third agate, the fourth emerald, the fifth onyx, the sixth ruby, the seventh chrysolite, the eighth beryl, the ninth topaz, the tenth turquoise, the eleventh jacinth, and the twelfth amethyst.

▣ The foundations of the city walls were decorated with every kind of precious stone' means that the twelve apostles have been transformed into precious stones and become the foundations of the city (verse 14).

※ Following the apostles, the saints who have been redeemed and transformed will be changed into jasper (verse 18), and will become the wall of the city that reveals God's glory. Every day, we must follow the Spirit's leading, go through the cross, and be changed into jasper that reveals the glory of God.

Verse 21-22 The twelve gates were twelve pearls, each gate made of a single pearl. The great street of the city was of gold, as pure as transparent glass. I did not see a temple in the city, because the Lord God Almighty and the Lamb are its temple.

1. Each gate of the city is made of a single great pearl, symbolizing the son who defeated death and rose again to give life. Only those who defeat death and live by the life of resurrection can pass through these gates (these gates are guarded by angels).

※ On the gates were written the names of the twelve tribes of Israel' means that only those who have fulfilled the Law and the Commandments may pass through these gates. Anyone that has overcome death and received the life of resurrection must live a life of fulfilling the commandments in order to pass through these gates (Mt 5:17, Ro 8:3～4)[602].

---

602)Mt5:17 "Do not think that I have come to abolish the Law or the Prophets; I have not come to abolish them but to fulfill them.
Ro8:3 For what the law was powerless to do in that it was weakened

2. The great street of the city is of pure gold, like transparent glass. What this says is that anyone who lives without having the divine nature of God in him cannot walk on the street, and anyone who is not within God's divine nature cannot dwell in the Holy City.
3. In the city there is no temple, the reason being that the entirety of the New Jerusalem is one big Most Holy Place, and that God and the Lamb in the Most Holy Place are the temple. In the end, the head of the church, which is Christ, and His body, that is, the church will be united and come to complete God's eternal dwelling place, the Most Holy Place, the New Jerusalem.

※ Before Moses built the Tabernacle, God showed him the temple and made him build it (Ac 7:44, Heb 8:5)[603]. God has built this temple from generation to generation and has obtained the New Jerusalem.

Verse 23-25 The city does not need the sun or the moon to shine on it, for the glory of God gives it light, and the Lamb is its lamp. The nations will walk by its light, and the kings of the earth will bring their splendor into it. On no day will its gate ever be shut, for there will be no night there.

1. The city is full of God's glory and because the light shines

---

by the sinful nature, God did by sending His own Son in the likeness of sinful man to be a sin offering. And so He condemned sin in sinful man,

Ro8:4 in order that the righteous requirements of the law might be fully met in us, who do not live according to the sinful nature but according to the Spirit.

603)Ac7:44 "Our forefathers had the tabernacle of the Testimony with them in the desert. It had been made as God directed Moses, according to the pattern he had seen.

Heb8:5 They serve at a sanctuary that is a copy and shadow of what is in heaven. This is why Moses was warned when he was about to build the tabernacle: "See to it that you make everything according to the pattern shown you on the mountain."

through the Lamb, inside the city, there is no sunlight or moonlight, but they live by the light of Gods glory. While we live on this earth, we must be inside the light of God's glory and live a life inside this light.

※ God is the light and the Lamb is its lamp' means that God is in His son, and through His son, He is revealed as light. So, we must come to realize that without the Lamb, we cannot do anything.

2. In the nations (the New Earth), the sun and moon will exist (Rev 22:2), but the nations will walk by the light of God's glory.
3. The kings of the earth, those who reign over the nations on the New Earth, will come and go to and from the city, bringing their splendor with them. They will have gained authority to pass through the pearl gates.
4. The New Jerusalem will be a place in which there is no night, and on no day will its gates ever be shut. There will, however, be limited access through these gates because angels will be guarding them.

Verse 26-27 The glory and honor of the nations will be brought into it. Nothing impure will ever enter it, nor will anyone who does what is shameful or deceitful, but only those whose names are written in the Lamb's book of life.

1. Among the people, only those who have the glory and the honor of the nations will be brought into the city. In other words, only those whose names have been recorded in the Lamb's book of life can enter the New Jerusalem.
2. Among the nations that still dwell outside the city, there will be those who are worldly, shameful, and deceitful. However, in a life where Satan does not exist, they will gradually be changed to be worthy of entering the city with glory and honor. In an eternal world, nations will endlessly change, and those who receive the life of the Lamb will keep increasing in number.

Chapter 22 The River of the Water of Life and the Tree of Life

[The River of the Water of Life]

Verse 1-2 Then the angel showed me the river of the water of life, as clear as crystal, flowing from the throne of God and of the Lamb down the middle of the great street of the city. On each side of the river stood the tree of life, bearing twelve crops of fruit, yielding its fruit every month. And the leaves of the tree are for the healing of the nations.

1. The throne of God and of the Lamb: This does not mean that there are two thrones, but only one throne for God and the Lamb, meaning that God and the Lamb are one: God-the-Lamb, that is, the God who redeems. The God that sits on the throne for eternity is the God who redeems us, and from that throne flows the river of the water of life that fulfills our needs and satisfies (Jn 7:38～39, Ex 17:6)[604].

※ How is it possible that God and the Lamb can sit together on one throne? This can be answered in chapter 21:23[605] where it says that God is the light and the Lamb is its lamp. The light and its lamp cannot be separated, nor can they stand side by side. The light shines from within the lamp, therefore God, who is the light, is inside the lamp, which is the Lamb (Heb 12:2, 1Pe 3:22)[606]. Due to the

---

604)Jn7:38 Whoever believes in Me, as the Scripture has said, streams of living water will flow from within him."

Jn7:39 By this He meant the Spirit, whom those who believed in Him were later to receive. Up to that time the Spirit had not been given, since Jesus had not yet been glorified.

Ex17:6 I will stand there before you by the rock at Horeb. Strike the rock, and water will come out of it for the people to drink." So Moses did this in the sight of the elders of Israel.

605)Rev21:23 The city does not need the sun or the moon to shine on it, for the glory of God gives it light, and the Lamb is its lamp.

light being inside the lamp, they are of one true nature that has two different sides. That is, the God who is seated on the throne is now the God of creation and the Lamb who has redeemed. We can call Him God-the-Lamb.

2. God gives Himself to us through the river of the water of life flowing from the throne (Ex 17:5~6, Eze 47:8~9, Jn 7:38~39, 1Co 10:4)[607].

※ The water of life represents God in Christ, flowing Himself into them as the Spirit to be the life supply of God's redeemed people. It is foreshadowed in type by the water that came out of the split rock (Ex 17:6, Nu 20:11)[608], and symbolized by

---

606)Heb12:2 Let us fix our eyes on Jesus, the author and perfecter of our faith, who for the joy set before Him endured the cross, scorning its shame, and sat down at the right hand of the throne of God.

1Pe3:22 who has gone into heaven and is at God's right hand--with angels, authorities and powers in submission to Him.

607)Ex17:5 The LORD answered Moses, "Walk on ahead of the people. Take with you some of the elders of Israel and take in Your hand the staff with which you struck the Nile, and go.

Ex17:6 I will stand there before you by the rock at Horeb. Strike the rock, and water will come out of it for the people to drink." So Moses did this in the sight of the elders of Israel.

Eze47:8 He said to me, "This water flows toward the eastern region and goes down into the Arabah, where it enters the Sea. When it empties into the Sea, the water there becomes fresh.

Eze47:9 Swarms of living creatures will live wherever the river flows. There will be large numbers of fish, because this water flows there and makes the salt water fresh; so where the river flows everything will live.

Jn7:38 Whoever believes in Me, as the Scripture has said, streams of living water will flow from within him."

Jn7:39 By this He meant the Spirit, whom those who believed in Him were later to receive. Up to that time the Spirit had not been given, since Jesus had not yet been glorified.

1Co10:4 and drank the same spiritual drink; for they drank from the spiritual rock that accompanied them, and that rock was Christ.

608)Ex17:6 I will stand there before you by the rock at Horeb. Strike the

the water that flowed from the side of the Lord Jesus when He was pierced with a spear (Jn 19:34)[609].

※ This water of life will be the river coming from the throne of God and the Lamb that sustains all of the New Jerusalem and saturates it. This river is the flowing spirit of God, the life-giving Spirit. Therefore, we see the Triune God in Revelation 22:1[610].

※ God is the source, the Son, the Lamb is the redeemer, and the river is the Spirit which gives us life.
Today, we hold the throne within us. Every time we obey the head of authority over this throne, we can feel something flow in us. Even now, the throne of God works in us so that streams of living water may flow from within us (Jn 7:37~39)[611].

3. The river of the water of life flows down the middle of the street. This is a street of gold, which means that we can obtain the flowing of this river when we act according to

---

rock, and water will come out of it for the people to drink." So Moses did this in the sight of the elders of Israel.

Nu20:11 Then Moses raised his arm and struck the rock twice with his staff. Water gushed out, and the community and their livestock drank.

609)Jn19:34 Instead, one of the soldiers pierced Jesus' side with a spear, bringing a sudden flow of blood and water.

610)Rev22:1 Then the angel showed me the river of the water of life, as clear as crystal, flowing from the throne of God and of the Lamb

611)Jn7:37 On the last and greatest day of the Feast, Jesus stood and said in a loud voice, "If anyone is thirsty, let him come to Me and drink.

Jn7:38 Whoever believes in Me, as the Scripture has said, streams of living water will flow from within him."

Jn7:39 By this He meant the Spirit, whom those who believed in Him were later to receive. Up to that time the Spirit had not been given, since Jesus had not yet been glorified.

the nature of God (seen as going on the road). In other words, divine life flows as we live according to the divine path, living by the divine nature.

4. 'The river of the water of life is clear as crystal' means that the river is clear and pure, not opaque or cloudy. When this water flows in us, it makes us pure and clear. The more the living water flows in us, the more of what makes us blind flows out. It gives us a discerning heart to make our existence, situation, and everything that has to do with us become crystal clear.
5. 'On each side of the river stood the tree of life' shows that the creation intended by God from the beginning (Ge 2:9)[612] will have been completed forever. The tree of life was denied to man because of the fall (Ge 3:22~24)[613], but opened to believers by the redemption of Christ (Heb 10:19~20, Jn 6:35, 57)[614]. In the Millennial Kingdom, the overcomers will

---

612)Ge2:9 And the LORD God made all kinds of trees grow out of the ground--trees that were pleasing to the eye and good for food. In the middle of the garden were the tree of life and the tree of the knowledge of good and evil.

613)Ge3:22 And the LORD God said, "The man has now become like one of us, knowing good and evil. He must not be allowed to reach out his hand and take also from the tree of life and eat, and live forever."
Ge3:23 So the LORD God banished him from the Garden of Eden to work the ground from which he had been taken.
Ge3:24 After He drove the man out, He placed on the east side of the Garden of Eden cherubim and a flaming sword flashing back and forth to guard the way to the tree of life.

614)Heb10:19 Therefore, brothers, since we have confidence to enter the Most Holy Place by the blood of Jesus,
Heb10:20 by a new and living way opened for us through the curtain, that is, His body,
Jn6:35 Then Jesus declared, "I am the bread of life. He who comes to Me will never go hungry, and he who believes in Me will never be thirsty.
Jn6:57 Just as the living Father sent Me and I live because of the

enjoy Christ, the tree of life, as their reward (Rev 2:27)[615], and in the new heaven and earth, all who are redeemed will enjoy an eternal inheritance (Rev 22:14, 19)[616].

※ This tree of life is Christ, who supplies life to us. Christ was first the Lamb for our redemption (Jn 1:29)[617], then the tree of life that supplies us with life (Jn 6:35)[618]. The redemption of Christ is to supply us with life through Himself. He is the Lamb of God, the tree of life, the bread of life.

※ The tree of life grows on each side of the river, meaning that the life of Christ comes from where the Spirit flows. Every time we submit to the headship of God's redeeming being, a river of life flows from His throne.

※ This river of life flows in the middle of the street of gold and there is a tree of life, which grows along the river as our rich life supply. Where there is a river, there is a tree of life that supplies us. The throne, the golden road, the water of life, and the tree of life must be enjoyed through our life and experience.

Father, so the one who feeds on Me will live because of Me.

615)Rev2:27 'He will rule them with an iron scepter; he will dash them to pieces like pottery'--just as I have received authority from My Father.

616)Rev22:14 "Blessed are those who wash their robes, that they may have the right to the tree of life and may go through the gates into the city.

Rev22:19 And if anyone takes words away from this book of prophecy, God will take away from him his share in the tree of life and in the holy city, which are described in this book.

617)Jn1:29 The next day John saw Jesus coming toward him and said, "Look, the Lamb of God, who takes away the sin of the world!

618)Jn6:35 Then Jesus declared, "I am the bread of life. He who comes to Me will never go hungry, and he who believes in Me will never be thirsty.

6. The fruits of the tree of life will be food for the redeemed of God forever. The fruit will always be fresh and produced monthly, yielding twelve crops throughout the year. The twelve crops mean that the fruit of the tree of life is rich and sufficient for the completion of God's eternal administration.
7. Every month indicates that the moon will still exist in the New Heaven and the New Earth, dividing the year into twelve months. The sun will also exist and divide day and night into 12 hours each, but for those who dwell in the light of God, they will not see darkness of night.

※ 12 is the number of the New Jerusalem, symbolizing God's unity with man in His eternal economy (12 Apostles, 12 tribes, 12 gates, 12,000 stadia, 144 cubits, 12 months in time, 12 hours of day, 12 hours of night).

8. The leaves of the tree are for the healing of the nations. The leaves stand for the acts of men (Ge 3:7)[619]. The leaves of the Tree of Life represent Christ's achievements. The born-again believers will internally eat the fruits of the Tree of Life through Christ, so that they may enjoy divine life forever. <u>On the other hand, the restored nations are healed through the leaves of the Tree of Life, because they live the life of mortals forever.</u>

Verse 3-4 No longer will there be any curse. The throne of God and of the Lamb will be in the city, and His servants will serve Him. They will see His face, and His name will be on their foreheads.

1. In the New Heaven and the New Earth there will be no more corruption, so no more curse. Hatred, accusation, backbiting, and all things of that nature are all seen as a curse, so if there is no more curse, there can only be tenderness, joyfulness, life, brightness, pureness, and wholeness.

---

619)Ge3:7 Then the eyes of both of them were opened, and they realized they were naked; so they sewed fig leaves together and made coverings for themselves.

2. For eternity, we will enjoy the throne of God and of the Lamb. The throne seen in Hebrew 4:16[620] is a throne of grace, but the throne seen in Revelation chapter 4 is a throne that holds authority over judgment. Again, however, the throne in Revelation chapter 22 is a throne of authority AND of grace (God-the-Lamb).
   This throne in chapter 22 is for God's government (his reign) as it is the throne of authority. However, what comes out of this throne is not authority, but the river of the water of life; this is indeed grace, not authority.
3. Serving God and the Lamb in eternity is a grace given to those who have been redeemed. In chapter 4 the four living creatures served God, and in 7:15[621] the saints clothed in white robes served God in the temple, but in the New Jerusalem, the new heaven and the new earth, they will no longer worship God in the temple as priests, but face to face.
4. For eternity, on the foreheads of those who have been redeemed by God, there will be not two names, but one: God-the-Lamb. This sealing is the Lord's declaration: "you are mine" (Isa 43:1), meaning that we will no longer be in Him, but be one with Him.

[The glory of God shines]

Verse 5 There will be no more night. They will not need the light of a lamp or the light of the sun, for the Lord God will give them light. And they will reign for ever and ever.

---

620)Heb4:16 Let us then approach the throne of grace with confidence, so that we may receive mercy and find grace to help us in our time of need.

621)Rev7:15 Therefore, "they are before the throne of God and serve Him day and night in His temple; and He who sits on the throne will spread His tent over them.

1. In the New Jerusalem there will be no more night. They will not need the light from the sun, because they will live in the light of God's glory. They will be kings who rule the nations forever. For eternity, when we reign as kings, we must not rule by force, but by the flow of life.
2. The nations have stayed faithful and are born again, and will be restored to the original condition that God first created. The faithful overcomers will become kings (Rev 20:4~6)[622], while the remnant of Israel who have received salvation (the 144,000) will become priests of the earth (Ex 19:6, Zec 8:20~23)[623]. They will be the citizens (the people) of the nations.

※ At the end of the Millennial Kingdom when Satan is released from the Abyss, some of the nations will again be tempted

---

622)Rev20:4 I saw thrones on which were seated those who had been given authority to judge. And I saw the souls of those who had been beheaded because of their testimony for Jesus and because of the word of God. They had not worshiped the beast or his image and had not received his mark on their foreheads or their hands. They came to life and reigned with Christ a thousand years.

Rev20:5 (The rest of the dead did not come to life until the thousand years were ended.) This is the first resurrection.

Rev20:6 Blessed and holy are those who have part in the first resurrection. The second death has no power over them, but they will be priests of God and of Christ and will reign with Him for a thousand years.

623)Ex19:6 you will be for Me a kingdom of priests and a holy nation.' These are the words you are to speak to the Israelites."

Zec8:20 This is what the LORD Almighty says: "Many peoples and the inhabitants of many cities will yet come,

Zec8:21 and the inhabitants of one city will go to another and say, 'Let us go at once to entreat the LORD and seek the LORD Almighty. I myself am going.'

Zec8:22 And many peoples and powerful nations will come to Jerusalem to seek the LORD Almighty and to entreat him."

Zec8:23 This is what the LORD Almighty says: "In those days ten men from all languages and nations will take firm hold of one Jew by the hem of his robe and say, 'Let us go with you, because we have heard that God is with you.'" An Oracle

by the devil and turn against God; they will be swallowed by the fire of heaven (Rev 20:7~9)[624]. Meanwhile the others will be moved into a new land and live as a nation surrounding the New Jerusalem, living by the light of God's glory (Rev 21:24)[625]. After the devil is thrown into the lake of fire, in a state where death is no more and the life of our bodies is eternal, they will be cured by the leaves of the tree of life and enjoy eternal life as in the beginning of creation; there will be no more death (Rev 21:4)[626].

3. Receiving light from God is a blessing given to the redeemed. We will no longer need the sun or any lamps as we will live by the light of God Himself. Today, we - those who live in the age of the church - are eager to experience, enjoy, and live this light.

Verse 6-7 The angel said to me, "These words are trustworthy and true. The Lord, the God who inspires the prophets, sent His angel to show His servants the things that must soon take place." "Look, I am coming soon! Blessed is the one who keeps the words of the prophecy written in this book."

---

624)Rev20:7 When the thousand years are over, Satan will be released from his prison

Rev20:8 and will go out to deceive the nations in the four corners of the earth--Gog and Magog--to gather them for battle. In number they are like the sand on the seashore.

Rev20:9 They marched across the breadth of the earth and surrounded the camp of God's people, the city He loves. But fire came down from heaven and devoured them.

625)Rev21:24 The nations will walk by its light, and the kings of the earth will bring their splendor into it.

626)Rev21:4 He will wipe every tear from their eyes. There will be no more death or mourning or crying or pain, for the old order of things has passed away."

1. The Lord says "I am coming soon" in chapter 22:7, 12, 20[627]. This is the Lord's warning to us. See the situation of the day, because we do not know what tomorrow will bring. In this day and age, things come and go rapidly (Da 12:4)[628] and are forgotten very quickly as well. As time passes, this phenomenon will become more severe. We must be awake and prepared.

[Blessed is he who keeps the words of the prophesy in this book]

2. It is said in Revelation 1:3[629], "Blessed is the one who reads the words of this prophecy, and blessed are those who hear it and take to heart what is written in it", but in chapter 22:7[630], it is written, "Blessed is he who keeps the words of the prophecy." We know that those who read and hear the words of the Revelation are blessed. However, for some reason, many people refuse to listen to this gospel and do not understand even when they read it. Those who read, understand, hear, and are moved to live these observances of the word will be truly blessed. Hallelujah!

---

627)Rev22:7 "Behold, I am coming soon! Blessed is he who keeps the words of the prophecy in this book."
Rev22:12 "Behold, I am coming soon! My reward is with Me, and I will give to everyone according to what he has done.
Rev22:20 He who testifies to these things says, "Yes, I am coming soon." Amen. Come, Lord Jesus.

628)Da12:4 But you, Daniel, close up and seal the words of the scroll until the time of the end. Many will go here and there to increase knowledge."

629)Rev1:3 Blessed is the one who reads the words of this prophecy, and blessed are those who hear it and take to heart what is written in it, because the time is near.

630)Rev22:7 "Behold, I am coming soon! Blessed is he who keeps the words of the prophecy in this book."

Verse 8-9 I, John, am the one who heard and saw these things. And when I had heard and seen them, I fell down to worship at the feet of the angel who had been showing them to me. But he said to me, "Don't do that! I am a fellow servant with you and with Your fellow prophets and with all who keep the words of this book. Worship God!"

1. When John saw and heard the words of this prophecy, he thought these words were so impressive and precious that he was about to fall down and worship the angel.
2. The angel was the same rank as John, the prophets, and those who obey the words of this book (the overcomers).
3. All worship must be to God and all glory also must only be to God.

[Do not seal up the words of the prophesy of this book]

Verse 10-11 Then he told me, "Do not seal up the words of the prophesy of this book, because the time is near. Let him who does wrong continue to do wrong; let him who is vile continue to be vile; let him who does right continue to do right; and let him who is holy continue to be holy."

1. Daniel's prophecy about the time of the end was sealed. God decided that the prophecy of Daniel would be opened in the end time (Da 12:9)[631]. However, the words of this book of prophecy (Revelation) should not be sealed because the end is imminent. In other words, the opening of the book of Revelation implies the end is near.
2. Those who live in the time when the book of this prophecy opens will live in a time when the Lord's coming is so near that all who don't open their hearts will fall into a pitiful state; because the time is so near, it will be hard to be healed.

---

631)Da12:9 He replied, "Go Your way, Daniel, because the words are closed up and sealed until the time of the end.

[I am the Alpha and the Omega]

Verse 12-13 "Look, I am coming soon! My reward is with Me, and I will give to each person according to what they have done. I am the Alpha and the Omega, the First and the Last, the Beginning and the End.

▣ When the Lord comes, He will reward everyone according to what he has done. This will be given to them after our rapture before the throne of Christ (Mt 16:27, Ro 14:10, 2Co 5:10)[632].

Verse 14-15 "Blessed are those who wash their robes, that they may have the right to the tree of life and may go through the gates into the city. Outside are the dogs, those who practice magic arts, the sexually immoral, the murderers, the idolaters and everyone who loves and practices falsehood.

1. Washing robes represents the cleansing of the deeds of the faithful (Rev 19:7～8)[633]. Washing our robes means keeping them pure (Rev 7:14, 1Jn 1:7)[634]. Through these deeds, we

---

632)Mt16:27 For the Son of Man is going to come in His Father's glory with His angels, and then He will reward each person according to what he has done.

Ro14:10 You, then, why do you judge Your brother? Or why do you look down on Your brother? For we will all stand before God's judgment seat.

2Co5:10 For we must all appear before the judgment seat of Christ, that each one may receive what is due him for the things done while in the body, whether good or bad.

633)Rev19:7 Let us rejoice and be glad and give Him glory! For the wedding of the Lamb has come, and His bride has made herself ready.

Rev19:8 Fine linen, bright and clean, was given her to wear." (Fine linen stands for the righteous acts of the saints.)

634)Rev7:14 I answered, "Sir, you know." And he said, "These are they who have come out of the great tribulation; they have washed their robes and made them white in the blood of the Lamb.

may obtain the right to the tree of life and the right to enter through the gates of the city.

※ To wash our good deeds with the blood of the Lamb is to confess and repent, because even among our good deeds, there may always be dirtiness, boastfulness, pride, and selfishness (1Jn 1:7～9)[635].

2. The tree of life is our everlasting supply of life. This tree will make us full, fresh, and new.
3. We cannot enter this city just wearing white robes, we must wash our white robes before entering so that they are absolutely clean.
4. The dogs, those who practice magic arts, the sexually immoral, the murderers, the idolaters, and everyone who loves and practices falsehood will be left outside the city. The faithful are saved, but during the Millennial Kingdom, those who still sin will be left outside the city.

Verse 16 "I, Jesus, have sent My angel to give you this testimony for the churches. I am the Root and the Offspring of David, and the bright Morning Star."

1. This book of Revelation is the testimony of Jesus Christ through the angels for the churches. Churches should be strengthened by these words and be able to cope wisely with the end times.
2. Christ is the root or source of David in divinity and the Son of David in humanity (Mt 22:42～45, Ro 1:3, Isa 11:1)[636].

1Jn1:7 But if we walk in the light, as He is in the light, we have fellowship with one another, and the blood of Jesus, His Son, purifies us from all sin.

635)1Jn1:7 But if we walk in the light, as He is in the light, we have fellowship with one another, and the blood of Jesus, His Son, purifies us from all sin.

1Jn1:8 If we claim to be without sin, we deceive ourselves and the truth is not in us.

1Jn1:9 If we confess our sins, He is faithful and just and will forgive us our sins and purify us from all unrighteousness.

636)Mt22:42 "What do you think about the Christ? Whose son is he?"

3. When Christ first came as the Lamb, He came as the sun (Lk 1:78~79, 2:32)[637], and even when He comes again, in the eyes of His ordinary people, He will come as the sun (Mal 4:2)[638], but to His saints that stay awake, He will be their bright Morning Star. This will be a reward given to the overcomers (Rev 2:28)[639].

※ The Morning Star is seen only by those who are awake early before the break of day, but the rising sun is seen by many a few hours later.

[Disaster when adding or subtracting what is written in this book]

Verse 17-19 The Spirit and the bride say, "Come!" And let the one who hears say, "Come!" Let the one who is thirsty come; and let the one who wishes take the free gift of the water of life. I warn everyone who hears the words

---

"The son of David," they replied.

Mt22:43 He said to them, "How is it then that David, speaking by the Spirit, calls Him 'Lord'? For he says,

Mt22:44 "'The Lord said to my Lord: "Sit at My right hand until I put Your enemies under Your feet." '

Mt22:45 If then David calls Him 'Lord,' how can He be his son?"

Ro1:3 regarding His Son, who as to His human nature was a descendant of David,

Isa11:1 A shoot will come up from the stump of Jesse; from his roots a Branch will bear fruit.

637)Lk1:78 because of the tender mercy of our God, by which the rising sun will come to us from heaven

Lk1:79 to shine on those living in darkness and in the shadow of death, to guide our feet into the path of peace."

Lk2:32 a light for revelation to the Gentiles and for glory to Your people Israel."

638)Mal4:2 But for you who revere My name, the sun of righteousness will rise with healing in its wings. And you will go out and leap like calves released from the stall.

639)Rev2:28 I will also give him the morning star.

of the prophecy of this book: If anyone adds anything to them, God will add to that person the plagues described in this book. And if anyone takes words away from this book of prophecy, God will take away from that person any share in the tree of life and in the Holy City, which are described in this book.

1. In chapters 2 and 3, the Spirit speaks to the churches, but in this verse, the Spirit and the bride speak as one. This means that the church has been united with the Spirit.
2. The Spirit and the bride say, "Come!" and to those who hear the words of Christ, let him say, "Come!" Whoever is thirsty, let him come; and whoever wishes, let him take the free gift of the water of life as his inheritance (Rev 21:6~7)[640].
3. Do not add anything to this book; one's ideas, thoughts, opinions, doctrines, teachings, theology. If one does so, he will suffer the plagues written in this book, the plagues of the seals, of the trumpets, and the three plagues of the Great Tribulation.

[Blessed is he who keeps the words of this book]

4. If for some reason one thinks that some of things written in this book are unnecessary, too difficult, or whatever the case may be, and takes words away from the prophecy of this book, God will take away from that person any share in the tree of life and in the Holy City.

※ Whether you will experience disaster or share in blessings depends on how you communicate the prophecy of this book and how you receive it. We must not add anything beyond this book. It must be communicated and accepted as recorded.

---

640)Rev21:6 He said to me: "It is done. I am the Alpha and the Omega, the Beginning and the End. To him who is thirsty I will give to drink without cost from the spring of the water of life.
Rev21:7 He who overcomes will inherit all this, and I will be his God and he will be My son.

Verse 20-21 He who testifies to these things says, “Yes, I am coming soon.” Amen. Come, Lord Jesus. The grace of the Lord Jesus be with God’s people. Amen.

1. In the end, the Lord Jesus warns us for the third time about His second coming. The latter part is John’s prayer and response to the Lord’s warning. After reading (receiving) this book, we must also pray like this, "Amen, Come, Lord Jesus." The Bible ends with a longing for the Lords coming, revealed as a prayer.
2. As our faith blossoms, we must be patient saints longing for the Lord Jesus' coming.
3. For us to receive, obey, and live according to this book, we must live and act following this vision and prophecy in the grace of Jesus Christ.
4. Not only this book, but the whole Bible ends with this grace. This grace lets us experience Christ, who holds together all things in the universe, and be part of the God of the Trinity. Therefore, He makes all of us an eternal corporate expression for the accomplishment of His eternal purpose. And let us enjoy contentment and rest, with Him and with each other, forever! Hallelujah!

Editorial Review

Testimony

I died.

When I was 33 years old, serving as a major in the army, full of bloody passion, I tried to catch a moving train. I missed my step and got sucked under the train because of its terrific speed.

I escaped death by a whisker, and as the clanging sound of the train receded into the distance I stood up, dusted myself off, and exclaimed "That was lucky!". Of course, it wasn't luck. If God hadn't saved my life I would have been dead.

Even on the day that I couldn't move a finger tip because of the severe pain caused by 8 hours of myocardial infarction...

Even on the day when I was in a coma in the intensive care unit and my brain was dying because of a sudden stroke.

Even on the day when my back was broken after suffering optical illusions in a car accident going down the Daegwallyeong Hill, Gangwon-Do..

I would have died long ago if He hadn't saved me···

But He saved me like that in order to let me die.

He wanted me to die.

His will for me was to crucify the thoughts and sensations of soul, my emotions, will, strength, greed, pride, guile, impatience, lewdness, envy, unrighteousness, murder, deceit and foolishness.

For if you live according to the flesh, you will die; but if by the Spirit you put to death the misdeeds of the body, you will live (Romans 8:13).

I face death every day-yes, just as surely as I boast about you in Christ Jesus our LORD (1 Corinthians 15:31).

Now I die every day

Please try to be the person who can eat the Word of Revelation!

Eating the Word is directly connected to our lives. The heart of the person who eats the Word begins to be handled on the cross. I begin to experience death on the cross. The life of the cross is the tribulation of Jesus.

The Apostle John introduced himself to the Seven Churches he loved as follows:

I, John, Your brother and companion in the suffering and kingdom and patient endurance that are ours in Jesus.

If you eat the Words of this book of Revelation and live the life of Your soul dying on the cross then please introduce yourself like me!

I, Sung-no Yoon,
am Your brother and companion in the suffering and kingdom

and patient endurance that are ours in Jesus

The 7 Churches of this era who have ears to hear what the Holy Spirit says to them!

Blessed is the one who reads aloud the words of this prophecy, and blessed are those who hear it and take to heart what is written in it, because the time is near (Revelation 1:3).

For the work of translation of this English version of my teaching on the Book of Revelation, I would like to express my sincere gratitude to Pastor Man-geun Kwak, Evangelist Chan-so Choi, Brother Ji-hyung Song, and for the work of revision, Hyang-jin Yoon, Matthew Oakley and Hyun-su Cha, and for the work of editing, Evangelist Hyung-woo Choi.

Through the publication of this [Revelation of the Revelation], I would like to give glory, gratitude, and appreciation to the Triune God, together with co-workers from all over the world who love and preach the life of the cross.